Communication Before Speech

Development and Assessment

Second Edition

Judith Coupe O'Kane
and Juliet Goldbart

with Chapter 8 written by
Jane Jolliffe, Barbara Rossington and Ruth Miller

and with acknowledgement to
the following contributors to the first edition:
Mark Barber, Linda Barton, Jane Jolliffe
Chris Kiernan, Debbie Murphy, Sue Walker

Routledge
Taylor & Francis Group

LONDON AND NEW YORK

First published 1998 by David Fulton Publishers Ltd.

Published 2016 by Routledge
2 Park Square, Milton Park, Abingdon, Oxon OX14 4RN
711 Third Avenue, New York, NY 10017, USA

Routledge is an imprint of the Taylor & Francis Group, an informa business

Note: The rights of Judith Coupe O'Kane and Juliet Goldbart to be identified as
the authors of this work have been asserted by them in accordance with the
Copyright, Designs and Patents Act 1988.

Notices
Practitioners and researchers must always rely on their own experience and
knowledge in evaluating and using any information, methods, compounds, or
experiments described herein. In using such information or methods they should
be mindful of their own safety and the safety of others, including parties for whom
they have a professional responsibility.

Product or corporate names may be trademarks or registered trademarks, and are
used only for identification and explanation without intent to infringe.

British Library Cataloguing in Publication Data
A catalogue record for this book is available from the British Library.

ISBN-13: 978-1-853-46486-7 (pbk)

Contents

Dedication

For their unstinting support to us in updating *Communication Before Speech*, we thank our husbands, Mike O'Kane and Alick Rocca. Our offspring too have had the experience of us needing to work extended hours in writing this book and they have been wonderful (but forget the support and patience bit!). We do thank Simon and Martin, and Daniel and Eleanor for their cooperation.

Acknowledgement

This book is dedicated to two people who have particularly influenced our personal and professional determination to enhance the communicative competences of children and adults with severe, and profound and multiple, learning difficulties.

Louise Carter, in her short life, inspired us in our commitment to understand, interpret and address the potentially 'closed' world of a child, or adult, with serious communicative and intellectual delay. Throughout her life at Melland School and at home, Louise's smile, laughter and appreciation of things she liked brought much, both to and from those who knew her. She fired us to seek ways to facilitate a rich quality of life in a responsive, social and communicative environment.

Rick Brinker, until his untimely death, was a good friend, a keen critic and a source of much intellectual stimulation to us. His great ability was in synthesising innovative theory, research and practice. His work underpins much of our approach, both in the first edition and in this volume. Such was his perceptiveness and creativity that he will continue to be influential for many years to come.

Introduction

The first edition of this book evolved during 1987 out of a series of one-day conferences which we instigated under the auspices of the (now) British Institute of Learning Disabilities, BILD. The content of some of the papers was based around the activities of a multidisciplinary working party established by Manchester Education Committee, involving teachers, a speech and language therapist and psychologists. Others developed out of in-service work with teachers on aspects of assessment and intervention.

At the time we were astonished at the popularity of these conferences. There seemed to be a great interest in early communication and in a broadly developmental approach to working with children and adults at pre-verbal stages. However, few publications seemed to focus on this area. As a consequence, Croom Helm published a book of chapters based around the conference papers. The book, *Communication Before Speech*, was well received in the UK, Australia and North America, and was even translated into Finnish!

When the book went out of print a couple of years ago, we were surprised at the number of requests we received to bring out a second edition. Clearly, the need for such a book still existed and we are delighted that David Fulton agreed to take on this project so readily.

In the ten years since the first edition the fields of language acquisition and learning disabilities have moved on. Pragmatics, the functional use of communication, has become central to much communicative intervention. Resettlement of people with learning disabilities into the community has been associated with an increased interest in work with adults, particularly those with behaviour that challenges services. We have been particularly excited by the work on early learning and early communication by Sheila Glenn, Jean Ware, Mel Nind and Dave Hewett, and the many writers we have been privileged to work with in the books we have edited since the first publication of *Communication Before Speech*. Readers will find reference to much of this work throughout the chapters in this volume.

Partly because of the extent of rewriting to update *Communication Before Speech* to include contemporary developments, and partly because of the present commitments of the previous authors, we decided to take over responsibility for authorship of the second edition. However, we want to thank and acknowledge the enormous contribution to our thinking made by our co-authors from the first edition: Mark Barber, Linda Barton, Jane Jolliffe, Chris Kiernan, Debbie Murphy and Sue Walker.

The inclusion of the Early Communication Assessment (ECA), developed since the first edition, is intended to meet the needs of readers requiring a detailed assessment. As with the first edition, it is hoped that the chapters and the assessment stand on their own. Together, however, they should provide the basis of a curriculum for the early stages of communication development which, in England, will complement the Programmes of Study for those working within Level 1 of the National Curriculum, *English: Speaking and Listening*.

There is one exception to our authorship. While our focus in this book is communication *before* speech, we have come to feel that stopping the book at the point where the learner starts to use some conventional form of communication – speech, signs or symbols – creates an artificial discontinuity. We therefore invited Jane Jolliffe and her colleagues to write a final chapter on their development of our joint work on the Manchester Pragmatics Profile. Through our shared initiatives, a means of profiling the pragmatics skills of both verbal and pre-verbal communicators has evolved, and this, we feel, takes *Communication Before Speech* a step beyond its original brief.

Chapter 1

Re-examining the development of early communication

During the last 20 to 25 years there has been an enormous expansion in research on how normally developing infants and young children acquire language. This research has resulted in new theories of language and communication acquisition; more detailed accounts than we can give here may be found in Harris (1992) and Nadel and Camaioni (1993). We have found these theories exciting, even inspiring, in our attempts to devise intervention strategies for impaired communicators. Our own research has concerned mainly children and adults with severe and profound learning difficulties. However, we are confident that our approaches are relevant to many other individuals at very early stages of language acquisition.

When the first edition of this book was published it could be argued that those of us working in more applied areas had been slow to respond to the implications of this new research. In the intervening ten years there has been a steady trickle of publications on language and communication in children and, to a lesser extent, adults with severe learning disabilities, aimed at making research accessible to and usable by practitioners (see, for example, Beveridge *et al.* 1989/97, Calculator and Bedrosian 1988, Harris 1990, Linfoot 1994).

Until the early 1970s, the study of language and language development was dominated by two main theories: Chomsky's grammarian theory (e.g. Chomsky 1957, 1965) and Skinner's behaviourist theory (e.g. Skinner 1957). It seems likely that any delay in the application of more recent theories and research stems more from the dominance, in published approaches to intervention, of these prevailing theories than from any lack of interest in new work.

These two approaches (behaviourist and grammarian), which will be discussed in greater detail in Chapter 4, led to a very large number of intervention studies with children and adults showing a wide range of types of language delay or disorder. Many of these studies concerned children and adults with severe learning difficulties, in particular those who were functioning at the one- and two-word stage. As we will see later, these studies were not always very successful. The scope of more recent research on normally developing infants and young children has been extremely broad and encompasses such areas as:

- Adult–infant interaction (e.g. Trevarthen 1979, 1993);
- The type of language input received by young children (e.g. Galloway and Richards 1994, Nelson 1973, Snow 1972);
- Early gestures and vocalisations (e.g. Bates, Camaioni and Volterra 1975, Bruner 1975);
- Different approaches to categorisation of first words and phrases (e.g. Benedict 1979, Bloom and Lahey 1978, Harris 1992).

The findings of these studies can be unified, quite logically, into two new theoretical approaches. These theoretical approaches are usually described as the *psycholinguistic* approach – a semantic-cognitive theory – and the *sociolinguistic* approach – a socio-cultural theory. These are, in fact, quite different approaches, but are by no means contradictory. Indeed, Harding (1983) argues that the development of intentional communication is built upon both cognitive ability and social experience. In order to see how each of these theories has influenced the research and practice that we will be discussing in later chapters, it is important to consider their underlying principles.

The psycholinguistic approach

This has four major underlying principles.

1. Some level of cognitive intentionality is required for the development of intentional communication (e.g. Camaioni 1993, Schweigert 1989).
2. The child's early utterances, which may precede recognisable words, are expressions of semantic relationships, where semantics involves those aspects of language which are to do with the meaning and content of words or protowords (the fore-runners of words).[1] Thus, the first words or protowords that children produce express things to do with meaning and content. Bloom and Lahey (1978) propose the following as the first semantic relations expressed:

   - Existence: The child comments on or acknowledges the existence of an object or entity, for example, 'What's that?' 'Shoe', 'This'.
   - Non-existence: The child comments on the absence of an expected object or entity, for example, 'Gone', 'Sock' with rising intonation.
   - Disappearance: The child comments on or requests the disappearance of an object or entity, for example, 'All gone', 'Bye-bye'.
   - Recurrence: The child comments on or requests that an object, entity or event reappear, reoccur or replace one that has gone, for example, 'Again', 'More'.

3. Semantic relations, these expressions of meanings and content, are an encoding of the child's existing knowledge about the world. So, when a child uses a word or a protoword they are, in fact, making some comment about something they understand about the world, some action or event in the environment. However, it must be remembered that the meanings do not exist out there in the world; they are imposed on events and object relations by the child (Palermo 1982).
4. Arising out of the first three points, we can see that language development is built, at least in part, on cognitive development; that is, on the child's actions on and knowledge about objects and the environment and the relationships between them.

The psycholinguistic theory can thus be seen to offer much in explanation of what we observe in the early utterances of young children. The approach also suggests certain intervention strategies, particularly the idea that children need experience of acting on objects and events in their environment, and that these experiences can be gained through interaction with people, with objects and, of course, through play (this topic will be considered in greater detail in Chapters 3 and 4). However, this theory does not explain *why* language and communication develop. Why should a child feel the need to express a cognitive relationship? Why should a child feel the need to tell you 'Ball gone'? For an explanation of this aspect, to find out why children learn to communicate, it is necessary to turn to the second theory.

The sociolinguistic approach

In the sociolinguistic approach, a socio-cultural theory, the emphasis is on the child in a social setting. This approach has five fundamental principles.

1. Language is acquired only if the child has reason to communicate (e.g. Harris 1992). We see this as a crucial point, and it will underpin much of what is discussed later in this book. The implication is that a child or adult with language and/or learning disabilities is only going to learn to communicate, or be motivated to communicate, if they have a reason, a purpose, for that communication. This reason could of course be personal, social or material.
2. As the child matures and produces more complex expressions, linguistic structure is initially acquired through decoding and understanding incoming linguistic stimulation. Hence, interactions between the language learner and more mature language users are likely to be very

important (e.g. Galloway and Richards 1994).

3. Language is learned in dynamic social interactions involving the child and mature language users. This emphasises the importance of positive contacts with linguistically competent people, since it is they who provide the input to be decoded and understood (e.g. Harris 1992).

4. Language is first acquired as a more effective means of obtaining things that the child could previously get, or do, by simpler communication (e.g. Bruner 1985).

5. Children are active participants in the process of learning communication, and bring to this learning situation a set of behaviours, both social and cognitive, which allow them to benefit from the adults' facilitating behaviours. Whilst adults play their part in this dynamic interaction, the language learner needs certain social and cognitive skills if they are to benefit (e.g. Camaioni 1993).

Again, this theory has provided a number of clues which we have found particularly helpful in devising intervention strategies. The first is the importance of the child as an active participant in learning language and communication. The notion of the child as an active learner has prompted us to make use of Piaget's (1952) account of development in the sensori-motor period, the first two years of normal development. Although we acknowledge the difficulties in establishing the precise relationship between cognition and language acquisition (see e.g. Kamhi and Masterson 1989), we have taken the view that certain cognitive and perceptual prerequisites are necessary, but not sufficient, for the development of language and communication. As the language learner becomes older, however, it seems increasingly likely that a mismatch may arise between cognitive level and language level. This may well be the case for some adolescents and adults with severe and profound learning disabilities and is a matter which requires considerable further investigation.

The second issue to emerge is the importance of giving the language learner real opportunities to communicate with mature language users. This theme will be addressed in some detail later in the book.

It will be apparent from the key points, above, that the psycholinguistic and sociolinguistic theories are not mutually exclusive. There is overlap within them, and it is our view that they can be used in a complementary fashion to inform assessment and intervention on communication and language for many client groups. We recognise that there are risks inherent in applying research findings from normally developing children to children and adults with severe learning difficulties who may not follow normal developmental sequences (Greenwald and Leonard 1979, Miller and Chapman 1984). However, unless there is evidence to the contrary and in the absence of comprehensive alternative accounts, the established developmental route seems the best to follow. Therapists, teachers and others planning or implementing intervention in this area need to exercise some caution, particularly if the clients concerned do not seem to be following typical and parallel developmental sequences in social, cognitive and communicative skills.

Development according to the psycholinguistic approach

Let us now examine the stages in development according to the psycholinguistic approach, summarised in Table 1.1. These will include aspects of cognitive, semantic and symbolic development. The ages are, of course, approximate and it cannot be assumed that having the cognitive behaviour necessarily implies that the semantic or symbolic behaviour will be established. The stages are drawn from Piaget's findings on the sensori-motor period (Piaget 1952, Uzgiris and Hunt 1975).

As can be seen from Table 1.1, during the first month there is only a limited amount that can really be described as cognitive development, certainly nothing that could be classed as semantic or symbolic development. Reflex exercise can be observed; if, for example, the tip of a finger is put in the groove of a baby's tongue, a reflex sucking response can be elicited. It is also suggested (Haith 1980) that infants at this stage show selective looking, that is, babies have certain strategies which make their visual activity far more than random. Hence, if babies are awake and active, they will open their eyes; if they encounter darkness they will make a broad search of the environment; if they find light but no edges or contours they will again make a broad search. In areas of high contrast, a narrow search is made. Thus, it does seem that infants are 'preprogrammed' in such a way that they can demonstrate some cognitive behaviour even at this very early stage.

Table 1.1   Cognitive, semantic and symbolic development in Piaget's sensori-motor period

Stage label	Approx. age (in months)	Cognitive, semantic and/or symbolic development
First habits	0–1	Infants engage mainly in reflex exercise, sucking, rooting. Selective looking.
Primary circular reactions	1–4	If babies do something with their own bodies, e.g. thumb-sucking, that they find pleasurable, they learn to repeat the action. Early undifferentiated schemes: e.g. mouthing, looking, and holding.
Secondary circular reactions	4–8	If babies do something external to themselves that they find pleasurable, they learn to repeat the action. Shaking, banging and other differentiated schemes (cognitive roles are being established).
Coordination of secondary schemes	8–12	Cognitive roles expand. Babies' use of familiar objects becomes conventional or 'appropriate'. Goals are established prior to initiation of activity (cognitive intentionality is fully established). Semantic roles start to be conveyed.
Tertiary circular reactions	12–18	Babies demonstrate tool use and new means of achieving ends through experimentation. They demonstrate relational play, then self-pretend play. First words are used, readily categorised by semantic role.
Beginnings of thought	18–24	Toddlers can predict cause-and-effect relationships. They show decentred pretend play, then sequenced pretend play. Complex series of gestures are used, then two-word utterances, with increasing syntactic development.

Over the following three months infants engage in a small range of undifferentiated schemes. These are actions which are performed on a whole range of objects irrespective of what, to adults, the properties or functions of the objects are. Thus they can be seen as generalised and repeatable responses to things in the environment. Typically, these schemes include looking, mouthing and holding. During this stage, Piaget describes the infant as engaging in primary circular reactions. In other words, if babies start a behaviour involving their own bodies which is found to be pleasurable, strategies are developed to keep that behaviour going, but the goals are not set before the action sequence is begun and it is questionable whether the notion of a goal is at all appropriate at this stage. Research (e.g. by Watson and Ramey 1972) has shown that, under experimental conditions, babies can learn a connection between their actions and a consequence by around three months of age. This might involve moving an arm round which has been tied a thread which, if pulled, switches on a flashing light display. However, this simple learning only occurs when the time between actions and consequences is less than three seconds, a situation which is unlikely in the normal environment. This learning of a link between action and consequence is called 'contingency awareness'. It has been studied in children with severe and profound learning disabilities by Brinker and Lewis (1982a and 1982b) and O'Brien, Glenn and Cunningham (1994) among others, and has been used as a basis for teaching very early communication skills (e.g. Schweigert 1989, Schweigert and Rowland 1992).

During the third stage the baby is increasingly able to combine early schemes in, for example, visually directed reaching, but goals are still not set before starting action patterns. There is, however, heightened interest in event outcomes and it seems that goals are set once action sequences have started. Furthermore, these action patterns (or manifestations of cognitive roles) can now involve objects and events external to the baby. These are known as secondary circular reactions. This first establishment of a connection between means and ends is of paramount importance, since it is during this stage, at about the six-month developmental level, that the infant acquires intentionality, the establishment of purposeful action on the environment.

Stage 4 sees cognitive roles expanding. The infant now has greater experience with objects and a wider range of actions on objects. Familiar objects start to be used appropriately; the first evidence of this, typically, involves the recognition that a cup is something you drink out of. In relation to the connection between means and ends, the child now establishes a goal prior to the start of an activity. The very beginnings of the communication of semantic roles can now be observed; having established a diversity of cognitive roles, the child starts to communicate them to other people. Bloom and Lahey's (1978) account of the first semantic roles to be communicated has been given above. To communicate these semantic roles or early meanings at this stage, the child uses looking, actions, gestures and/or vocalisations.

During stage 5, which lasts from around one year to 18 months, the child starts to engage in relational play. Children begin to put objects into containers and take them out and to relate objects together in play, putting spoons in cups, bricks in boxes and so on. In the second half of the stage, this develops into self-pretend play, feeding self with a spoon, pretend brushing own teeth. This is also the stage where children could be expected to produce their first words. Initially, these are likely to reflect the very early semantic categories described by Bloom and Lahey, but, during this stage, these categories expand to include a wide range of meanings which the child can now convey. Leonard (1984) has proposed the list of semantic roles or notions in Table 1.2 as being those expressed at the single-word and early two-word stage.

Table 1.2   Semantic notions

Semantic notion	Meaning being expressed
Nomination	Naming
Recurrence	Awareness of potential for reappearance or re-enactment
Denial	Rejection of a proposition
Non-existence	Recognition of the absence of an object that was present
Rejection	Prevention or cessation of an activity or appearance of an object
Action + object	An animate receives the force of an action
Location	Spatial relationship between two objects
Possession	Object is associated with someone or something
Attribution	Properties not inherently part of the class to which the object belongs
Experience + experiencer	Animate affected by event
Action + instrument	Inanimate causally affected in an activity

Adapted from Leonard (1984: 144)

Stage 6 is really a transitional stage; a link into the pre-operational period. In this stage, symbolic play starts to develop, with the child showing decentred pretend play, for example feeding dolly or brushing teddy's hair. These actions then become sequenced, for instance feeding dolly, daddy and teddy or, a little later in the stage, undressing dolly, putting it in the bath, washing it, taking out of the bath and drying it and putting it to bed. These longer play sequences are echoed in the child's complex sequences of gestures, or gestures plus single words and then, towards the end of the stage, in two-word utterances and the beginnings of syntactic developments. Our interest in this book, however, is largely with what happens up to and including stage 5; communicative development up to first words.

Development according to the sociolinguistic approach

It is now necessary to turn our attention to development according to the other theoretical approach, the sociolinguistic approach. Here, our interest is in the way in which language learners come to acquire a functional use of language and communication. As indicated earlier, the psycholinguistic and sociolinguistic approaches are in many ways complementary. Relevant cognitive points will, therefore, be added to the account below, to try to give a more complete picture of the development of early communication. The account is summarised in Figure 1.1.

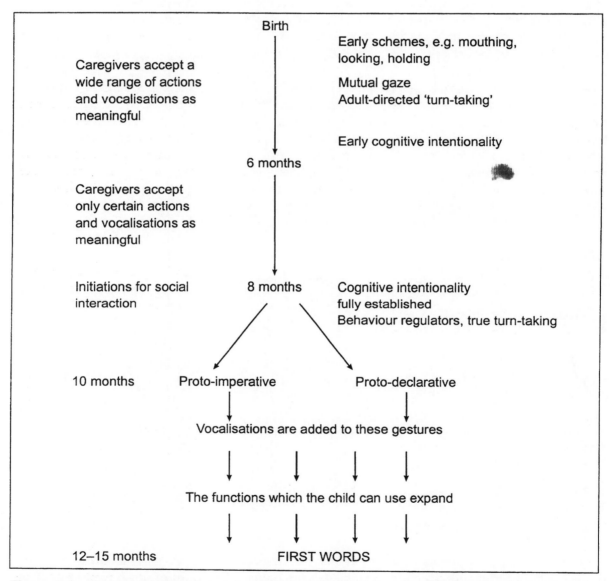

Figure 1.1   The integration of social and cognitive developments in the acquisition of early communication skills

It is well accepted that babies are born with a range of characteristics and skills that predispose them to be social beings. For example, they may orient to a human voice (Alegria and Noirot 1978), or even engage with the gentle handling of an adult (e.g. Trevarthen 1993). They can also express affective, or emotional, states (e.g. Stark 1981).

From birth onwards, looking and motor behaviours become an increasing part of the baby's repertoire of social interactive behaviours. Up to about six months, caregivers accept a wide range of these actions and vocalisations as meaningful. For example, when the caregiver is changing the baby's nappy the baby might blow a raspberry, to which the caregiver might say, 'Does that feel better then?' or if the baby, having been taken out of her cot and put on the floor, kicks her legs, the caregiver might say, 'Yes, you like it down here, don't you?' So the adult is attributing meaning to, or richly interpreting, the infant's actions or vocalisations. Interactions between the infant and caregiver at this stage usually take the form of periods of mutual gaze, baby and caregiver spending periods of time in eye contact and adult-directed turn-taking, where the adult talks to the baby and leaves spaces for the baby to fill, with sounds or actions. The baby's action is taken as a response and the 'dialogue' continues.

At around six months, as demonstrated in Figure 1.1, the baby is demonstrating some level of intentionality; the beginnings of intentional actions on the environment. Caregivers are reportedly becoming much more selective in their interactions with the baby (Harding 1983). From this stage they interpret only *certain* actions or gestures as meaningful and do their best to see that their babies achieve whatever the caregiver assumes to be the baby's objective. Hence, by accepting only more and more clearly defined behaviours as conveying meaning *and* treating them as communicative, they are shaping, or building in, for the infant, intentional communication; the concept that you can affect other people's behaviour by your own actions or vocalisations. Thus, a transition has taken place from purposeful action on the environment, i.e. intentionality, to intention to transmit some message, which would be intentional communication. At this stage the infant engages in true turn-taking interactions with caregivers.

As with cognitive intentionality, communicative intentionality seems to develop in stages. This is not an uncontentious area, but some of the contradictions seem to be over terminology rather than substance. For example, Bruner (1981) proposes three types of early intentional communication:

- initiation for behaviour regulation;
- initiation for social interaction; and
- initiation for joint attention.

Behaviour regulators, which are communicative acts used to regulate the behaviour of other people in order to get things or experiences or to prevent them, seem to be analogous to 'proto-imperatives' as described by Bates *et al.* (1975). Initiations for social interaction would appear to correspond to the communicative intentions with respect to interaction with a partner which Tronick (1981) suggests are established by six months. This seems to be a little earlier (perhaps two months) than Bruner would support. If we conceptualise these as 'person-directed actions' and the behaviour regulators as a complex type of 'object-directed actions' (e.g. Sugarman 1983), both can be classed as perlocutions.

Initiations for joint attention are communicative acts used to direct the communicative partner's attention with the aim of sharing the focus of an entity or event as opposed to obtaining something. For Camaioni (1993) only these initiations are genuinely intentional communication. According to this model, behaviour regulators can be viewed as a type of 'tool use', with the other person as the tool used to obtain for the learner the desired object or outcome. Initiation for social interaction would be classified as a social rather than intentional communicative act. This is a complex issue which has a bearing on the way we work on communication skills with people with profound learning disabilities. On the one hand we would support the valuing of pre-intentional or unintentional communication (see Chapter 2, this volume, and the National Joint Committee for the Communicative Needs of Persons with Severe Disabilities 1992) as necessary if the individual is to become an intentional communicator (e.g. Newson 1979). However, our own experience suggests that it is over-optimistic to anticipate the development of initiations for joint attention once initiations for social interaction have been established in individuals with profound multiple disabilities (Barber *et al.* 1995).[2]

Communicative intent can only ever be a theoretical construct, inferred from behaviour, but, as can be seen from the above discussion, these behavioural criteria can be set at somewhat different levels. It is probably true to say that our criteria have become more stringent since the publication of the first edition of this book. As a result, we want to emphasise the importance of the various points along the route towards intentional communication: contingency awareness, goal-directed behaviour, behaviour regulators, initiations for social interaction etc. However, we want to view the illocutionary stage as requiring something more, suggesting that the learner sees the communication partner as a partner, a person whose interest can be engaged and directed. This would seem to require initiations for joint attention, or, to use Bates *et al.*'s (1975) terminology, 'proto-declaratives' or more sophisticated behaviour regulators where the other person's attention has to be drawn to the desired object by the learner prior to indication that it is being requested. Perhaps only these are properly regarded as proto-imperatives (Bates *et al.* 1975). It is also likely that sophisticated initiations for social interaction, such as gaining attention and then greeting, come into this intentional category.

Stephenson and Linfoot (1996) neatly summarise the criteria that Bates and others (e.g. Bates *et al.* 1975, Harding 1982, 1984, Sugarman 1983) have described for communicative acts to be deemed intentional:

- non-verbal behaviours coordinating object-directed actions with people-directed actions,
- persistence until the (inferred) desired goal is achieved,
- repair, i.e. repetition or modification of strategies if the correct goal is not achieved,
- satisfaction on achievement of inferred goal.

From the infant's perspective, he or she has from about four and a half months been using a 'reach-for-real', that is, reaching for something within reach in order to get hold of it. The baby's actions on objects may be interpreted by others as having communicative content, but not as being intentional. Subsequent to this, the baby starts to coordinate actions on objects with actions on people, through the stages described above, using initiations for social interaction and behaviour regulators. These behaviours are treated by others as being intentional communication, though, as we have seen from the discussion above, they probably do not strictly meet these criteria. As the baby starts to incorporate attempts to direct the attention of others into these communicative acts we can start to view them as intentional communication. The reach-for-real continues, of course, but the baby also uses a 'reach-for-signal', reaching for something which is out of reach. By incorporating looking from the desired object to the adult and back again into the reach-for-signal, the baby communicates to the adult that he wants the thing he is reaching for and knows that the adult can obtain it for him (proto-imperative), or that he wishes to direct the attention of the adult towards something of interest in order to share this experience (proto-declarative).

In the next stage these proto-imperatives and proto-declaratives would also incorporate a vocalisation. For example (proto-imperative), the baby reaches with an open hand gesture towards a banana in the middle of the table, looks from it to you repeatedly and says 'Uh! Uh! Uh!' until the adult gives her a piece of the banana. The proto-declarative works in a rather different way. For example, the baby reaches, or, later, points to the family cat who has jumped on to the table and says 'dah!', looking back and forth from the cat to the adult until the adult turns to look at the cat and acknowledges their shift in attention, perhaps by saying 'Oh! Naughty cat!' Hence, the proto-declarative can be defined as using an object or event to gain joint attention with the adult or other communication partner. Once this development has been achieved, babies are more active, directive and clearly intentional partners in interactions, being able to direct others' attention to things about which they want to communicate.

The use of proto-imperatives and proto-declaratives starts at around ten months. In the following month or two, these two functions diversify further to enable the child to communicate a wide range of communicative functions to people in their environment. These functions will be discussed in some detail in the third and fourth chapters of this book. From around 12 to 15 months, of course, these functions start to be communicated as words, though the use of gesture for communication does continue.

From 15 or 18 months, children and their caregivers engage in joint action routines (Snyder-McLean *et al.* 1984). These are frameworks for joint attention or joint action, formulated routines, based around caregiving or play, engaged in first by adult and child or adult and children, but later by *declarative language.*

small groups of children on their own. In the early routines the adult comments on the child's actions, thus mapping appropriate language on to what the child is doing. The sequences also provide an opportunity for the child to try out a wide range of communicative functions in a familiar and facilitative context. At this point it is clear that the findings of the two approaches have merged. From this sociolinguistic, socio-cultural approach, we have seen that the baby becomes an increasingly active and directive partner in communication, with progressively less of the burden of interpretation falling on the adult. The young child is showing increasingly sophisticated ways of communicating, from looking to gesture, to gesture plus vocalisation, to words (or signs or symbols), and, finally, it can be seen that the child is able to do increasingly varied things with this skill of communication.

The information gathered from the two more recent approaches to communication development can now be drawn together as an initial stage in planning a sequence for intervention. Some of the points can be implemented immediately in their own right, others will form the subject matter of later chapters.

First, and most obviously, it must be ensured that all learners are given a diversity of experiences to enable them to develop a range of schemes for acting on the environment. Some early work on the relationship between sensori-motor cognition and the development of communication was carried out by Kahn (1984). The development of social interaction and interest in other people, leading to the desire to initiate for joint attention, is also crucial. Two recent approaches that have addressed this somewhat neglected area are 'intensive interaction' (e.g. Nind and Hewett 1994) and Ware's work on responsive environments (e.g. Ware 1996).

The transition from actions relating to self to actions relating to objects and people seems to be particularly problematic for individuals with profound and multiple handicaps. Individually tailored and highly salient environmental feedback from small actions may facilitate this development. This approach has been well documented by Schweigert (Schweigert 1989, Schweigert and Rowland 1992). On the part of parents, teachers and other significant people in the language learner's environment, there is a need to develop sensitivity in order to recognise the point where the learner appears to have developed intentionality, and then to start shaping intentional communication. An assessment tool and intervention methods appropriate to this stage form the content of the following chapter.

The establishment of intentional communication is, of course, just a beginning. In addition to working with individuals, it is necessary to consider how to foster the use of communication in everyday settings, at home, in social and educational centres or workshops, at school or college and in the wider community. It cannot be assumed that skills taught in one setting will automatically generalise to other contexts. This needs to be planned for and involves a consideration of very general strategies for promoting communication which will be discussed in the third chapter. In moving towards the communication of semantic roles and the eventual use and understanding of single words, it is important to provide input to help learners encode their cognitive experiences. A detailed approach to teaching first meanings will be presented in Chapter 5.

An assessment leading to an early communication curriculum, which provides a foundation for all the ideas expressed in this book, will form the penultimate section. Amongst these chapters, which are arranged roughly in a developmental sequence, there should be some assessment and intervention ideas to meet the needs of any 'communicators before speech'. The book ends with a step beyond the title into the communicative use of language. This chapter has been written especially for the book. Its authors demonstrate how many of the principles described in the earlier chapters can be applied to people using spoken (or otherwise conveyed) language albeit at a range of levels.

Notes

1 A protoword is the individual's own consistent pattern of sounds which stands for a person, object, action or event but is not the same as the adult word. See also Crystal (1976), Owens (1984) and Nelson (1973).
2 A useful paper by Stephenson and Linfoot (1996) continues this discussion with particular reference to the acquisition of use of graphic symbols.

Chapter 2

The Affective Communication Assessment: ACA

When given a taste of salad cream Louise reacts. To an observer, most of her responses to the taste are centred around her face. Her mouth, and especially her tongue, become more active. Her tongue seems to push the salad cream forwards, lip activity increases, as does the movement of her eyes, and a slight frown appears. On a second presentation of the salad cream her lips close to prevent the spoon from entering her mouth.

However, when Louise is given chocolate sauce she responds quite differently. Again her eye activity increases, as does the activity around her mouth, but in this instance her mouth movement is different. Rather than pushing the sauce away she appears to be spreading it around her mouth. In fact, on a second presentation she readily accepts the spoon full of chocolate sauce.

How do we conclude that Louise likes the chocolate sauce and dislikes the salad cream?

Our assessment suggests that she is functioning at a stage of pre-intentional communication and it is we who interpret her responses to stimuli and place meaning on them. When she is given salad cream to taste she reacts by frowning and increasing her tongue, lip and eye movements and we interpret this as conveying, 'I don't like it'. Louise is not intentionally communicating that she does not like it. She is simply reacting to salad cream itself. On the other hand, we can recognise from her behaviours that she likes the chocolate sauce. It is quite possible for us to interpret these responses and place consistent communicative meaning on them.

Pre-intentional communication

For years, teachers, speech and language therapists and psychologists have struggled to understand and apply appropriate assessment and intervention strategies for those who function at a very early stage of communication. They may be young infants with some form of communication delay, but a high proportion are children and adults who have severe learning difficulties which are often combined with sensory and physical disabilities. Results of a survey by Leeming *et al.* (1979) indicated that just over a quarter (26.5 per cent) of pupils with severe learning difficulties are not yet imitating single words. Until recently there has been little in existence to sensitise teachers and other professionals to the level of functioning of these pupils, and adults with similar needs. Of course, detailed knowledge of the child, or adult, is important and provides much information, but difficulties have arisen in utilising this information to plan subsequent teaching intervention strategies.

A need was identified, initially in a school context, to develop a sensitive assessment for such pupils which would inform intervention. At the point when this work was carried out there was little available research on the early communicative development of children with severe learning difficulties. Our theoretical background, therefore, has necessarily incorporated findings of studies of normally developing infants. The works of Bates (1976), McLean and Snyder-McLean (1978), Snow (1972) and Thoman (1981) have been of significant value. It was felt important to examine social interaction prior to the establishment of intentional communication. Also, we were concerned with the relationship between this and cognitive development. Finally, we needed suggestions for intervention strategies.

Thoman (1981) identified the notion of affective communication where the adult interprets and places meaning on the infant's responses to the environment. Bates' (1976) theory of pre-intentional communication is concerned with children who have not yet reached sensori-motor stage 4, particularly in the areas of means for obtaining a desired environmental event, object-related schemes and the development of visual pursuit and permanence of objects. (For further information on sensori-motor stages see Coupe O'Kane and Levy 1996, Dunst 1980, and Uzgiris and Hunt 1975.)

These theoretical principles formed the foundation for the Affective Communication Assessment (ACA) devised by Coupe *et al.* (1985). Although speculative in concept, the data obtained from the ACA opens up channels for teaching and monitoring development.

The Affective Communication Assessment (ACA)

Given that the child or adult with SLD exhibits a plausible range of behaviours, for example facial expressions and body movements, it is likely that these will regularly occur in response to certain external stimuli. For the person who is functioning at a pre-intentional level, for reasons discussed in Chapter 1, it is important for communicative partners to be sensitive to these responses, to attach meaning to them and to respond as if they were a communicative signal. Thus a two-way process of communication can be facilitated which will incorporate some consistent responses to the person's feelings of like, dislike, want and reject. Through observations of the person's behaviours it is possible for the communicative partner to identify those consistent repertoires of behaviours which express feelings and responses. This information can then be utilised to draw up and implement relevant and specific programmes of intervention.

To assess affective communication we are essentially concerned with interpreting or placing communicative meaning on individuals' responses to a variety of internal and external stimuli. Sensitive interpretation is necessary and we have concentrated on four crucial meanings: like, dislike, want and reject, which seem to be reliably identified (Coupe O'Kane 1994). Of course many variations and extremes can be interpreted, as can other meanings such as distressed, hungry, tired, frustrated, surprised and so on (Izard 1978, Ricks 1979). Throughout this stage of pre-intentional communication a developmental sequence can be taken into account which progresses through three levels:

Level 1 (pre-intentional): reflexive level

Social significance is assigned by the communicative partner, who is generally familiar, to a small range of very early behaviours, sounds and reflexes produced in response to a limited range of internal and external stimuli. The person may receive and orient to input from all available sensory channels. Communicative partners tend to respond instinctively to the person's behaviours and attend to the relationship rather than the caregiving activity, e.g. intense periods of eye-to-eye, face-to-face contact. The person is more likely to orient to events which are controlled by another person.

Level 2 (pre-intentional): reactive level

Social significance is assigned by the communicative partner to repertoires of changes in behaviour, reactive behaviours, produced in response to a wide range of stimuli. These include events and people within the environment and the person is receiving and distinguishing input from all available sensory channels (McLean and Snyder-McLean 1987). The communicative partner tends to concentrate on aspects of the caregiving activity and, within a turn-taking interaction, the person is encouraged to fill a turn with increasing vocalisation and movement of the head, body and hands. The communicative partner will also follow the person's line of visual regard. At this level, the person will respond to some familiar, non-verbal communication by the communicative partner such as following their line of regard, and begins to respond to affective messages such as tone of voice, facial expression.

Level 3 (pre-intentional): proactive level

Repertoires of behaviour become signals to the communicative partner who then assigns communicative intent and meaning. Communicative partners become increasingly selective in the behaviours they respond to. They still respond to vocalisations but also looking and reaching behaviours. First, they interpret the 'behaviour as an "intention" to carry out some "action"' and secondly they interpret the behaviour as 'trying to "find out about" something' (Bruner 1977). The communicative partner shapes the person towards intentional communication and tends to reference an object, person or event in close proximity. At this level, efforts are made to physically explore and act on the environment and the reach is for real. The general focus of attention shifts from caregiving activities towards a focus on objects and toys. The person can now abstract meaning from the adult's intonational patterns, voice and facial expressions.

Whilst the ACA was initially developed as a tool for guiding us to determine stimuli which might elicit strong positive and negative responses from children, it was quickly seen as an appropriate tool for use with adults. Information gained will thus provide the basis for extending the person's repertoire of affective communication and lead towards intentional signalling. Indeed, through assessing the person in such detail it is possible to accumulate much information about their responses to a wide range of stimuli. These stimuli should take into account all sensory channels, that is auditory, visual, tactile, taste, smell as well as the environment itself. With knowledge of the setting conditions and systematic observation, responses can be sensitively interpreted, and further observational checks can be made to determine the pattern, frequency and consistency of these behaviours. From this wealth of information predictions can be made regarding the person's repertoire of affective communication, and appropriate programmes of intervention can be planned.

The ACA has supported the basis for much development for teachers and speech and language therapists, e.g. the Redway School (Latham and Miles 1997) and the Severe Communication Impairment Outreach Projects in Australia (Bloomberg and West 1996), where the range of communicative interpretations at the pre-intentional stage of development have subsequently influenced both assessment and intervention. Discussion of its use in combination with cognitive and social assessment can be found in Goldbart (1994).

ACA stage 1: observation

An individualised set of stimuli and experiences to which the person is already known to respond are identified in discussion with familiar people. Using the Observation Recording Sheet (Figure 2.1), these stimuli are presented in turn and any responses noted using either the categories of behaviour listed or others, as appropriate to the individual. This may require video recording or joint observation by two people. At the same time, the adult interprets the meaning thought to be conveyed by the person in response to each stimulus. These can usually be understood as 'I want' / 'I don't want', or 'I like' / 'I don't like'. However, we have also interpreted a neutral response along with others such as surprise.

During this initial stage, as many observations of the responses as possible, to as wide a variety of stimuli as possible, should be collected. It is important to ensure that the person is alert and comfortable and that optimum time of day, the context and so on are considered. A period of time must be allowed between the presentation of successive stimuli, and, for many people with severe learning difficulties and severe sensory impairment, it is necessary to allow time for the stimulus to be registered in order subsequently to observe a response.

Stimuli can be presented twice in succession, with a pause in between to see, for instance, whether the second presentation is rejected though the first was accepted in ignorance of its taste or smell.

ACA OBSERVATION Recording Sheet NAME:		STIMULI												DATE:				
HEAD	Turn - R/L U/D																	
	Activity ↑↓																	
	Rotating																	
	Other																	
FACE	Frown																	
	Smile																	
	Anguish																	
MOUTH	Activity ↑↓																	
	Open/close																	
	Tongue activity ↑↓																	
	Contact																	
EYES	Activity ↑↓																	
	Open/close																	
	Gaze																	
	Localise/search																	
HANDS	Activity ↑↓																	
	Finger activity ↑↓																	
	Contact																	
ARMS	Reaching																	
	Activity ↑↓																	
LEGS	Activity ↑↓																	
BODY	Activity ↑↓																	
VOCALISATION	Utterance																	
	Cry																	
	Laugh																	
	Other																	
AFFECTIVE COMMUNICATION **Interpretation of behaviour**																		

↑ = increasing　　↓ = decreasing　　R = right　L = left　U = up　D = down

Coupe *et al.* 1985

Figure 2.1　Observation Recording Sheet

ACA stage 2: identification

Having collated and interpreted observations of the responses to a variety of stimuli, it is important to check for the consistency and quality of the behaviours. From the stage 1 Observation Recording Sheet it is possible to go on to identify the strongest responses of like, dislike, want and reject, and thus gain further, more detailed information through the Identification Recording Sheet (Figure 2.2). This Identification Recording Sheet should be used by:

1. selecting the strongest responses;
2. listing those behaviours exhibited;
3. re-presenting the stimuli and contexts to which the person exhibits strong responses and other qualitatively similar stimuli to which similar responses might be expected;
4. recording the behaviours;
5. interpreting the responses.

Quite sensitive information can be gathered during this stage of identification in terms of whether certain behaviours or clusters of behaviours are reliably (or fairly reliably) associated with specific interpretation of the person's responses; e.g. Louise responded as she did to several tastes of the salad cream, all of which were interpreted as her disliking the taste. Typically, clusters of responses, e.g. facial expression, head movement and legs pulled up, yield more information than single responses.

ACA stage 3: intervention

At this stage, potentially communicative behaviours have been identified along with the stimuli and settings in which they are likely to occur. It therefore becomes easier to create optimum setting conditions through which the person can communicate effectively, using a predicted repertoire of behaviours. This is also used to sensitise staff and carers so that they can then respond in a relevant and consistent way throughout the day (Ware 1996). Thus, through this shaping process, the frequency of the communicative behaviours is likely to increase. It is essential for opportunities to be presented where the person is in a position to control or have an effect on the environment and the people within it. In this way, the person, however unintentionally, can initiate and respond to communication. The learner receives reliable feedback for their own actions through them being treated as communicative.

Indeed, creating a responsive environment for those who function within these early stages of communicative and intellectual development is crucial, for personal and social development. Ware (1996) stresses the importance of social interaction and turn-taking where the communicative partner should provide opportunities for the person to respond to the actions of others, allowing time to do so, and also give opportunities for them to take the lead in an interaction. There is a good deal of evidence to indicate that caregivers find it more difficult to respond to a child with a disability and are more likely to experience negative or unsatisfying interactions (Ware 1996). However, the information collated through the ACA can greatly assist communicative partners in nurturing more positive and successful interactions.

By extending existing repertoires and capitalising on new behaviours we feel it is possible to generalise and shape the affective communication towards intentional signalling. It is important that intervention lays stress on a two-way process of communication and that a warm, consistent social context is provided. We have found it useful to consider the following seven aspects of interaction with respect to both the person and the communicative partner.

1. Vocalisation: e.g. respond to the person's vocalisations; say their name using different vocal tones and modes such as whispering, calling or singing.
2. Facial expression: e.g. react to a personal interpretation of the individual's facial expressions; initiate smiling, laughing, frowning and so on, looking for responses.

ACA Identification Recording Sheet	STIMULI											DATE:						
NAME:																		
AFFECTIVE COMMUNICATION Interpretation of behaviour																		

Coupe *et al.* 1985

Figure 2.2 Identification Recording Sheet

3. Body proximity: e.g. generally it is important for the teacher or carer to be close to the child or adult when interacting, particularly with their face near and clearly visible. The person's general body tone, in terms of tension and relaxation, is a useful source of information. However, we need to be sensitive to the individual's feelings about personal space.

4. Eye contact/orientation of visual regard: this needs to be considered when initiating interaction, responding or introducing an object into the interaction; e.g. if necessary, the person's head or face can be moved to aid eye contact with the communicative partner, or joint regard of a relevant object.

5. Physical contact: this can be useful but the extent to which it is a part of an interaction will depend on knowledge of the person and their apparent likes and dislikes; e.g. touch or stroke the person's face or body, prompt the person to touch the communicative partner.

6. Imitation: e.g. imitate the person's own sounds or facial expressions back to them during an interaction.

7. Turn-taking: e.g. give the person time to respond to the communicative partner who can, in turn, respond with an imitated or novel behaviour.

The data collated from the ACA could also be utilised to foster and develop the caregiver interactive style described by Nind and Hewett (1994), where caregivers, as communicative partners, could

- mediate the physical environment;
- be warm and affectionate;
- touch, rock and hold the person;
- share control of the activity with the person;
- allow selves to be controlled by the person;
- enjoy the interaction;
- allow their style of interpersonal behaviour to be modified by the person;
- employ visual regard, mutual gaze, mutual vocalisations, touching etc.;
- exaggerate facial expressions;
- use motherese – slower, simpler speech;
- verbalise in short bursts, allowing gaps for the person's coos and murmurs;
- believe that the person is capable of reciprocal communication and act accordingly;
- use games and playful ritualised routines;
- synchronise tempo with that of the person;
- watch, wait, and hold self ready to act at the appropriate time;
- keep the person's level of arousal and involvement within certain optimum limits;
- balance the agenda with that of the person;
- respond contingently to the behaviour of the person;
- be very sensitive to the person's signals and feedback;
- use imitation, especially of actions regarded as communicative;
- let the person take a turn;
- provide social stimuli;
- adjust their input as the person progresses.

Implementing the ACA

Matt is a year 8 pupil, aged 12. He has profound and multiple learning difficulties, multisensory impairment and significant health care needs. His teacher, Prior (1997), has recently utilised the ACA to assess Matthew and develop an appropriate programme of intervention.

From the ACA (stage 1 and 2) assessment of Matthew (see Figures 2.3, 2.4 and 2.5), it is evident that he is demonstrating extremely strong responses at the first two levels of communicative functioning:

ACA OBSERVATION Recording Sheet ① — NAME: MATT	warm water	cold water	soap lather	loud clap (close)	salt	salad cream	tickle	shaving foam	aftershave	fibre optics	'name'	loud laugh	brush teeth	whisper	chocolate	mustard	sand
HEAD — Turn - R/L U/D	U/D	R-L			U/D												
Activity ↑↓			↓				↑							↓			
Rotating																	
Other																	
FACE — Frown				✓	✓	✓						✓	✓	✓		✓	
Smile	look of pleasure		relaxed														
Anguish		✓					✓										
MOUTH — Activity ↑↓						↑	↑		↑				↑	↑			
Open/close	open	open	open														
Tongue activity ↑↓					sucking ↑											✓	
Contact																	
EYES — Activity ↑↓				↑			↑		↑								
Open/close	open				O/C							O/C	O/C	blink	✓		
Gaze		✓	✓	✓						✓							✓
Localise/search																	
HANDS — Activity ↑↓									↑			↑					
Finger activity ↑↓	↓	none	↑				↑						↑	↑ s		↑	↑
Contact																	
ARMS — Reaching																	
Activity ↑↓	↑↓	pulled away	↑ s						↑				↑				
LEGS — Activity ↑↓																	
BODY — Activity ↑↓																	
VOCALISATION — Utterance		✓	✓		✓	✓			✓								✓
Cry																	
Laugh																	
Other	nice moan						moan					✓		soft moan			
AFFECTIVE COMMUNICATION — Interpretation of behaviour	pleasure	extreme dislike	enjoyment	anxiety	extreme dislike	curiosity – not keen	hard tickle – discomfort		quiet lack of interest		attention	dislike	irritation	attention		anxiety – dislike	some interest

Figure 2.3   Matt's Observation Recording Sheet 1

ACA OBSERVATION Recording Sheet ②
NAME: MATT
STIMULI
DATE: APRIL '97

		lighted match	joss stick	jam	soft jazz	lively jazz	flowers	foot-spa	hand massage	scalp massage	soft music (headphones)	lively music (headphones)	deflating balloon (noise)	inflating balloon (touch)	ball pool	shaving foam	water balloon	
HEAD	Turn - R/L U/D										R	R						
	Activity ↑↓													↑				
	Rotating																	
	Other			still				L	head on side	head T-L	gazing							
FACE	Frown			✓	V.R	V.R							✓	✓	✓			
	Smile				RELAXED	RELAXED			V R	V R	R							
	Anguish																	
MOUTH	Activity ↑↓	↑			↑	↑												
	Open/close			close	TWITCH	TWITCH			open	open	open	open						
	Tongue activity ↑↓			✗														
	Contact																	
EYES	Activity ↑↓										↑	very active						
	Open/close				SLEEP								c	o c				
	Gaze	✓		✓		✓			✓	✓								
	Localise/search	some							very brief	very brief								
HANDS	Activity ↑↓																	
	Finger activity ↑↓	↑		sl. wriggle		sl.			↑		NIL	sl. more-ment		↑				
	Contact								enj. this									
ARMS	Reaching																	
	Activity ↑↓	sl. ↑							sl. ↑									
LEGS	Activity ↑↓																	
BODY	Activity ↑↓																	
VOCALISATION	Utterance												✓	✓				
	Cry										LIKE	DISLIKE						
	Laugh																	
	Other			✗					cooing noises	cooing noises	↑	↑						
AFFECTIVE COMMUNICATION Interpretation of behaviour		curiosity but not much interest		not a lot of interest – no sounds	very relaxed pleasure	very relaxed pleasure			very relaxed some eye contact	enjoyed very much	listening – no noises	lots of frowning	soft vocalisation relaxed – like	only looked – for feel – dislike				

Figure 2.4 Matt's Observation Recording Sheet 2

ACA IDENTIFICATION Recording Sheet NAME: **MATT**	STIMULI											DATE: 26 August '97					
	lighted match	jam	soft jazz	lively jazz	hand massage	scalp massage	soft music (headphones)	lively music (headphones)	deflating balloon (noise)	inflated balloon (touch)	warm water	cold water	soap lather	loud clap (close)	salt	salad cream	tickle
Head turn R / L							R	R			↑	√					
Head activity ↑↓										↑			↓		↑		↑
Head (other)					To one side	To one side											
Face frown		√						√	√	√		√		√	√	√	√
Face relaxed			√	√	√	√	√				√		√				
Mouth activity ↑↓	↑		↑	↑											↑		↑
Mouth open / close		c			o	o	o	o				o	o	o			
Eye activity ↑↓							↑	↑ very						↑	↑		↑
Eye open / close			c	c					c	o/c	o					o/c	
Gaze	√	√			√	√						√	√				
Search	√																
Finger activity ↑↓	↑	↑			↑			↑		↑	↑	↓	↑				↑
Arm activity ↑↓	↑				↑						↑	↓	↑				
Utterance									√				√		√	√	
Other (voice)									soft		soft		moan				
AFFECTIVE COMMUNICATION Interpretation of behaviour	curiosity	no interest	very relaxed	very relaxed	relaxed and alert	enjoyment	listening	dislike	interest (like)	dislike / reject	pleasure	dislike / reject	enjoyment	anxiety	dislike	curiosity	discomfort

Figure 2.5   Matt's Identification Recording Sheet

Reflexive level: The assessment has shown clearly how Matthew responds to a variety of stimuli, with some strong responses being shown to warm water and cold water.

Reactive level: Staff have interpreted these responses to mean strong 'like' and 'dislike' and, accordingly, have been able to interpret Matthew's responses to other situations and activities.

From the assessment, the intervention now focuses on the third level:

Proactive level: To develop Matthew's responses of 'like' and 'dislike' and for them to be consistently interpreted as meaning 'more' and 'stop'. Initially, it is intended to build on his strong preference for warm water. From this, staff hope to develop his ability to anticipate the consequence of an enjoyable activity. The continued use of the ACA is seen as an important means of building an extensive profile of Matthew's 'likes' and 'dislikes'.

ACA: A Study of Louise

Louise is a six-year-old child with severe learning difficulties and additional physical and visual impairment. She is also on medication to control epilepsy.

Vision

She is cortically blind, has nystagmus with a left divergent squint and an underdeveloped optic nerve. She responds to light stimulation but her functional vision is very limited.

Hearing

Louise has an acute sense of hearing. She responds positively to vocal and non-vocal sounds. Thus, hearing is a crucial sensory channel for her.

Physical competence

She has hypertonic cerebral palsy and is non-ambulant. Her movements are predominantly involuntary and reflexive in nature. Poor head control and a lack of trunk control inhibit functional position. Active, voluntary control is difficult to accomplish due to her primitive reflexes. Any voluntary movement is limited to head turning to her left (due to asymmetric tonic neck reflex her head turns to her right). This is important to consider as stimuli should be presented to her left. A check needs to be made to determine whether any apparent localising response is actually reflexive or voluntary.

Communication skills

Louise is functioning at a stage of pre-intentional communication. She is an extremely sociable child and it is relatively easy for adults to interpret her likes and dislikes, wants and rejections. Louise uses strong repertoires of facial expressions, vocalisations and body movements. However, because of her sociability and pleasant disposition there is a danger that adults will over-assume her level of functioning; that is, her responses are often interpreted as signals.

Cognition

Louise's extreme physical and visual limitations make it difficult to assess her level of cognitive functioning. Many of her behaviours are reflexive and others link up to stages 1 to 4 in the sensorimotor period (see Uzgiris and Hunt 1975). She has undifferentiated schemes and her basic behaviours incorporate grasping, mouthing, turn to light source.

Discussions with Louise's teacher and nursery nurses enabled us to identify several situations where Louise had strong like or dislike, want or reject responses. By observing her in a structured way using Observation Sheet 1, we wished to obtain an indication of any current repertoires of behaviour which corresponded to these strong feelings. All stimuli were presented to her left side and we expected many of her observable behaviours to be centred around her head.

Observation

When given a taste of salad cream Louise reacted immediately by drawing her face into a wince (recorded as anguish on the left-hand side of the Observation Recording Sheet 1). Her mouth and especially her tongue were seen to become more active (recorded with a vertical arrow in the corresponding places). The tongue activity was apparently an attempt to push the cream forward in her mouth. Lip activity increased and an increase in the rate of eye movement was recorded, along with a slight arm bend. On second presentation of the salad cream, Louise's lips closed before the spoon passed between them. These behaviours were recorded as 'strong dislike' and 'rejection' respectively in the Affective Communication section of the sheet (see Figure 2.6).

On presentation of chocolate sauce, she behaved quite differently; again there was a noticeable increase in eye activity and lip and tongue movement, this time apparently attempting to position the sauce for swallowing. Her facial expression remained passive. Seen alongside the previous presentations of salad cream, Louise's recorded behaviours to the taste of chocolate sauce were quite similar, but the quality of reaction was very different and the chocolate sauce was obviously more welcome. Her response was interpreted to mean 'I like it'.

For a different stimulus, Louise was positioned on a soft floor mat while a member of staff banged her hands on the surface near her head. Louise immediately turned her head. Smiling, she slightly moved her arms, fingers and legs and produced an utterance. Her body also moved to the left. The initial increase in head activity was recorded as a surprise reflex, but subsequent recording showed that her head consistently moved to the left when she vocalised.

On presentation of the smell of her father's aftershave, Louise opened her mouth, and an increase in eye activity was observed. Her facial expression remained passive and this was recorded as a gaze. When after three presentations she had shown the same behaviours it was felt that she had noticed the smell, but that her reaction to it was neutral.

Numerous other stimuli incorporating all senses were presented. These included a staff member sneezing which produced what was interpreted as a 'like' response, involving right-to-left movement of her head, a smile, increase in eye and mouth activity and a vocal utterance similar to that produced in the mat-banging situation. On the recording sheets, after numerous stimuli had been presented, noticeable similarities began to appear, particularly in behaviours involving strong likes and dislikes. In her repertoire of behaviours which showed likes and wants, utterances and head rotations occurred along with smiles and increased eye activity. Her repertoires of behaviours which showed dislikes or rejections involved slight arm and leg flexions, lip closures and appropriate facial expressions of 'frown' and 'anguish'.

Identification

Those repertoires of behaviours which were interpreted as conveying strong likes, dislikes, wants and rejections were checked for consistency. Louise's repertoires of behaviour were listed down the left-

ACA OBSERVATION Recording Sheet / NAME: LOUISE	chocolate sauce	tartare sauce	Space Dust	'Sneeze'	slapping surfaces close by	herb + spice salts	whisper	drink of water	salad cream	garlic granules	mustard	'name'	honey	peanut butter	lemonade	father's aftershave	tickle
HEAD Turn - R/L U/D		L→R	L	R→L	L	L→R	L	L→R	L→R	L→R	L→R	L	U		F	L→R	R→L
Activity ↑↓			↑		surprise		↓		↑		↑	↑	↑	↑			↑
Rotating							√					√					
Other			√		√						back √						
FACE Frown						√											
Smile		√	√	√	√		√					√	√		√		√
Anguish							√		√			√					
MOUTH Activity ↑↓	↑	↑	↑	↑			↑		↑	↑	↑		↑	↑	↑	↑	↑
Open/close	O	C			O	C	O	C	C	C	C	O	O		O	O	O
Tongue activity ↑↓	↑	↑	↑			↑			↑	↑	↑		↑	↑	↑	↑	↑
Contact															√		
EYES Activity ↑↓	↑	↑	↑	↑	↑		↑	↑	↑	↑	↑	↑	↑	↑	↑	↑	↑
Open/close			O + C														
Gaze			√												√	√	
Localise/search	√		√		√			√	√	?	√	√		√			√
HANDS Activity ↑↓					↑			↑				↑	↑				
Finger activity ↑↓					↑										↑		
Contact																	
ARMS Reaching																	√
Activity ↑↓	↑	↑	↑		↑	↑		↑	↑		↑			↑	↑		↑
LEGS Activity ↑↓		↑			↑	↑			↑	↑							↑
BODY Activity ↑↓					↑ L												↑
VOCALISATION Utterance			√	√	√		√					√					√
Cry																	
Laugh					√										√		
Other																	√
AFFECTIVE COMMUNICATION Interpretation of behaviour	like	dislike	aware	strong like	strong like	mild dislike	like	reject	strong dislike	dislike	dislike	like	want	like	like	neutral	strong like

Figure 2.6   Louise's Observation Recording Sheet

hand side of the Identification Recording Sheet (see Figure 2.7). The stimuli which had provoked these reactions, along with other similar stimuli suggested by classroom staff, appeared at the top of the list. The anticipated responses were observed. Furthermore, a consensus of agreement was reached by several observers. As with the initial observations, care was taken with the order of presentations so as to avoid the satiation of one sense (such as taste). Also, periods of settling-down time were given especially after strong reactions to presented stimuli. In this way responses would not intrude on each other. Louise was found to vocalise strongly in situations involving movement when swung from side to side by a staff member, and in the mat-slapping situation vocal utterances were consistently given. These situations appeared to give her strongest 'like' responses. Her most emphatic 'reject' responses occurred in situations where certain smells and tastes were presented to her. Reactions centred around her mouth and arm movements. From the wealth of information gained about Louise's likes, dislikes, wants and rejections, it was possible to determine a strategy of intervention.

Intervention

Once the identification of Louise's repertoire of behaviours had been checked for consistency, strategies of intervention were designed. She was felt to be functioning at the proactive level where social significance could be assigned to the way she reacts to events and people within her environment. Also, Louise's efforts to act on her environment have become signals to adults who can then assign communicative intent. However, as yet she shows no evidence of signalling communicative intentions to others. The information collated enabled us to capitalise on her efforts to act on people and events within her environment and shape those signals towards a stronger, more intentional two-way process of communication. The seven aspects of interaction, identified above, were considered.

Vocalisation

Louise was found to 'like' and enjoy strong physical contact and movement. In these contexts we know that she will vocalise and smile consistently. It was felt important that a strategy should be identified to develop her vocalisation into a 'want' signal. For instance, an adult should hold Louise in her arms and swing her from side to side, then stop. Louise could be predicted to vocalise in response to this, which would be interpreted as 'like'. However, in order to shape this vocalisation towards a communicative signal for 'want', the adult should wait for Louise to vocalise, at which point she will receive a further swing. This same sequence could be generalised to a variety of situations thus; vocalisation would be given a consistent and highly rewarding consequence.

Facial expression

Louise's facial expression is her most effective channel of affective communication, giving as it does a consistent indicator of her likes and dislikes, wants and rejections, particularly in relation to tastes and smells. It is very responsive but of little value in initiating. As previously discussed, on a second presentation of salad cream and other undesirable tastes, Louise pursed her lips so that a further presentation was impossible. This was felt to be a strong 'reject' reaction. Our intervention strategy would be that after Louise had been given an initial taste of, for instance, salad cream, it would be offered a second time, in which case Louise's pre-intentional, or affective but proactive, communicative responses would be interpreted as a refusal. Staff would consistently acknowledge the signal, and hence Louise would have more control over her environment. This experience will provide Louise with feedback which will continue her progression towards intentional communication.

ACA IDENTIFICATION Recording Sheet NAME: LOUISE	STIMULI											DATE:					
	slap mat close to her	water	name	salad cream	swing	honey	whisper name	vigorous tickle	rocking	lift above head	mild drink	garlic granules	father's or dad's aftershave	squeaky toy	torch in eye	sneeze	mustard
Head turn L/R / O/D	R →L	L →R		L →R		R →L		RO-TATE		RO-TATE	L	L →R		R →L		R →L	L →R
Head activity	↑	↑	↑	↑	↑	↑	↑	↑	↓		↑	↑		↑	↑	↑	↑
Frown		√		√								√					√
Smile		√				√				√				√		√	
Mouth activity	↑		↑	↑		↑		↑	↓	↑	↑	↑	↑	↑		↑	↑
Mouth open / close	O	C		C	O	O	O	O		O	O	C	O			O	C
Tongue activity	↑			↑		↑		↑	↓	↑	↑	↑	↑			↑	↑
Eye activity	↑	↑	↑	↑	↑	↑	↑	↑	↓	↑	↑	↑	↓	↑	↑	↑	
Localisation search		√				√	?					√		√	√	√	
Hand activity	↑				↑			↑	↑			↑		↑			↑
Arm activity	↑	↑		↑	↑			↑									
Utterance	↑		√		√			√		√				√		√	
Laugh	√				√			√		√						√	
Leg activity	↑	↑		↑								↑					↑
AFFECTIVE COMMUNICATION Interpretation of behaviour	strong like	reject	like	strong reject	strong like	want	like med. → strong	strong like	like	strong like	want	reject	neutral	like	neutral	like	strong reject

Figure 2.7   Louise's Identification Recording Sheet

Body proximity

Louise cannot control the distance between herself and others. It is important, therefore, to design a pattern of body positioning which allows adults to see and feel her reactions to stimuli. In this way an optimum setting for interaction can be created.

Eye contact

Prior to completing this assessment Louise's vision was considered to be too limited to be considered as a priority for intervention. However, her responses indicate that she has a level of competence which enables her to respond to light sources, moving shapes and the presence of people. Perhaps, as yet, this cannot be considered a priority channel for intervention, but close observation of her responses to visual stimuli should be monitored. Certainly all Louise's communicative partners need to be given this new information.

Physical contact

Although physical contact is difficult for Louise to initiate, it was felt to be most important. Louise is very aware of the presence of an adult. Indeed, because of her strong responses to physical contact and being cuddled, this was felt to be important in eliciting and responding to her 'like' and 'want' responses.

Imitation

Louise vocalises and produces cooing sounds. Whenever possible staff will imitate these vocalisations, giving time for her to respond. This relates very closely to the final aspect of intervention – turn-taking.

Turn-taking

Through vocal play or more physical activity Louise can be taught to establish a more controlled sequence of turn-taking. While being pulled to a sitting position by her hands Louise shows an increase in shoulder movements. This can be established as a turn-taking play routine where, after a few sequences of pulling into a sitting position and lowering again, the adult can pause to allow Louise to move her shoulders as her turn in the routine. Similarly, a play routine can be established when Louise is lying down where the adult bangs on the mat near to her head. Louise will be predicted to vocalise and laugh in this situation and these behaviours can be utilised as Louise's turn.

A parent's perspective

Louise's mother felt that for the first time they have a summary of her abilities in writing.

> I feel as if we have known this all along but the Affective Communication Assessment has brought it to the forefront. It will help to explain her level to family and friends. It is true that a lot of people expect too much of her; now we can explain about interpreting her behaviour.

Louise's father works away during the week and he has seen the progress which, although slight, is noticeable. To capture her on video and have the assessment documented is important.

She has come on more this year than any other year. As far as I can see, this assessment must have helped to sensitise all the staff who work with her to get the best out of her. She responds so much more. I have always been able to get a smile out of Louise but now she can shout. She joins in with people around her and it matters, it helps with friends and family because now we know how to get a response from Louise and how to interpret it. We can tell them what to do with her to get a good response. Before, friends always used to pick her up and talk to her but they did not get the response which they are getting now.

Louise has a wide range of likes and wants but few dislikes. As these are mainly to do with food, her mother felt that it was difficult always to respond to the dislikes and rejects because she must eat. However, where she can she gives Louise a choice. 'For instance, we know that Louise doesn't like water, so we might give her this, and if she doesn't want it, we'll give her a cup of tea instead.' The seven considerations for intervention have helped her greatly:

I can now incorporate imitation with turn-taking, using her own vocalisations. When she shouts, I shout and vice versa. We are using eye contact, physical contact, body proximity and facial expression. Bedtime is good for this as it is the one time of day when we are alone together. This is a lovely time where I spend ages using all aspects of communication.

In planning where to go next, Louise's mother felt confident:

Now if I am not in the room with Louise she shouts, whereas before she would just lie or sit and be quite happy where I put her. She is initiating much more and not just responding. I think she is definitely trying to join in; for instance, if I talk to her sister Emily, Louise will join in the conversation. I know that she is not intentionally communicating anything yet. It is still a matter of other people having to interpret everything for her. With her being so disabled her main form of signal can only be vocal or facial expression. We want more of this and can now see how it can be developed.

Louise's mother felt that all the parents of those with profound and multiple disabilities would be keen for such an assessment to be used with their children. A workshop incorporating the use of videoed observations of her daughter had assisted her understanding of affective communication, and she promoted this as a means of enabling other parents to understand and see the value of affective communication, In fact, whatever the child's level of development, she felt it would be helpful for parents if video was used during assessments. In this way parents and staff could see how each child had improved. Indeed, for Louise: 'It seems to just all slot together now. Just like a jigsaw puzzle and we have captured it all on video.'

Chapter 3

Communication for a purpose

In the preceding chapters, much of the discussion has involved the assessment of children or adults at very early stages in the development of communication and suggestions about the content of intervention programmes appropriate to their needs. However, this chapter and the one that follows are concerned rather more with the *how* than the *what* of teaching communication skills. In other words, we will try to address some of the ideas and approaches we have found useful in developing the skills and strategies a student needs to transmit successfully some message to another person or persons. In doing so we will also be making frequent reference to an approach to assessment which fits neatly with these ideas; the Pre-Verbal Communication Schedule (Kiernan and Reid 1987a, 1987b). Components of this approach are also represented in the latter two stages of the Early Communication Assessment (see Chapter 6).

In the discussion in Chapter 1 of the sociolinguistic approach to language acquisition, it was argued that children will only learn to use language if they have a reason to do so; that is, if they have something about which to communicate or if the communication is embedded in something which is enjoyable. We have extrapolated from this a general principle which underpins our whole approach to intervention: we are more likely to be successful in teaching an adult or child to communicate if what we teach is functional or has some value for that individual.

To see whether this approach to teaching is embodied in currently available approaches to language intervention we need to examine commonly used sources and materials. The majority of commercially available language teaching kits and programmes and language intervention studies published in the last 30 years are based on the language acquisition theories of either Chomsky (the grammarian account) or Skinner (the behaviourist account), or a combination of the two (see Goldbart 1985, Harris 1984a). Where both approaches were employed, teaching techniques were usually influenced by the behavioural approach and the selection of target behaviours by the grammarian approach. Both of these approaches have been criticised for their focus on theory and their neglect of actual child language data in their development of theories of language acquisition (McLean and Snyder-McLean 1978). It was claimed in Chapter 1 that these intervention approaches had not proved to be particularly successful. We will now address that claim, and the studies themselves, in greater detail.

From the mid-1960s to the late 1970s, a considerable number of papers on language intervention with children showing a wide range of difficulties were published. These covered children with hearing loss (e.g. Bennett 1973), language delay (e.g. Hedge and Gierut 1979, Leonard 1974), language disorder (e.g. Gray and Fygetakis 1968, Zwitman and Sonderman 1979), autism (e.g. Carr *et al.* 1975, Hargrave and Swisher 1975) and severe learning disabilities (e.g. Bricker and Bricker 1974, Halle *et al.* 1979). We will concern ourselves mainly with those involving children diagnosed as having either autism or severe learning disabilities.

Despite great differences in the behaviourist (Skinnerian) and the grammarian (Chomskian) approaches to language acquisition, the majority of the intervention studies based on these approaches have certain features in common. The most obvious of these is that the focus of interest of the whole intervention is often on what happens in the immediate teaching context. This can be seen by looking at the extent to which these studies look for generalisation to spontaneous use; that is, whether targets which are achieved during teaching are subsequently used outside the teaching context. In only 59.8 per cent of 39 studies of autistic children, 58.3 per cent of 12 studies of children with language disorder, language delay or hearing loss, and 36.4 per cent of 55 studies of children with severe learning difficulties, was an attempt made to see whether generalisation had been achieved (Goldbart 1985). This difference between studies of children with and without severe learning difficulties suggests that researchers working with subjects who had learning difficulties had lower expectations of generalisation than those working with other subjects.

Even in those studies which have been influenced by the grammarian perspective, the teaching techniques are drawn mainly from behaviour modification. These techniques include shaping, modelling and imitation, prompting and fading, forward and backward chaining and training and the use of tangible reinforcers. Whilst such techniques are highly applicable to much teaching, in particular within a special education framework (Porter 1986), the way they have been used in language teaching tends to limit the opportunities for conversational interchange and true communication. Typically, the teacher or therapist presents a verbal and/or a visual (such as a picture or object) stimulus and the learner is required to produce a predetermined response, often a label, for example: 'What's this?' 'Drink.' 'Yes, drink.' Thus, there is a non-maintenance of communication. There is not very far you can go with that conversation!

If we examine the reinforcement used in many of these studies, there is often little relation between the reinforcer used and the language being taught; for example: 'What's this?' 'Drink.' 'Yes, drink'; reinforcement – a piece of apple. Even if social praise is used as a reinforcer, the options for conversation are limited: 'What's this?' 'Ball.' 'Yes, good talking!' What is the appropriate 'next turn' in this conversation?

There seems, furthermore, to be an excessive concern with the teaching of object labels. This assumes that once the learner has acquired a particular word for a particular use, it will automatically be used in all other relevant contexts. For example, if we teach the student to label a cup as 'drink', this will subsequently be used for requesting a drink, commenting that another student has a drink and telling someone else to finish their drink. We do not have evidence that this is true of delayed or impaired language learners, and, as Mittler and Berry (1977) suggest, this excessive teaching of object labels may in fact negatively affect language learning.

Selection of target behaviours is determined by the perspective of language acquisition adopted by the researcher. In the case of a Skinnerian approach, this may even be by task-analysing a word (e.g. Lovaas 1977). For example: to teach 'mummy', the child might be taught to say the sounds *m, u* and *y*; these are then chained together to make 'mummy'. It is hard to envisage how the learner is to make the connection between this string of sounds and, for example, the person who puts them to bed at night.

Despite what we might expect, the Chomskian approach, with its emphasis on grammatical structures, did not always lead to a more sensible selection of targets. For example, the emphasis on teaching object labels, which will be discussed further in the following chapter. Furthermore, since English is a notoriously irregular language, attempts to highlight grammatical categories sometimes created major difficulties for researchers. For instance, it would have been confusing to teach irregular past tense forms. Hence 'This is the baker, today he bakes, yesterday he baked. This is the flier, today he flies, yesterday he flied'!

By 1978, the success of these studies in facilitating development of language and communication was being questioned. For example, Guess *et al.* (1978), who had invested much time and energy in such studies, were saying: 'Little is known about the extent to which spontaneous functional language can be taught to mentally handicapped children', and Rutter (1980), in relation to children with autism: 'It is clear from a host of studies that operant treatments have often been followed by improved speech production, but have they specifically influenced the development of language in the sense of a symbolic code that allows the generation of normal messages?' It seems, therefore, that despite a large number of studies, no clearly successful route to increasing spontaneous language and communication had been established.

As a response, and as a result of research on language acquisition in normally developing children, the last ten to fifteen years have seen several attempts to approach language intervention in more ecologically valid ways (e.g. Campbell and Stremel-Campbell 1986, Halle 1984, Martin *et al.* 1984, Warren and Bambara 1989). These studies have been concerned with making more use of the language learner's social environment and drawing more on what is known about normally developing children's language acquisition and communicative interactions. To do this we need to know more about the existing language environments of delayed or impaired communicators. The studies of interactions between people with learning disabilities and others in their environment fall into three categories: studies of parents and their young children, of teachers and students in the classroom and of adults with learning disabilities and staff in residential settings.

There is much controversy surrounding research on the language input received by young children with severe learning disabilities. Rondal (1976) finds that, in most respects, the language of mothers to their children with Down's syndrome is the same as that of mothers to children developing normally, matched on mean length of utterance. In contrast, Matsuo-Muto and Kato (1994) found mothers' utterances to their children with Down's syndrome to be less responsive, to be more negative and to contain fewer nouns signifying objects. Conti-Ramsden (1997) is a useful source for discussion of both the contradictory findings and methodological problems in the area.

There are two studies of classroom interactions, which yield quite similar results. The first is by Beveridge and Hurrell (1980), who recorded teachers' responses to 2,000 initiations from four children in each of ten classes in SLD schools. The responses they observed are given in Table 3.1, and it can be seen that the most common responses that the children receive are 'brief acknowledgement', 'ignoring' and 'simple immediate response'. Within these interactions, therefore, there is very little that is going to maintain conversation. The only category which seems to be truly facilitative in terms of providing an opportunity for teaching or practising language or communication is 'verbalisation expanding the child's idea or content' which is the response to about one in six of the children's initiations.

Table 3.1   Teachers' responses to children's initiations

Responses which did not maintain the interaction	%	Responses which maintained the interaction	%
Ignoring: not seeing/hearing initiation, no response	23.3	Simple immediate response, inviting further interaction, e.g. 'Yes' or 'Good'	20.3
Brief acknowledgement, but then moves away or redirects attention	33.4	Verbalisation expanding the child's idea or content	15.6
Negative verbalisation: 'Stop it' or 'Go away'	1.7	Verbalisation changing the child's idea or content	1.5
No verbalisation and interaction not maintained, but positive gesture or action	2.8	Continuous referral, e.g. 'Come and show me when you've done it'	0.5
Negative non-verbal, e.g. smack or rough removal of an object	0.05	Non-verbal but positive action or gesture which maintains the interaction, e.g. joins in game, smiles	0.85

(Adapted from Beveridge and Hurrell 1980)

Similarly, Goldbart (1985), looking at school-age children with severe learning difficulties and pre-schoolers with and without severe learning difficulties (five in each group), recorded the number and success of initiations directed by children to classroom staff in a time period. Successful initiations were those after which the child received undivided attention from the adult (the figures are presented in Table 3.2). Although the differences are not large, the children with severe learning difficulties appear to initiate less frequently and less successfully than typically developing pre-schoolers.

Table 3.2   Number and success of initiations by children towards adults

Children	Number (1)	Number (1*)	Per cent (1*)
Pre-school SLD	79	19	24.1
School age SLD	79	20	25.3
'Normal' pre-school	91	36	39.6

(1) = Initiation directed to adult
(1*) = Initiation receiving undivided adult attention

(Adapted from Goldbart 1985)

A study of young adults with SLD in a hospital setting by Prior *et al.* (1979) had similar results. They found that staff used instruction-type language most frequently and conversation-type language least frequently. Again, there was a high frequency of staff ignoring initiations from residents. Similarly, Pratt *et al.'s* (1976) study of a large institution for 'mentally handicapped adults' showed that staff talking to residents used controlling language more often than informative language. This is important because Tizard *et al.* 1972) found that speech types defined as informative were better for residents' language development than those defined as controlling.

All these studies suggest that if we want to promote the kind of interactions which we know to facilitate language development in normally developing children, we need to think about ways of restructuring the interactions between people with impaired communication skills and their teachers and carers. Interestingly, Felce and his co-workers (Felce *et al.* 1987) found staff in small community houses significantly more responsive to residents' appropriate behaviours than those working in institutions or larger community settings. The reasons for this are unclear and it seems likely that obtaining wide-ranging changes would necessitate two areas of planning. First, the target behaviours identified for individuals' language and communication programmes and the contexts chosen for teaching must reflect the purposes for which language is used. A second aim must be to engineer more opportunities for children and adults with severe learning difficulties to experience the kind of interactions typically developing toddlers have with their caregivers, albeit in age-appropriate ways. This would include more opportunities to affect and control their environment. In order to do these things, we need to know the purposes to which language is put, in particular in interactions between young or impaired communicators and others. What do we need to be able to *do* with the communication skills we have? How can these functions of communication be best portrayed? A detailed account of this area of the study of communication (pragmatics) with particular reference to work with adults is given in the final chapter. We will focus here on one aspect of pragmatics: communicative intentions.

In Chapter 1 of this volume, typically developing children's acquisition of the earliest communicative functions, proto-imperative and proto-declarative, was described. These are conveyed using gestures and/or vocalisations. The range of functions gradually expands and, by the time children are using a few single words (12–18 months), these are used to convey a diverse set of communicative functions. Many different authors have produced broadly similar taxonomies of these early functions and those expressed at later stages of language acquisition (e.g. Dore 1977, Halliday 1975, Roth and Speckman 1984a, 1984b). These provide a useful way of identifying what children can do with their language skills. Definitions of Halliday's functions, based on his longitudinal study of one child, are given in Table 3.3. Similar use of functions has been described in people with severe learning difficulties by Cirrin and Rowland (1985, re adolescents) and Kiernan and Reid (1987b, re children, adolescents and young adults). There is considerable agreement between the three sets of categories as shown in Table 3.4, although Halliday's list extends into rather more advanced communicative functions (for further discussion see Kiernan *et al.* 1987 and for discussion of more advanced functions, or 'intentions', see the final chapter of this book).

Table 3.3 Halliday's functions

Instrumental	–	satisfying one's needs
Regulatory	–	controlling others' behaviour
Interaction	–	you and me, greetings, names
Personal	–	awareness of self
Heuristic	–	seeking information
Imaginative	–	pretend and make believe
Informative	–	telling others things

The first four functions develop before the later three.

(Halliday 1975)

If we want impaired communicators to develop truly effective communication skills they will need to have the opportunity to communicate, at least, all the functions described by Kiernan and Reid. The need to restructure the environments of people with severe learning difficulties, as outlined above, is part of this process.

Table 3.4 Communicative functions according to three different authors

Kiernan and Reid (1987a, 1987b)	Cirrin and Rowland (1985)	Halliday (1975)
Seeking attention	Directs attention to self	Personal
Needs satisfaction	Requests object	Instrumental
Needs satisfaction	Requests action	Regulatory
Simple negation	Protests	Personal
Positive interaction	Directs attention for communication	Interactional
Negative interaction	–	–
Shared attention	Directs attention to object	Regulatory / Informational
–	Requests information	Heuristic
–	Answers	–
–	–	Imaginative

Kiernan and Reid's identification of the communicative functions used by people with severe learning difficulties formed part of the development of their Pre-Verbal Communication Schedule (PVCS) (Kiernan and Reid 1987b). This assessment, which runs parallel to much of the Early Communication Assessment (see Chapter 9), comprises 28 sets of questions concerning aspects of communication grouped into three categories: pre-communicative behaviours, informal communicative behaviours and formal communicative behaviours. These are answered by people who know the child or adult with SLD well, through their knowledge and observations. The section on pre-communicative behaviours addresses behaviours described within this book as 'pre-intentional' and there is some overlap with the Affective Communication Assessment (see Chapter 2). The section on informal communication includes a wide range of borderline and early intentional communicative skills such as communication through looking, gesture, vocalisation, objects and pictures. The third section incorporates communication through any formal system: words, signs and symbols.

The responses to the questions are analysed in two ways, each yielding valuable data for intervention. Answers to some of the questions contribute to scores on the seven communicative functions, giving an indication of the learner's ability to, for example, communicate their needs to others (needs satisfaction). A more qualitative picture emerges from a communication profile (see

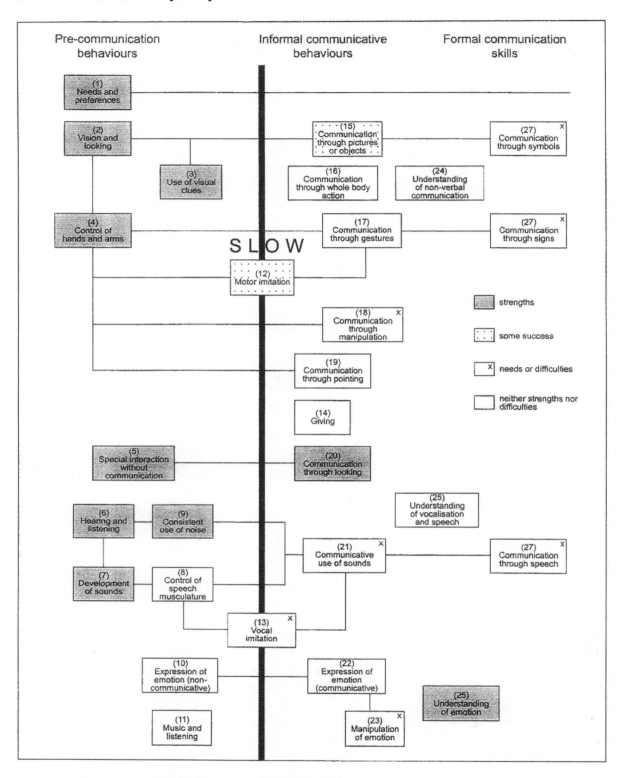

Figure 3.1   Al's PVCS profile (Al at 16 years 7 months)

Figure 3.1) on which can be indicated the extent to which the learner has succeeded in each of the 28 sets of questions, thus giving a picture of relative strengths and needs in routes to acquiring increasingly formal communication skills. Brief details on comprehension are also elicited within the schedule. The communicative functions scores and a profile sheet for Al, a young man of 18, are given in Table 3.5 and Figure 3.1 respectively.

Table 3.5 Al's scores on the PVCS categories

Seeking attention	1/5
Needs satisfaction	4/8
Simple negation	1/5
Positive interaction	3/6
Negative interaction	0/6
Shared attention	1/5
Understanding of non-verbal communication	7/10
Understanding of verbal communication	10/14

Al has a mild hemiplegia which affects his control of one side of his mouth and one hand. This may partly account for his not having acquired spoken language. It also slows down his hand movements, making signing a difficult option for him. He is a very gentle young man who only occasionally demonstrates frustration at not being able to communicate his thoughts and wishes. Al is soon to move on to adult services. A review of his communicative needs and skills using the PVCS suggested that he was not making the anticipated progress using a signing system, though he appeared to have learned a small number of relevant signs. Two communicative functions were identified as priorities for Al: needs satisfaction and simple negation. As can be seen from Table 3.5, Al does have some skills in the first of these, so it was decided to build on existing strengths while working in parallel on a relatively new area. Having an acceptable way of communicating negation to others was seen as a major priority, especially since Al would soon be moving to a relatively unfamiliar setting.

From the communication profile we can see that Al already has some skills in 'communication through pictures or objects' and 'communication through looking', but particular difficulties in 'communicative use of sounds'. He shows some ability to use the communicative functions of 'needs satisfaction' and 'positive interaction', but few strengths in other areas. His comprehension level, which would require rather more detailed assessment, suggests that he might be able to move quite rapidly on to a formal symbol system, with the use of a voice output communication aid as one of a range of possible long-term objectives.

Two programmes were established for Al, based on the results of the PVCS assessment. One involved developing with him a communication book: a photograph album containing pictures of activities, people and things available to him on a particular day. Al quickly learned to request activities by showing the appropriate picture to family members or staff, initially at their prompt 'What do you want to do, Al?', then spontaneously. A second programme involved giving Al a means of rejecting things or events that he did not want. The first step was to use naturally occurring opportunities to give Al choices between two fairly desirable options. This was necessary because Al found rejecting a single item very difficult.

Head shaking (a distal gesture²) was modelled as a way of indicating rejection. Eye pointing (a current strength) plus reaching (also a distal gesture) were used to indicate the preferred item. Only brief practice was required to establish these skills, which had been observed in his current repertoire. The next step involved choices between one preferred and one undesirable item, for example between tea (disliked) and coffee (preferred) at morning break, or between trampolining (disliked) and helping with the laundry (preferred). It took longer for Al to seem confident in dealing with this communicative activity. However, once he seemed free of anxiety, he was offered, at appropriate points in the day, items or activities he was not expected to want. This was carried out at first only by people who knew Al well, but, eventually, by a range of people in various contexts. At this point we felt fairly confident that Al had a means of conveying to others that he did not want something; a vital protection as well as a valuable communicative skill.

It could be argued, in relation to children, that the organised and well-run classroom is not a good place to learn to communicate or to affect your environment. Apart from the points outlined earlier on staff–student interactions, students are provided with food at meal-times, and a drink at break-time, they routinely go to the toilet, or are changed at regular intervals, lessons and material are changed regularly, and students are not allowed to remain at one activity or in one position for too long. Each student is engaged in periods of intensive one-to-one or group teaching alternated with periods of play or leisure time, as appropriate to their needs. Even the start and end of the day is controlled by organised transport. *What need is there to communicate?*

Using the concept of communicative functions, we can devise some general strategies for trying to improve opportunities for real communication at home or in the classroom, college or social and educational centre; in particular, communication to have an effect on the environment and the people within it. Hence, as Seibert and Oller (1981) state, 'the primary goal of intervention becomes the facilitation of generalised communicative functions for which syntactic structure and semantic content are only the tools'. The case for this type of intervention, with particular emphasis on children and adolescents using at least a few words, has been well argued by Bell (1985), Harris (1984b), Newton (1981) and Snyder-McLean *et al.* (1984). The latter three studies also include some evaluation of their proposals.

General strategies for promoting communication

Seeking attention

In terms of communication this can be rather an 'empty' function. There are many individuals with severe learning disabilities who will gain other people's attention with an apparently functional question or request, for example gaining adult attention by smiling and vocalising or saying a phrase like 'Is it Thursday today?' However, when they receive a response this interaction or discourse goes no further, and the original actions or phrase may be repeated. It becomes clear that the sentence or non-verbal initiation is being used not meaningfully, but solely with the function of gaining attention. In this case, if the person is using speech, signing or a symbol system in this way, we would argue that the other early functions (needs satisfaction and simple negation) should be introduced as a matter of priority. It is likely that other people will over-estimate their communication skills, leading to them receiving inappropriate input. However, there are people with very limited communication skills, engaging in these behaviours at the non-verbal level, who would benefit from consistent responses from significant others in their environment to develop their social interaction skills (Nind and Hewett 1994, Ware 1996).

Jade has profound and multiple learning disabilities. She is not independently mobile. She tends to track people as they move around the room, but not to initiate to them in any more proactive fashion. She enjoys attention and can activate a single switch to operate a tape player. Jade has been given a single switch-operated buzzer which acts as a signal for a designated staff member to go immediately to Jade and to give her 15 seconds attention, which can be extended if Jade appears to be maintaining the interaction. Jade is, therefore, learning a means of gaining social interaction from others and gaining experience of being the initiator. The staff are learning to be more responsive to Jade's social interaction skills. For further details of an evaluation of this type of intervention see Schweigert (1989) and Schweigert and Rowland (1992).

Needs satisfaction

This means giving individuals the opportunity to express real *choices, needs* or *preferences:* for example, offering a choice between milk and orange juice, or asking 'Which apple do you want?' The response to this could be a reach or other simple gesture[3], with or without a vocalisation, or it could be more sophisticated, for example the name of the preferred item, or 'That!'

Chris, an independently mobile eight-year-old with severe learning difficulties, shows very limited skills in either 'seeking attention' or 'needs satisfaction' on the Pre-Verbal Communication Schedule. He has been given opportunities to choose between toys and items of food and drink by reaching towards and making contact with the hand of the adult who is holding the thing he wants. Physical prompting has been necessary, but this is now a fairly well-established means of communication.

Simple negation

This means giving individuals the opportunity to *reject* or *refuse* objects or events: for example, asking, 'Do you want to go to the toilet?', or offering the option of moving on to another type of activity or more of an activity which they have just tried. Again, the response could be a gesture and/or a vocalisation, it could be a change in orientation or facial expression, or an eye-point.

Louise, for instance, demonstrates a wide range of interpretable responses on the Affective Communication Assessment, and is just starting to communicate intentionally. However, she is severely limited physically. Thus, a frown plus puckering of her lips indicates that she does not want a proferred drink of water.

Positive interaction

Here, the learner uses positive behaviours to maintain an interaction, without specific reference to objects or events. The aim is not to gain something (needs satisfaction) or to establish 'shared attention', but rather to engage another person socially. Activities would include greetings, turn-taking and, at a more sophisticated level, play routines. Play is discussed in greater detail in Chapter 4.

Saffiya and Lisa tend to be very socially isolated. Both convey needs satisfaction and simple negation through looking and informal gestures or vocalisations. They are being encouraged to engage with each other socially in turn-taking games, for example using 'pop-up cones' and other activities which require both to participate for the end result to be achieved.

Negative interaction

This involves behaviours that we would be unlikely to want to teach, for example, gradually moving a plate closer and closer to the edge of the table, while watching for the response from someone nearby. The intention is to initiate an interaction, but the vehicle for doing it is less than ideal! It is worth remembering that this type of communication is very much a feature of typical development and should not automatically be viewed as 'a problem'.

Shared attention

This involves setting up unpredictable events, or arranging the non-occurrence of normally reliable events, within a familiar and well-understood routine, which gives the person an opportunity to *comment* on or *communicate* with others about something unexpected; for example, an new mural or an unexpected piece of furniture in the room, taking the refills out of ball-point pens, omitting one person's cutlery when the table is laid for dinner, giving a student an empty jug and asking him or her to pour drinks for everyone. This concept will be developed further in Chapter 4 in the context of joint action routines.

Aysha, for instance, is asked to pour a drink for other members of her class at snack time. But the jug is empty. She attempts to pour from the jug, quickly notices that nothing is coming out, then looks into the jug. She shows the empty jug to her teacher, shaking her head, and then puts the jug down on the table, firmly, watching the teacher for a response.

Once learners are conveying this early set of communicative functions, we can consider ways of extending the communicative scenarios with which they can contend, incorporating more advanced communicative functions from the work of e.g. Dore (1977), Halliday (1975), and Roth and Speckman (1984a, 1984b). This can involve increasing the number and range of people with whom they communicate as well as the purposes for which communication is required. Important in this is the use of language and communication for problem solving.

Problem solving by individuals or groups

This problem solving may require the use of cognitive strategies only on the part of one individual, or may involve communication with others about how the problem is to be solved. For example, the person is given the opportunity to obtain a desired object which is within sight but out of reach. Clues can be provided, a chair to stand on or a stick to extend reach. Or three students together are asked to take an inflated paddling pool out of the classroom to the playground. Since the paddling pool is wider than the door, the three will have to work out between them a strategy for getting it out.

Billy's teacher wants him to solve a problem; she will help him if asked. The task is to retrieve a biscuit which is out of reach, on a chair which is on top of a table. The teacher asks who would like to get it, Billy puts up his hand as a request to be the agent and is given a stick. Having attempted to reach the biscuit while standing on the floor, he then positions and climbs on his own chair. With the stick he pushes the biscuit off the chair, but, unfortunately, it falls on the floor. Billy's teacher offers him another biscuit. He refuses this by shaking his head, then takes it, places it back on the seat of the chair. Then, using the stick, he retrieves it successfully.

In our experience these situations are highly motivating and greatly enjoyed, to the extent that it is not uncommon for people who successfully complete a task by accident to indicate that they want to do it again 'properly'.

The examples given for these strategies are ones we have found useful, mainly, but not exclusively, in a school setting. They can be readily adapted for pre-school or adult settings. Indeed, these contexts, not being based around the demands of a formal education system, may offer greater flexibility in the implementation of such strategies. The PVCS has been found to be useful in suggesting appropriate ways of using the general strategies, in identifying priorities for selection of communicative function and indicating strengths in *how* the individual might convey that function. Parents, teachers and other staff, knowing their children or the people with whom they work, will have many other ideas which are functional, real opportunities for communication, and fit naturally into the daily routine. Functional approaches to intervention and, as we shall see in the next chapter, joint action routines, can be built around everyday actions like leisure activities, self-care, washing up, shopping, dressing and meal-times, So they can be planned and carried out very successfully with adults in colleges, in social education centres and in their own homes (Jones 1986).

Finally, for some individuals, establishing the concept of communication will be the whole aim of intervention for some time, while for others a wide range of communicative functions can be taught in this way. There will also be people with good communication skills in certain settings, for whom these ideas may provide a means of generalising these already learned behaviours to a much wider range of contexts.

Notes

1 In the ten years since the first edition of this book was published the position has altered slightly, though not as much as one might have hoped. One approach to teaching communication has become very popular in schools for children with severe learning disabilities: the Derbyshire Language Scheme (Knowles and Masidlover 1982). This approach is based on part on psycholinguistic approaches to language acquisition, notably the 'semantic revolution' of the 1970s. However, the more recent development in pragmatics, the social use of language, do not feature significantly within the programme, leaving it open to many of the criticisms outlined above. It has been subjected to very little formal evaluation. Also, as yet, under-evaluated is the Hanen programme (e.g. Manolson 1992). However, this is an approach oriented specifically towards parent education. It incorporates many of the ideas described in this chapter, though it seems to be directed more towards children with less severe or less global delays.

2 McLean and Snyder-McLean (1987) have described the progression from *contact* gestures (e.g. pulling away, giving an object) through *distal* gestures (e.g. open-hand request, nodding for yes) to true linguistic forms (e.g. single words) in clients with severe developmental delays.

3 Ibid.

Chapter 4

Playing in the zone: using routines to develop early communication skills

This chapter' describes a successful and enjoyable approach to communication and associated skills which has proved so popular that one group wanted to give up Christmas dinner in order to engage in it! What is this wonderful, magical, motivating methodology? Nothing other, of course, than play.

For 'play' we can keep in mind all the routine social interactions – caregiving routines, social exchanges, joking, pretending and so on – that form the context within which typically developing children seem to acquire much of their language and communication (Bruner 1985). These are also, of course, the kinds of social transactions that take up much of our adult life. So, while we might be suggesting pretend play routines for young school-age children, social skills sessions, laying the table or discussion about what is to be cooked for dinner would provide a parallel context for work with adults. This view is supported by Butterfield (1994) who suggests assessing communication in the context of daily living routines and embedding intervention within age-appropriate leisure activities. Of course, according to the definitions below (Garvey 1991), these routines cannot be described as play. However, they offer valuable means of extending the approach in order to ensure age-appropriateness for a wide range of learners.

Garvey (1991: pp.4–5) provides us with a useful set of definitions of what constitutes play:

1. 'Play is pleasurable, enjoyable.' While players do not have to be laughing, the activity must be seen to be positively valued by the player.
2. 'Play has no extrinsic goals.' Its motivations are intrinsic, an enjoyment of means rather than ends. (Of course the teacher, therapist or other play partner may have objectives for a play activity but these are unknown and irrelevant to the player.)
3. 'Play is spontaneous and voluntary.' It must be, or appear to the players to be, freely chosen.
4. 'Play involves some active engagement on the part of the player.' It is worth remembering, however, that this may be hard to assess in relation to a person with severe physical disabilities.
5. 'Play has certain systematic relations to what is not play.' By this Garvey means that play has well-established links with, for example, language learning, cognitive development, problem solving, social role taking, etc. For our purposes, of particular interest are the links between play, particularly pretend or symbolic play, and language and communication.

The development of play

In her review of studies of symbolic play in children of between one and three years of age, McCune-Nicolich (1981, 1986) establishes the following sequence in the development of symbolic play:

Level 1: Recognition of objects or pre-symbolic schemes;
Level 2: Self-pretend or auto-symbolic schemes;
Level 3: Differentiated pretend or decentred symbolic games;
Level 4: Pretend combinations or combinatorial symbolic games;
Level 5: Planning or internally directed symbolic games.

Some writers, e.g. Lewis *et al.* (1992), do not consider a child's play to be truly symbolic until it meets three criteria:

a) the child uses an object or prop as if it were something else;
b) the child attributes to an object properties it does not have;
c) the child refers to absent objects as if they were present.

This conforms to McCune-Nicolich's Level 5 only. Levels prior to this Lewis *et al.* refer to as 'functional play'. (Lewis *et al.*'s assessment of symbolic play would be of use to anyone wishing to study this area.)

Play and language and communication

We can now examine how these developments relate to language and communication. Bates and her co-workers (1979), studying normally developing infants of 9–13 months, found, first, that development of combinatorial play correlated with development of symbolic play, and that both of these correlate highly with what Bates *et al.* call the 'gesture complex', i.e., the communicative gestures of giving, showing, communicative pointing and ritual requests. At this early stage, combinatorial play correlated highly with both comprehension and production of language. Symbolic play correlated with production and, to a lesser extent, comprehension. However, in a follow-up study at 18 months, only symbolic play was positively correlated with language development.

Correlations between McCune-Nicolich's levels of symbolic play and language have been identified by several authors; specifically McCune-Nicolich herself (1981, 1986), Kelly and Dale (1989) and, with reference to Japanese rather than English, Ogura (1991). These correlations have been summarised by Ogura in Table 4.1.

Table 4.1   Ogura's correlations

Level	Play	Language
1	Recognition of objects	Pre-language communication
2	Self-pretend	Single words, global reference
3	Differentiated pretend	Reference to broader range of single words
4	Pretend combinations	Simple language combinations
5	Planning	Development of language combinations

To what extent are these correlations found in children with learning difficulties? There is rather limited research in this area, with the focus of most studies of play being the style adopted by mothers in free play or a structured teaching session with their child with learning difficulties.

At the early (pre-symbolic or sensori-motor) stage, the sort of play behaviours we would want to examine are often viewed as cognitive behaviours; for example in the object-related schemes scale of Uzgiris and Hunt's (1975) assessment, which consists of six ordinal scales based on Piaget's account of sensori-motor development (brief details of this account have been given in Table 1.1).

Mundy *et al.* (1984) found correlations between object-related schemes and communication in infants and young children with severe and profound learning difficulties both at mental ages between two and seven months and at mental ages between 8 and 13 months. At developmental levels beyond this, there are several useful studies. In their research on normally developing children and children with severe learning difficulties at mean lengths of utterance (MLUs) less than 1.5, and 1.5 to 2.0 morphemes, Casby and Ruder (1983) found higher levels of play in children with higher MLUs irrespective of developmental status. In other words, the correlations between language level and level of symbolic play hold for the children with severe learning difficulties just as they do for the children without learning difficulties. These relationships were found also by Westby (1980) with children with moderate and severe learning disabilities.This finding holds for children with autism too (McHale *et al*. 1980, Mundy *et al*. 1987). Mundy *et al*. (1987) found that both play variables and non-verbal communication correlated with language development while not themselves being correlated. In contrast, it is important to note that Kennedy *et al*. (1991) found some variations in the relationship between language and play in their sample of six developmentally delayed children.

Wing *et al*. (1977), in a rather different type of study, appear also to have found a correlation between language comprehension and the development of symbolic play. Their finding of no symbolic play in children with comprehension below 20 months (rather later than in normally developing children) is surprising. It may, perhaps, be accounted for by the global measure of language comprehension used in contrast with more specific aspects of production used in other studies, and also, perhaps, the very heterogeneous nature of the sample. These studies, however, suggest that we can have some confidence that the progressions in symbolic play and language proceed in similar ways in children with and without learning difficulties.

Play and cognition

We will continue with a consideration of the relationships between play and cognition. In addition to the arguments made in the first chapter of this book about the relationship between cognition and play, many authors include play in their measures of cognition, i.e. play is assumed to be an aspect of cognition. This is most evident at the pre-symbolic level, where the child's actions on objects or people can obviously be described as evidence of play and/or cognition. As Ogura (1991) states, 'Implicit in most studies, and explicit in some, is the notion that play with objects reflects cognitive development during infancy.' There is also evidence of this assumption at later, symbolic, stages, where researchers' interest is in the sequence of development and its age relationships (e.g. Fein 1975).

An exception to this is the 1979 study by Bates *et al*. referred to earlier. Bates and her colleagues found correlations at the 9–13-month age range between combinatorial play and symbolic play, between combinatorial play and object permanence, combinatorial play and imitation, and, to a slightly lesser extent, combinatorial play and means-ends relationships. Symbolic play, they found, correlates with imitation and means-ends relationships but not object permanence. This was despite the finding that imitation and means-ends relationships do not correlate with each other. The correlation between symbolic play and means-ends relationships was supported in children between 12 and 24 months by Kelly and Dale (1989).

Piaget, in his book *Play, Dreams and Imitation in Childhood* (1962), described the development of symbolic activity in play as characteristic of stage 6 of the sensori-motor period, i.e. the transition stage leading into the pre-operational period. Rubin *et al*. (1983) review the relationship between play and age and play and cognitive development in this period. These correlations are found, but there is also some suggestion that construction play in pre-school children correlates with intelligence test scores and socio-dramatic play with measures of social competence.

Studies in relation to children with learning difficulties have centred on the relationship between play level and mental or developmental age, identifying positive correlations between the two (see Table 4.2). This is true both of studies looking only at symbolic play (Jeffree and McConkey 1976, Wing *et al*. 1977, Hill and McCune-Nicolich 1981 and Cunningham *et al*. 1985) and of the study by Gowen *et al*. (1992) which looks longitudinally at pre-symbolic and symbolic play. The correlation holds for studies of children with Down's syndrome and for those with subjects of varying etiologies.

To summarise, there seems to be good reason to accept that there are strong correlations between play and language and communication in children with and without learning difficulties, and correlations between rather more general measures of cognitive development and play in children with learning difficulties.

Table 4.2   Correlations between play and (develop)mental abilities in children with learning and other developmental disabilities

Authors	Subjects	Test used
	Symbolic play	
Jeffree & McConkey 1976	normal & SLD	Griffiths
Wing *et al.* 1977 *	SLD & autistic	various
Hill & McCune-Nicolich 1981	Down's syndrome	Bayley
Cunningham *et al.* 1985	Down's syndrome	Bayley
	Pre-symbolic and symbolic play	
Gowen *et al.* 1992	normal, SLD & physically disabled	Bayley & Stanford-Binet

* Wing *et al.* found no evidence of symbolic play in children with M.A.s of 19 months or below.

Intervention through play or role play routines

Having established these correlations, why might a parent, teacher, therapist or other professional wish to use play, in its loosest sense, as a vehicle for intervention in the areas of language and communication? Two sets of reasons can be addressed, the first relating to the opportunities afforded by the play context itself and the second relating to the role of an adult or cognitively more advanced peer. One major opportunity that the play context offers relates to the nature of the language and communication used and taught. Specifically, the play situation provides a communicative context for the language targets and opportunities for the genuine transmission of information.

As suggested in the previous chapter, in non-play contexts it is all too common for the teacher or therapist to request a series of predetermined responses from the learner:

'What's this?' 'An apple.' 'Yes, an apple.'
'What is teddy doing?' 'Sleeping.' 'That's right, he's sleeping.'
'Show me the girl sitting on the table.' 'Yes, that's right, the girl is sitting on the table.'

These exchanges are characterised by certain features which are not typical of normal conversation:

- they are asymmetrical: one of the partners asks all the questions;
- they do not involve genuine transmission of information: the answers are predetermined and already known to the questioner;
- they are not dynamic: the exchange is complete after the teacher or therapist's feedback;
- the topic is not negotiable: it is determined by the dominant partner, though the other's interests may be taken into account.

Furthermore, apart from satisfying the other person, the learner has no purpose, no pragmatic function (see previous chapter) for his or her reply. All this, despite the findings of Cheseldine and McConkey way back in 1979 that language acquisition in children with Down's syndrome is facilitated by parents modelling desired behaviour using non-directive statements rather than attempting direct elicitation of the response through questions or demands. Similarly, in relation to normally developing children Bruner (1985) argues, 'It is almost always in the interest of fulfilling his communicative intentions that the child recognises and picks up new structural tricks relating to language' (p.27).

One example of an approach which uses play to facilitate the development of cognition and language is presented in McConkey and Price's 1986 book *Let's Talk*. Price (1997) reiterates their ethos: 'Language can only be learned within the context of familiar and routine situations. Where the situation is unfamiliar, the child relies upon interaction with his or her care giver to make the situation meaningful' (p.211). We will return to the role of the caregiver shortly.

The second issue in relation to intervention concerns the support afforded by the play context. Donaldson (1978) argues that when we abstract a task from its purposes, take it out of its context, we make it more difficult for young children to succeed. Donaldson uses this argument to explain pre-operational children's failures on standard Piagetian tasks exploring, for example, class inclusion and decentration, compared with their relative success on related tasks which provide a 'human sense' context (e.g. Donaldson and McGarrigle 1974, Mossler *et al.* 1976). She suggests that 'embedding' a task in a context, as opposed to presenting it in an abstract, context-free format, provides support for the child to make sense of the task. This, presumably, allows the child to bring to the task any relevant previous experience or strategies. Clearly, a play routine has the potential for providing just this sort of supportive context for the learner, whether the task be cognitive or linguistic. A framework for planning such play routines will form the final part of this discussion.

The third aspect of the play context which offers advantages in teaching cognition or communication relates directly to the studies surveyed earlier. The strong impression gained from the correlational data is that both language development and at least some aspects of cognitive development are related to symbolic development. The opportunity to work directly on symbolic activity, for example through McCune-Nicolich's stages, is available within the play context. One direct approach to intervention in play is presented and evaluated by McConkey (e.g. McConkey *et al.* 1982). However, Butterfield (1994) argues that, for children with significant developmental delays, intervention based on play alone is not sufficient to extend language skills. Rather, specific intervention aimed at developing language *through* play is necessary. In the case of adolescents or adults with very severe delays she recommends a focus on daily interaction situations demanding functional communication. This would seen to support the ideas expressed in the previous chapter.

Going back to the second aspect of intervention through play, we are interested in the role of adults or cognitively more able peers in promoting development and learning. Bruner makes the point forcefully when he argues that the fundamental vehicle for education is social transaction rather than solo performance (Bruner 1985). The process by which this comes about is called, by Bruner, scaffolding. We can see a specific example of this in language acquisition, which Bruner claims takes place in 'familiar and routinized settings'. The child and adult pair are acting within a known domain, where the likely intentions are predictable and therefore more easily recognised. What the child cannot do is 'filled in . . . by the mother's scaffolding activities' (Bruner 1985). Scaffolding can be seen as a support system which is tailored to match the child's current acquisition processes.

A very early account of this role of adults or cognitively more advanced peers in mediating children's development comes from the work of Vygotsky, written in the 1930s, but readily accessible in English language only from the 1960s onwards. In *Mind in Society*, he describes the 'zone of proximal development'. This is 'the distance between the actual developmental level as determined by independent problem solving and the level of potential development determined through problem solving under adult guidance or in collaboration with more capable peers' (Vygotsky 1978: 89). Bruner and Vygotsky, then, are agreeing that children learn through experience mediated by a more advanced tutor who, using language to explain the task, structuring of activities and other strategies, enables the child to succeed in a task in which success could not have been achieved independently. Children gradually take over these strategies to the point when they can use them independently. The gradual internalisation of language is an important component of this.

How do we engineer experiences in this zone of proximal development? Bruner provides us with an answer: 'It is very obscure how an adult gets a child to venture into the zone. I think it is easiest when the venture is seen as play' (Bruner 1985: 29). A valuable account of the application of these approaches to the education of children with mild or moderate learning difficulties is presented by Mitchell (1994). To draw all these proposals together, it would seem that learning takes place most effectively in familiar, routine contexts involving play with an adult or more able peer. In relation to peer group activities, Connolly *et al.* (1988) found longer interactions, greater involvement and increased cooperation when the activity was social pretend play rather than an activity without social pretend play like drawing or jigsaw puzzles. This reinforces the suggestion that pretend or symbolic play is a particularly useful context. In relation to the use of adults versus more able peers, the evidence is interesting. Beckman *et al.* (1993) studied interactions between toddlers with disabilities and a variety of partners. The play materials were not particularly symbolic, but the findings may have some relevance. The frequency and complexity of social exchanges was greater with mothers than with the normally developing peers, but the results from older peers become progressively more like those of the mothers. However, the subjects initiated more with their peers than with their mothers and the closer the pairs were in age, the more the toddlers initiated. The content of the exchanges were similar for all pairs. It seems, then, that there are advantages from both types of interaction partner, and it may be that interactions involving both an adult and one or more peers would carry both advantages.

Very little discussed thus far about play and language or communication intervention is truly innovative. Butterfield (1994) summarises a range of approaches based, in various ways, on the ideas described in this chapter. In general they have been positively evaluated by researchers, but there is little evidence that they are used extensively in the UK. The approaches can be divided into those appropriate for learners at pre-intentional stages of communicative development and those appropriate for learners who are already intentional communicators (see Chapter 1). Other writing on related themes is referred to in parentheses.

Approaches appropriate to learners at pre-intentional stages of communicative development (from Butterfield 1994)

- Scaffolding for cognitive schemes: enabling learners to experience engagement in diverse ways with a wide range of objects, hence developing object-related schemes (Uzgiris and Hunt 1975; see also Coupe O'Kane and Levy 1996, Goldbart 1994);
- Contingent responding: predictable and differentiated responding by others to learners' initiations (see also Nind and Hewett 1994, Ware 1996);
- Promoting turn-taking: engaging in ritualised games to promote reciprocal interaction (see Chapter 4, this volume, and Kiernan and Reid 1987a, 1987b);
- Referencing: directing the learner's attention to a (presumably) desirable object, then to the other person who can assist in obtaining it, i.e. teaching proto-declaratives (see Chapter 1, this volume);
- Scaffolding for communication: imitating back to the learner their own vocalisations and gestures, then modelling slightly more advanced examples (see also Nind and Hewett 1994).

Approaches appropriate for learners who are already intentional communicators (from Butterfield 1994)

- Incidental teaching: arranging the natural environment to elicit initiations from the learner (e.g. Halle 1984; see also Chapter 4, this volume);
- The mand-model technique: developing learners' responses to other people's requests. This could be seen as more directive than the other approaches described here, depending on how much the environment has to be rigged in order to elicit the response (see e.g. Rogers-Warren and Warren 1980);
- Delay procedures: providing learners with opportunities to respond to cues *other* than adult verbal input. In practice, this involves introducing a delay into a familiar routine, providing the learner with opportunities to initiate within a known context (e.g. Halle *et al.* 1979). This relates closely to variations in joint action routines, described below;
- Milieu teaching: integrating incidental teaching, mand-model teaching and delay procedures, according to the extent to which the learner initiates (see e.g. Brinker 1978, Warren and Bambara 1989). The aim of milieu teaching is three-fold: for the natural environment to be the teaching context, to enhance the quality of the interaction between the learner and significant others, and to use play to develop cognitive and social development. These aims are further developed in the final approach to teaching language and communication to be described in this chapter.

Joint action routines

The final objective of this chapter is to present an approach to planning 'joint action routines' as vehicles for teaching or therapy in a way which conforms to guidance from Bruner and Vygotsky and which is firmly rooted in pretend or social role play. It comes from the work of Snyder-McLean *et al.* (1984). Snyder-McLean *et al.* describe an approach to teaching language and communication skills within a framework of joint action involving an adult and peers, which is carefully tailored to the existing levels of communication and cognition of the participants. Their idea has been adapted and formulated as a content-free proforma for planning which allows a wide diversity of routines to be devised according to the ages, abilities and interests of the participants (Kiernan *et al.* 1987).

Joint action routines are formulated play routines which can be built around everyday events like dressing or having a bath, or play routines like pretend tea parties, taking turns with simple toys or very sophisticated routines like rescuing someone from a burning house. In many ways they parallel the pretend play or role play sequences engaged in by normally developing pre-schoolers. Like a lot of pretend play, joint action routines have set routines with opportunities for variation, a plot or purpose and scope for a variety of different roles. They can be adult-devised so that opportunities for expressing a range of communicative functions can be built in. Hence, the learner gains experience in communicating in different roles, for different purposes, but within a clearly understood familiar framework with an adult model when needed. The routine should seem relatively unstructured (non-directive) to the learners. However, it is actually carefully designed so as to provide a scaffold or framework within which learners gradually acquire relevant and appropriate language, communication and other behaviours at least in part from the models of more able participants. This facilitates their increasing participation in and control of the routine.

These ideas can be used at very early developmental stages: for example, coaction with a familiar person or a turn-taking game, rolling a ball from adult to child and back again, with each participant communicating their readiness for the next turn. Some support for using routines as a vehicle for teaching communication comes from Reddy's (1990, 1991) research with typically developing infants. She found that infants violate the rules in well-known routines in a humorous manner, suggesting that even at the age of seven months to one year infants have a very well-established memory for their structure. Joint action routines can obviously be used in complex settings with many sub-routines providing the opportunity to teach complex language and communication.

The planning proforma is made up of a series of questions which can be summarised as follows:

- Is there a unifying theme or purpose?
- Is there a need for interaction?
- Are there a small number of distinct definable roles?
- Are the roles interchangeable?
- What is expected of each role in terms of what is to be said?
- What is expected of each role in terms of what is to be done?
- Is there an inherent, logical sequence to the routine?
- Are there clearly defined beginnings and endings?
- Are there frequent opportunities to respond?
- Is there an opportunity for repetition within the routine?
- What is the proposed frequency and duration of the routine?
- Are there opportunities for variation, e.g. choices, new events, errors, omissions, sabotage?

This last question provides scope for building in opportunities for generalisation of language or concepts learned *once the original routine has been mastered*. This involves planning carefully selected variations to the routine, initially just expanding the possibilities within the routine by adding choices, e.g. between items to buy, places to go, and additional events or sub-episodes within the known framework. Once it is clear that the learner can cope with and exploit these small variations, we can consider introducing other changes which may require problem solving skills as well as making demands on language and communication. Errors and omissions involve one participant, generally an adult or cognitively advanced peer, missing out an expected part of the routine or doing something incorrectly; for example, when biscuits are handed round, there is one fewer than the number of participants, or when the learner requests a book they are given an apple. This can provide some humorous contexts for learning and may stimulate initiations in learners who have become very passive after years of limited communication.

Finally, and closely related to errors and omissions, we can introduce sabotage, the deliberate disruption of some aspect of the routine, again often with very funny results. This might include blocking the end of a tube down which participants have taken turns to roll a ball, having the doll's head fall off during a bath-time play routine or having the top stuck on a ketchup bottle at dinner time (see Newton 1981 for an evaluation of some of these ideas under a different name). It is important to restate here that these variations, particularly the latter three, should only be introduced in familiar contexts within the framework of a known routine. The aim is to provide modest extensions to the opportunities provided within the routines, rather than major challenges.

We hope it will now be clear that joint action routines are appropriate for learners at a wide range of ages and levels of communication skills. Routines can involve early interaction activities, pretend play routines, more complex social role play leading into social skills training activities and leisure and daily living routines. Examples of joint action routines with both young children and young adults are given below.

The following is a transcript of an excerpt from a joint action routine involving the second author and two young boys, David and Gavin. Both boys could understand a range of single words. They were using a number of gestures and one or two single words for communicating a range of functions.

Joint action routine: putting dolly to bed

JG: Look! Here's dolly. (*Shows doll to both boys.*)
JG: She's going to have a bath.
       (*Gavin points to the bath and looks to JG for confirmation.*)
JG: Yes, in there.
JG: Who's going to take off trousers?
       (*Gavin and David point to themselves.*)
JG: David take off trousers! Pull, pull, pull!
       (*David takes off trousers while Gavin watches.*)
JG: Who's going to take off jumper?
       (*Gavin reaches for doll, takes off jumper while David watches.*)
JG: Jumper off, good boy.
       (*Gavin holds naked doll.*)
JG: Where's she going?
       (*Gavin puts doll in the bath, looks up for confirmation.*)
JG: In the bath. (*Nods to Gavin.*)
       (*Gavin turns doll round to face him.*)
JG: What are you going to wash? (*Models action of washing.*)
       (*Gavin rubs hands together, David imitates.*)
JG: Oh! Wash hands, yes, wash hands.
       (*Gavin looks up, reaches for flannel.*)
JG: Want flannel?
       (*Gives him flannel.*)
       (*Gavin washes doll's hands.*)
JG: Now David's turn.
       (*Gavin passes doll and bath to David a little unwillingly.*)
       (*David takes flannel and washes the doll's face and head.*)
JG: What are you washing?

(*David rubs his hands over his hair.*)
JG: Yes, hair, wash hair.

The following example is taken from a tape of a speech and language therapy (SLT) student working with a group of students at an FE college. The activity arose out of the SLT student's informal observation in the college's cafe. She found that the FE students, who experienced a diversity of communication difficulties, often received something other than what they had requested at the cafe but either did not have, or did not use, appropriate strategies for repairing the communication breakdown. For a few sessions the group decided that they would have their coffee break in their base room and practise skills and strategies for resolving these kinds of problems. Joint action routine planning sheets (Kiernan *et al.* 1987) were drawn up, based around the theme of ordering items in a cafe and repairing the typical breakdowns that might occur in this context. The group had been working on the routine for several sessions and a number of variations were being introduced.

Jo has good comprehension, but mild dysarthria[2] and moderate learning disabilities. As a result she tends to use short rapid sentences which unfamiliar people sometimes construe as rudeness. Ella has good comprehension and can use complex sentences to convey a wide range of communicative functions. However, she is very reserved, and will accept what she is given rather than challenge someone she perceives to be higher status than herself. Ketan uses a word board at times to support his speech, as unfamiliar people find him hard to understand. He is a wheelchair user with severe physical restrictions but is cognitively able. The SLT student is Beth. She is role-playing a member of the canteen staff.

Beth:	Whose was the coffee? (*Puts it in front of Jo who ordered tea.*)
Jo:	Not me, thanks. Her. (*Heavy emphasis on 'thanks', then points to Ella. Looks up at JG who is videoing the session.*) See, I remembered. (*Laughs.*)
Ella:	It's mine, thank you. Has it got sugar?
Beth:	Sugar's on the table. (*Eye-points to sugar.*)
Ella:	(*Quietly*) There's no spoon.
Jo:	(*Nudges Ella*) Ask her!
Ella:	Can I have spoon?
Beth:	Oh, sorry. Let me get one. (*Puts spoon next to Ella's cup.*) Now, one toast (*puts plate in front of Ketan*), one bacon buttie (*puts plate in front of Jo*) and a toasted tea cake (*puts plate in front of Ella, turns to go.*)
Ketan:	(*Loudly*) No! (*Waits until Beth turns back.*) Toast not mine. Mine tea cake, thanks.
Beth:	Sorry, which one was yours? (*Feigns misunderstanding.*)
Ketan:	(*Repeats, stressing both words and picks up the menu to indicate the correct item.*) TEA CAKE.
Beth:	Sorry, whose was the toast then? (*Swaps toast for tea cake and waits, looking at Ella.*)
Ella:	That's right.
Beth:	Good. Enjoy your meal.

When the group decided that they had practised the various alternative routines enough, they went back to the college cafe for their snack. Informal observation suggested that all three students were trying to put the strategies they had practised into effect, when appropriate. There was also some evidence of these strategies; politely correcting another person, requesting items and requesting information (not demonstrated above), generalising to other contexts. It was felt that this group had also benefited from the metalinguistic aspect of the activity, in other words from discussion about language itself.

Unfortunately, this approach is relatively unevaluated, but it is underpinned by the research and theory described earlier in this chapter. In our experience it is also enjoyable for all participants; as Fewell and Kaminski (1988) state, 'play is intrinsically motivating'. We conclude with a quote from Vygotsky which we hope will fire readers' enthusiasm: in play 'the child always behaves beyond his average age, above his daily behaviour. In play it is as if he were a head taller than himself' (Vygotsky 1978: 102).

Notes

1 An earlier version of this chapter appeared as J. Goldbart (1994) 'Playing the zone: communication and cognition in the classroom', *The SLD Experience* **10**, 12–14, Autumn.
2 Dysarthria is an impairment to the smooth control of oral and related movements associated with speech, eating and drinking. It affects intelligibility and may cause the person to have difficulty with, for example, chewing and swallowing. Severe dysarthria might be a reason for a person to use an alternative or augmentative means of communication, such as a symbol, word or letter board or a more high-tech communication aid.

Chapter 5

Teaching first meanings

This chapter describes a method of teaching early meanings to children and adults with severe communication delay, who demonstrate a range of appropriate actions with objects, and who understand and communicate about objects and events within their environment.

Early meanings are defined by Leonard (1984) as 'aspects of cognitive structure that the child may attempt to communicate about'. First meanings, therefore, are concerned with people, objects and events which are familiar to the person in the final stage of sensori-motor development. For Bloom (1973) the earliest of these meanings were:

- existence of entities;
- non-existence of items children expect to find;
- disappearance of things.

Our approach to teaching first meanings was developed in the light of results of a language survey carried out at Melland School (Coupe 1981) when 28.4 per cent of pupils were at or below the stage of imitating single words. This agreed closely with the results of the Schools Council Survey (Leeming *et al.* 1979) and the work of Kiernan *et al.* (1982). It seemed that many pupils were failing to develop functional communication at the single word level. Hence, we examined the content and approach of existing teaching methods and determined that, owing to a lack of accessible and sensitive research and intervention strategies, the teaching of comprehension and expression of single words tended to emphasise the use of nouns to identity objects and pictures. Mittler and Berry (1977) suggest that this undue emphasis on the teaching of labelling may be counterproductive to language development.

Whilst object names do constitute a high proportion of the first words young children use (Benedict 1979 – 50 per cent; Nelson 1973 – 51 per cent), intervention strategies seemed to neglect the meanings conveyed, that is semantic roles, and the uses intended, that is the functions of these single words. Thus, the underlying concepts were generally not taught and there was a lack of emphasis on teaching language skills in a communicative context. Research into the language acquisition of normally developing children demonstrates that the earliest words and protowords used by the children are usefully classified according to the semantic role, that is the underlying meaning of the utterance as opposed to its grammatical category or its function (Greenfield and Smith 1976, Leonard 1984, Nelson 1973). In view of the range of semantic roles described in these studies, it seemed likely that people with severe learning difficulties might have delayed or deficient development of semantic notions which therefore would require specific remediation. In the light of this rationale we developed the following three perspectives (Barton and Coupe 1985):

1. teach first meanings concepts rather than verbal labels;
2. place teaching in a setting where each person has something to communicate about;
3. provide opportunities for those who are not yet ready to use words to communicate intentionally with gestures, vocalisations and protowords.

This would follow the normal development sequence described in Chapter 1. Bates *et al.* (1975)

tentatively suggest that gestural and vocal signals gradually give way to increasingly word-like sounds before the use of verbal symbols at sensori-motor stages 5–6.

First meanings

We chose to teach the early meanings described below, which were influenced by the work of Bloom (1973), Bloom and Lahey (1978) and Leonard (1984).

Existence

Acknowledges that an object or event exists by look, gesture, vocalisation, sign or word. For example, when presented with an interesting object, Emma reaches and touches it, then looks to the person who is holding the object.

Disappearance

Comments on or requests the disappearance of a person or object by look, gesture, vocalisation, sign or word, such as 'no', 'gone' or 'away'. For example, when food is put away in the fridge, John gestures with upturned hands that it is gone.

Recurrence

Comments on, or requests, a representation of an object that existed but has disappeared, or a repetition of an action that occurred then stopped, either non-verbally by a point, gesture, vocalisation, or by a word or sign such as 'again', or 'more'. For example, a battery-operated car is activated by an adult. Claire looks at the adult and vocalises to request a repetition of the action.

Non-existence

Indicates that an object does not exist where it is expected to be, either non-verbally by a look, gesture, or vocalisation, or by a word or sign such as 'no', 'gone', or the name of an object. For example, Liam is given an empty biro and instructed to draw. Lack of results leads to him visually investigating the pen and showing it to the other person, accompanied by 'tuts'.

Location

Comments on the position of an object, person or event or the spatial relationship between two objects, or requests that an object be placed in a certain location by look, gesture, vocalisation, or a word or sign such as 'there', 'on', 'table'. For example, Sarah goes to get her coat which is on another person's coat peg. She visually searches, sees her own coat, looks at the communicative partner and points to it.

Possession

Conveys the relationship between an object or person and themselves or another, by a look, gesture, vocalisation, sign or word such as 'mine'. For example, Saima points to herself when asked 'Whose coat is this?'

Rejection

Communicates that an object, adult or event is not wanted or for an activity to cease by a look, gesture, vocalisation, or a sign or word such as 'no', 'stop', 'bye bye', 'gone'. For example, Michaela is offered a sticky cake. She looks at it, touches it and then pushes away the hand that is proffering it.

Denial

Denies a proposition by look, gesture, vocalisation, or a word or sign such as 'no' or 'didn't'. For example, Darren takes a crisp when the adult in charge of the activity is not looking. The adult accuses him and he, with a full mouth, shakes his head.

Agent

Is the person or object that causes an action to occur and can be conveyed by a look, gesture, or vocalisation, or a word or sign. For example, on presentation of a jug of orange juice and glasses, Karen points to herself and says 'me', to indicate that she wants to pour.

Object

Is the object or person that may be affected by an action and can be conveyed by look, gesture, or vocalisation, or a word or sign. For example, when shown a toothbrush, Mark points to his teeth, says 'teeth' and mimes a cleaning action.

Action

Is any observable activity or change of state and can be expressed non-verbally by a look, gesture or vocalisation or by a word or sign such as 'up', 'go', 'jump'. For example, when asked to activate a toaster, Emma says 'go' and presses the lever to cook the bread.

Attribute

Comments on, or requests, a property of an object or person by look, gesture, vocalisation or a word or sign such as 'big', 'hot', 'horrid', or 'nice'. For example, after mixing dough, Andrew holds up his hands and comments 'dirty'.

Assessing first meanings

Chapter 6 and Appendix A provide additional information for assessing the cognitive and communicative functions of first meanings. This is further supported by band 2 of the communication assessment produced by the staff of the Redway School (Latham and Miles 1997), where they address first meanings 'because the first communications are not clear words, but ideas or meanings which pupils wish to communicate'.

Prerequisites for teaching first meanings

We have determined three important prerequisites for the teaching of first meanings.

Cognitive

The person should be functioning at the end of sensori-motor stage 4 and entering into stage 5 in the following scales:

1. Means for obtaining desired environmental events.
2. Object-related schemes.
3. Visual pursuit and permanence of objects.

To determine the developmental stage of an individual pupil, see Coupe O'Kane and Levy (1996), Dunst (1980) and Uzgiris and Hunt (1975).

Communicative

The person should be communicating by gesture, looking or vocalisation and have acquired, at least, a small range of intentions.

Social interactional

The person should be capable of having their attention directed by communicative partners in giving joint attention to events and objects.

Teaching first meanings: an example lesson

The following transcript is of a lesson with five nursery-age pupils, a teacher and a speech and language therapist. The sequence of meanings taught was:

1. Existence: a toy car is presented and is acknowledged by each child.
2. Agent: who wants to make the car go?
3. Action: the agent makes the car go.
4. Recurrence: the agent arranges for the action to be repeated.
5. Action: the agent makes the car go.

First, the teacher modelled the play sequence with the toy car, emphasising the meanings involved. Pupils were then given the opportunity to nominate themselves as the agent. So that Christopher, for instance, pointed to himself and vocalised that he wanted his turn in acting upon the car. He took it from the teacher, put it on the floor and, after verbal prompting from the teacher, pushed it along the floor. When the teacher retrieved the car, he requested recurrence of the sequence by saying, 'Again'. He then repeated the sequence. On completion of Christopher's turn the teacher allowed opportunity for other children to nominate themselves as agent.

In this lesson, while the teacher worked with the pupils, the speech and language therapist recorded their behaviour. Of necessity, a quick and easy recording format is required. However, when possible, we do advocate that lessons are regularly videoed so that more detailed recording and identification of pupils' progress can be made from the tape. The sequence of meanings is noted and the pupil behaviours are then recorded as they occur in sequence. The objects used should be varied with repetition of the sequence so that, in this instance, after teaching the planned sequence of meanings with a toy car, the lesson was repeated using a ball and skittles.

Teacher

Existence	Teacher holds up car
	Teacher says, 'Car . . . look, look, look'
	Teacher puts car on floor
	Teacher says, 'Look'
Action	Teacher pushes car and says, 'Go'
Recurrence	Teacher picks up car, holds up, says, 'Again'
Action	Teacher pushes car and says, 'Go'.

Christopher

Existence	Teacher holds up car
	Christopher looks at car
Agent	Teacher asks, 'Who wants it?'
	Christopher points to self and vocalises
	Teacher says, 'Good boy, Chris', gives him car
	Christopher takes car, puts it on floor
Action	Teacher says, 'Go'
	Christopher pushes car
Recurrence	Teacher picks up car and holds it up
	Christopher takes car and vocalises an approximation to 'Again'
Action	Teacher responds by saying, 'Again, good boy'
	Christopher pushes car
	Teacher says, 'Go' and catches car.

Natalie

Existence	Teacher holds car
	Natalie looks
Agent	Teacher asks, 'Who wants it?'
	Natalie vocalises and points to self (gesture)
	Teacher says, 'Good girl', puts car in Natalie's hand
	Natalie drops car
Action	Teacher retrieves car and says, 'Go'
	Natalie prompted to push car
Recurrence	Teacher picks up car, holds it in front of Natalie
	Natalie vocalises for more
	Teacher responds, 'Again, good girl'
Action	Teacher puts in Natalie's hand
	Natalie prompted to hold car
	Teacher says, 'Good girl, Natalie, go'
	Natalie pushes car.

Martina

Existence	Teacher holds up car
	Martina looks
Agent	Teacher asks, 'Who wants it?'
	Martina vocalises
	Teacher acknowledges, 'Good girl, Martina'
Action	Teacher gives car to Martina
	Martina takes car
	Teacher says, 'Go'
	Martina prompted to push it
Recurrence	Teacher picks up car, places it in Martina's hand, asks, 'Again?'
Action	Martina, with prompting, pushes the car

Teacher picks up car, looks at Martina, says, 'Good girl'.

Joseph

Existence	Teacher shows car
	Joseph looks
Agent	Teacher asks, 'Who wants it?'
	Joseph vocalises
	Teacher repeats to Joseph, 'Who wants a go?'
	Joseph prompted to point to self and spontaneously says, 'Me'
	Teacher touches his face, says, 'Good boy'
Action	Teacher gives Joseph the car
	Teacher says, 'Go'
	Joseph places the car on the floor and pushes
Recurrence	Teacher retrieves the car, says, 'Again'
	Joseph retrieves the car and has a second quick go
Action	Teacher says, 'Go'
	Joseph takes car and pushes it
	Teacher picks up car and says, 'Good boy'.

Emma

Agent	Emma calls out, 'Me'
	Teacher responds, 'Good girl, Emma'
	(Teacher talks to scorer)
Action	Teacher gives Emma the car, says, 'Ready'
	Emma holds car, says, 'Go', then turns away from circle to push car
	Teacher comments, 'Ooh' as car stops, then, 'Go and get it'
	Emma goes to retrieve car, taking her time
Recurrence	Teacher says, 'Again Emma, again, again'
	Emma picks up car
Action	Teacher says, 'Go. Go. Hurrah'
	Emma pushes car.

Considerations for effective intervention

Teaching first meanings should be as enjoyable and functionally appropriate as possible within a structured framework which creates maximum opportunity for communication. To provide for this, the following strategies should be considered and utilised.

Management of learners

For many children or adults with severe learning difficulties, individual teaching can successfully take place in group contexts, the ideal numbers being four to six students to two adults. For others it will be more appropriate to work in a smaller group or a one-to-one situation. We have found it useful to involve a combination of teacher, support worker and speech and language therapist. The requirements of each lesson need not be the same for each person in the group. In this way, individual needs can be met through differentiation, in terms of level of experience, joint attention, vocalisations, gestures, words, signs and the degree of prompting. Group teaching provides much opportunity for modelling and imitation of the behaviour of others and allows much repetition and practise of meanings. Priorities can be determined for each learner and be effectively taught.

Sequencing meanings

Students can be involved in simple events which clearly exemplify specific meanings, for example activating mechanical objects, hiding themselves or objects, observing the location of objects. These meanings can then be sequenced to provide meaningful routines which the students are likely to encounter in their daily experience.

Generalisation

Generalisation of each sequence of meanings can be established by using a range of functionally appropriate objects, events, people and locations. For instance, the toy car was used in the demonstration lesson cited above and this was followed by a sequence using a ball and skittles.

Resources

The same sequence can be repeated using different resources. It is most important to aid the generalisation of the meanings being taught. The resources are important. They need to be carefully selected to be motivating and clearly illustrative of the meaning being taught. After any teaching session, materials can be left out to allow students to initiate and practise the sequences amongst themselves.

Presentation

Each meaning needs to be clearly presented and the language accompanying it should be economical but predetermined and should coincide exactly with the event or function being conveyed.

Reinforcement

Essentially this should be intrinsic. However, for some students strong social or other reinforcement will be a major factor.

Recording and evaluation

It is important to record the performance of individual students on a regular basis so that their progress can be evaluated. Evaluation should be concerned with the frequency of communicative behaviours but, most importantly, account for the behaviours themselves and the progression towards spontaneous communication of the meanings. A group recording sheet can be designed which allows for a record of individual students' behaviours. The behaviours to note particularly are look, gesture, vocalisation, word and sign. If prompting is required, and this includes imitation of a behaviour, then this should be noted. The same recording sheet could be adapted and used for an individual. Recording should be quick and simple to carry out. Sequences of meanings can be approached in two different ways:

1. An individual's performance may be recorded in detail while they take part in a group lesson;
2. The performance of all students in the group can be recorded as they take their turn during the lesson.

Sequencing and generalising first meanings

The teaching of first meanings is not an end in itself but a foundation upon which to generalise and build communicative strategies and abilities. It is possible to manipulate common, everyday situations and objects so as to teach sequences of meanings in a variety of functionally appropriate contexts. Essentially it is important to build up evidence that the person can spontaneously use and understand each concept taught and for this to be generalised to a variety of appropriate contexts.

It is possible for everyday situations to be utilised in order to meet the communicative needs of individual pupils. Martina and Emma were members of an infant class and during their milk break maximum opportunities for communication were created. Martina's priorities for communication were that she would use the first meanings of location, agent, action, recurrence and rejection in the following functionally appropriate situations: milk break, dressing, dolls' house play and fine and gross motor activities. Emma's priorities are similar, but extend to the meanings of location, agent, action, object, non-existence, denial, recurrence, attribute and disappearance.

For the staff or carers it is essential that the individual student is given opportunities to initiate and control the outcome of a situation, however structured these settings may be. The milk break for this infant class allowed individual sequences of meanings to be communicated by all the pupils daily. Furthermore, it proved to be a naturally social situation which was motivating for the whole class. The following two examples show how milk-time created opportunities for Martina and Emma to communicate.

Martina: First meanings used during milk break

Location	Looks at adult and points to milk on the table.
Agent	Nominates either herself or adult to pour by looking at adult and pouring herself, or looking at adult and placing their hand on the milk bottle. This is usually accompanied by vocalisation.
Action	If Martina pours the milk she usually requires prompts from the adult. If the adult pours she looks at the adult and their action of pouring.
Recurrence	Martina indicates that she wants more by look, vocalisation and a sign.
Rejection	If given water instead of milk, she will push it away and look at the adult.

Emma: First meanings used during milk break

Location	Obtains the milk from the corridor and communicates about its location by pointing outside the classroom, together with 'There'.
Agent	She indicates that she wants to pour and give the milk out by pointing to herself and saying, 'Me'.
Action	She pours the milk and gives it out, accompanied by eye contact with each child in turn and by saying, 'Here,' or the child's name.
Object	She labels 'milk', 'cup' and 'straw' at appropriate points in the milk-break sequence.
Non-existence	She communicates if the milk or cups are not in the expected place, usually by facial expression, look to the adult and sometimes, 'Gone' or 'Not there'.
Denial	If Emma spills the milk whilst pouring, she denies that she did it, sometimes by answering the accusation with a shake of her head and 'No', and often by pointing to the child closest to her.
Recurrence	Signs and says, 'More' when she wants more milk or 'Again' if she wishes to pour more for other children.
Attribute	She now comments about the attributes of objects – 'Nice' (about the milk) and selects the larger quantity for herself and looks at the adult whilst doing so.
Disappearance	Emma often teases adults or children by hiding a milk bottle or cup behind her back, accompanied by 'Gone'.

These examples demonstrate how the same context can be readily utilised to build up a varying complexity of sequences appropriate to the developmental level of each child or person with severe learning difficulties. It is also possible to highlight and teach one specific meaning at a time.

In the same infant class a group of four children were involved in putting their shoes on after a physical education lesson. All the meanings used, apart from denial, were well established and generalised; hence the teacher targeted this particular first meaning. The sequence of meanings consisted of:

1. Existence: Acknowledges shoes.
2. Location: Locates shoes in different positions.
3. Denial: Denies possession of shoes other than their own.
4. Agent: Nominates self or adult to put shoes on.
5. Object: Shows understanding of concept *shoe* and communicates about it.
6. Action: Puts shoe on.

The first meaning of denial was, in this instance, taught by the adult giving each child the wrong shoe and also by the adult insisting that the child's shoe was her own. In varying ways, sometimes with prompts, all four children denied possession of another child's shoe and denied the adult possession of children's shoes.

A further example of placing emphasis on one meaning is highlighted within the daily milk-break routine. The children in turn, or in pairs, were given the task of getting their milk but, unknown to them, the milk crate had been removed from its usual place in the corridor. To make functional use of the concept of non-existence the children were required to communicate that the milk was not where it was expected to be. Hajra understood the cognitive concept of non-existence so that, for instance, when the milk crate was not in its expected position she would search other locations to find it. The emphasis of teaching non-existence as a first meaning, however, was to teach her to communicate about this concept. With prompting, when necessary, she was taught to convey the non-existence of the milk. Indeed, during milk-break routines over a period of time she was presented with varying situations in which she could generalise and convey the meaning of non-existence. She was given an anticipated cup of milk – with no milk in it. She was asked to get the cups from the shelf but they were not where they should have been. These ideas can be embedded within a joint action routine: see Chapter 4.

Conclusion

Teaching first meanings can be practically applied to any situation, whether routine or novel. While the examples discussed here relate to children of school age, they amply serve to illustrate how well individual needs of all ages can be met. Intervention can take place in a small group context. For the students themselves, it is essential that opportunities for communication are created throughout the day. It is important for them to need to communicate and for them to see results from communicating about the environment and their effect on it.

Chapter 6

Assessment of early communication

Considerations for assessment

Assessment, in schools for pupils with severe learning difficulties, has played an essential part in what Lacey *et al.* (1991) refer to as a circular educational process, where it informs decisions on appropriate teaching objectives and strategies. Using the curriculum document for assessment purposes ensures that, rather than pupils being merely judged on their performance, a profile of individual strengths and needs can be determined and an individual scheme of work be drawn up to address these needs. While the emphasis of a syllabus might be more oriented towards life and social skills, the same principle of a circular process will apply to services for adults with severe and profound learning difficulties.

In the past, assessments were mainly developed to look at intellectual ability in relation to peers. These norm-referenced assessments consist of a range of tasks which are presented in turn; the performance of the person being assessed is scored according to predetermined criteria and compared with those obtained by the standardisation sample. These tended to be used to ascertain the mental age and/or intelligence quotient (IQ) of children with developmental delay for placement in appropriate educational facilities, such as SLD schools. While some may consider this appropriate for initial screening of children, information gained from such tests failed to provide adequate information from which to identify needs and plan for subsequent teaching.

In contrast, criterion-referenced assessments offer more relevant, utilisable information, particularly for those who teach pupils and adults with SLD. Here the performance is assessed, over time if necessary, and recorded. Behaviours to be assessed are generally identified sequentially in relation to developmental stages or through a logical analysis of the steps involved in a given task. Strengths and needs can be identified without reference to the performance of peers and, without mental age equivalent and IQs being mentioned, where relevant a person's developmental level of functioning may be determined and used constructively.

The purpose of assessment, according to the Task Group on Assessment and Testing (DES 1988), is:

- formative, so that the positive achievements of a pupil may be recognised and discussed and the appropriate steps may be planned;
- diagnostic, through which learning difficulties may be scrutinised and classified so that appropriate remedial help and guidance can be provided;
- summative, for the recording of the overall achievements of a pupil in a systematic way;
- evaluative, by means of which some aspects of the work of a school, an LEA or other discrete part of the educational service can be assessed and/or reported upon.

What do we mean by early communication?

Conventionally, communication is defined as an intentional transmission of meaning in a formal code between people who share that code (Sugarman 1984). However, to meet the needs of people who are often defined as pre-communicative we need a more flexible definition. Communication can be said to occur when one person's behaviour is interpreted or inferred as meaningful and understood by their partner in the interaction: 'Few if any would claim that all interaction is communication, although communication is recognised as taking place in interactional contexts' (Bullowa 1979). The behaviours produced act as signals or message carriers which are then received, processed and responded to. This broadening of the definition of communication allows us to view all children and adults as communicators. Indeed, by treating them as communicators they become communicators: '. . . the mother's inference of intent may precede and contribute to the development of intentional communication' (Harding 1983).

Much of the research and literature on the genesis of communication falls into two camps: those who believe communication is dependent on cognitive advances, and those who believe that affect and social interaction propagate communication (see Chapter 1 for detailed discussion). By identifying levels of communicative development which correspond approximately to Piaget's sensori-motor stages, we feel we have sensitised ourselves to important changes in 'a continuum of behaviours' (McLean and Snyder-McLean 1985) and to the emergence of intention and meaning. Whilst the relationship between communication and cognition is, as yet, unclear, a detailed understanding of cognition may provide us with a profitable area of investigation for communicative failure and strategies for remediation. By studying the structure of early interactions and the role of affect, we feel we have raised our sensitivity to the context and rules of communication and hence to possible causes of delay or failure and potential areas of intervention, '. . . assuming that affective forms of communication precede, influence and subsequently become integrated with linguistic (that is, cognitive) communication, disruption of early social-affective relations may be a prelude to later emotional and language disorders' (Thoman 1981).

Developing an Early Communication Assessment

On the basis of a survey on 1300 children in SLD schools in North West England, Leeming *et al.* (1979) found that 28.4 per cent of the pupils assessed were functioning at or below the one-word imitation level. In a partial replication of this survey, on children in South East England with PMLD (profound and multiple learning difficulties), Kiernan *et al.* (1982) found comparable results. Like teachers, parents of children and young people with PMLD have identified communication as a major area of concern (Hogg *et al.* 1987). Evans and Ware (1987) reported that out of 800 PMLD pupils, teachers identified 647 as having no communication skills. Furthermore, they indicate that not all PMLD pupils make the expected progress and draw the conclusion that the 'idea that all children are educable is again being seriously questioned'.

While the emphasis on assessment and teaching has traditionally been given to the development of receptive and expressive language, communication has come to be seen as the 'primary function of language' (Muma 1978). In the early 1970s the teaching of language was guided by developmental checklists such as those by Gunzburg (1973) and Sheridan (1973). The developmental milestones identified, however, did little to assist with assessment and subsequent intervention for children and adults who functioned within the very early stages of development. Indeed, the notion of communication seemed to be a somewhat misunderstood concept to the extent that many people with PMLD were considered to be non-communicative (Evans and Ware 1987). This is possibly due to an overly restrictive, linguistically orientated definition of what communication is, along with a lack of relevant available and accessible assessment materials based on sound theoretical perspectives.

As discussed earlier, a strong relationship exists between cognition and communication. Glenn and Cunningham (1984) support the view of Rogers (1977), suggesting that there is some indication that profoundly disabled children appear to progress through Piaget's sensori-motor stages in much the same sequence as non-disabled children. Indeed, in many schools and services for adults with SLD, staff have developed exciting early cognition curricula based on the sensori-motor stages which are supported in content and assessment strategies by Uzgiris and Hunt (1975) and Dunst (1980). Stephens' (1977) argument for a comprehensive curriculum for PMLD pupils which extends both horizontally and vertically, reflecting Uzgiris and Hunt's concept of ordinal scales, would seem viable for all people functioning within the early stages of development. It seems feasible, therefore, to develop an Early Communication Assessment which, while not necessarily having parity with, is parallel to, Piaget's (1952) sensori-motor stages. An Early Communication Assessment is therefore required which synthesises the relevant theories and available assessment materials to produce a detailed but clear assessment document.

An evaluation of the research literature would seem to indicate that people with severe, profound and multiple learning difficulties may progress through stages of communicative development in much the same way as normally developing infants, albeit at a slower rate. However, owing to developmental delay, often combined with additional physical and sensory handicaps, they may exhibit fewer, less apparent responses to caregivers, which are likely to result in communicative partners failing to read or interpret signals. Dunst (1980) and Yoder (1987) find that the presence of either severe cognitive impairment or severe physical impairment render pre-intentional and intentional communication less interpretable. This is further confirmed by the findings of Evans and Ware (1987) who indicate that 'overwhelmingly the most common responses to all children's initiations is a failure to respond at all'.

For those who strive to educate and enhance the development of these children and adults, and their caregivers, there is an apparent need for an assessment which will assist in sensitising observations and interpretations, enabling them to respond in a way which nurtures communicative competence. Hogg and Sebba (1987) point out that 'Extensive brain damage, epilepsy and failures of social development can disrupt sequences of development and may preclude further advances in a given area.' But they do go on to conclude that profound retardation and multiple impairment can, justifiably, be viewed within a framework of development for normal children. Hence, for these children and adults it would seem appropriate to use existing developmental frameworks as guidelines for intervention, but recognise the possible limitations of this approach (Glenn and Cunningham 1984).

The Early Communication Assessment (ECA)

It has been feasible to develop an assessment of early communicative functioning, the principles of which draw on the theories of early communication relating to normally developing infants, theories which highlight the child or adult with SLD actively developing through social and cognitive interactions with the environment and the people within it (Piaget 1952, Vygotsky 1962, Fischer 1980). Hence, six levels of communication are defined for this Early Communication Assessment, which correspond broadly with the six sensori-motor stages of cognition, and these are organised into 13 areas of communicative functioning. In this way, a vertical and a horizontal dimension at each appropriate level is also determined. It is worth noting, however, that research on sensori-motor development in children with severe and profound learning difficulties – e.g. Owens (1989) – has demonstrated that, while children with severe and profound learning difficulties develop through Piagetian stages in the same sequence as normally developing infants, this progression takes place at different rates in different domains of sensori-motor intelligence. Hence, a child may be within sensori-motor stage 3 in imitation but 4 in causality. If this is true in relation to cognition it would seem unsafe to presume that children and adults would progress through all areas of the ECA at the same rate. Thus, although levels of communicative functioning across areas have been identified for general descriptive purposes, it may not necessarily be the case that someone at level 4 in communicative intentions will be at level 4 in, for example, comprehension in context.

At the sixth level, the main form of communication will be referential and we will see a development to two element 'sentences'. Progress during this level is outside the remit of the ECA: however, Chapter 8 and Appendix C extend the nature of our work in providing a complementary assessment, the Manchester Pragmatics Profile. Much has been written on the importance and implications of pre-linguistic communication for the development of language and speech. For example, Bruner (1983) argues that

> primitive 'speech act' patterns may serve as a kind of matrix in which lexico-grammatical achievements can be substituted for earlier gestural or vocal procedures . . . If we make the reasonable assumption that at some point the child begins to develop some primitive notion of semanticity – that patterned sounds stand for particular things or classes of things in experience – then it is no great mystery that such sounds will at first accompany ostensive referential gestures and eventually even replace them.

Bates (1976) emphasises the role of cognitive growth in the emergence of language and speech: 'The prediction is made that while illocutionary processes can take place after certain sensori-motor developments, locutionary processes for constructing and projecting propositions must await the sixth sensori-motor stage with the development of the symbolic capacity.' This level is the final one in our hierarchy of communication development and has no finite end as children and adults continue to acquire new knowledge and competences in form, meaning and function throughout their lives as communicators.

The Early Communication Assessment or ECA (see Appendix A) was conceived in the classroom and it was considered important for it to involve practical, useful communicative landmarks and not be concerned with attempting to cover an extensive and exhaustive list of possible human communicative behaviours at particular stages. The selection of items is heavily based on experience of the communicative abilities of children and adults with severe, profound and multiple learning difficulties. In addition, the theoretical stance emergent from the last 20 years' work on 'rich interpretation' of communicative attempts and the functional, dynamic approach that is now so prevalent in the literature on early communication provides the necessary framework for supporting the development of the ECA.

In order to establish an assessment which is of use to teachers, therapists, care staff and relatives, it is considered important to include a broad view of communicative functions but also provide sufficient detail to allow for developmental progress to be ascertained. These requirements are established through the horizontal and vertical dimensions described below. Hence the Early Communication Assessment is organised into a matrix with five developmental levels and 13 areas of communicative functioning (see Appendix A).

Levels of communicative functioning

Level 1: Pre-intentional: reflexive level

The individual at this level has a limited repertoire of behaviours which can be interpreted by familiar people. A large part of this repertoire is made up of reflexes, such as sucking, grasping, Moro (startle) and rooting, cardinal points, stepping and so on (for further information see Gordon 1976). Other responses include cries, vegetative noises and facial 'expressions' which reflect the 'high degree of maturity of the facial neuromuscular system' (Owens 1984). Varying states of alertness on a continuum between fully asleep and fully awake, with concomitant changes in activity levels, are likely to be construed as communicative. This is also true of the sensations absorbed by the caregiver from the infant, for example body temperature, smells, body contact and position. The infant has the ability to fixate visually at distances of 8–10 inches and to track jerkily through 180 degrees. This early development of vision allows mutual regard to occur: 'since mutual gaze is the context for a great deal of communication in other modalities at the beginning as well as throughout life, it should be considered a very fundamental form of human communicative behaviour' (Robson 1967).

These behaviours are exhibited in response to internal as much as to external stimuli, which are received through all sensory channels – visual, auditory, tactile, gustatory and olfactory. At this level any behaviour which involves a change from a previous state, and which we can differentiate, can have signal value for a caregiver. 'The possibilities for human-to-human communication are limited only by human motor and perceptual capacities' (Bullowa 1979). In addition to producing behaviours, the child or adult is registering input from his sensorium with particular impact from auditory and visual stimuli. The individual appears to orient to or discriminate between different facial configurations, strange and familiar voices, and speech sounds over non-speech sounds. This is illustrated by the 'neonatal synchrony of movement to adult speech' (Condon and Sander 1974). These very early preferences have been seen as preprogramming infants for interest in and interaction with their caregivers. According to Newson (1979), infants are 'biologically tuned to react to "person-mediated" events'.

During this period, not only are the child's behaviours non-intentional but so are many of the care-giver's, as they respond instinctively to the child's output. Indeed, both partners are contributors: with the child shaping the caregiver's behaviour, the 'adult interactant becomes aware of his own involvement with the infant, as he too maintains an intense period of eye-to-eye, face-to-face communication' (Brazelton 1979). Thoman (1981) summarises this process: 'Their mutual adaptation is viewed as being achieved through a continuous feedback system resulting in mutual modification of behaviours. Thus the nature of this feedback system is basically that of a communication system.'

The main messages to be interpreted at this level are like, dislike, want, reject, known and not known. These meanings can be interpreted through varying states of comfort, distress, alertness and lack of interest (see Chapter 2). The content of the adult's communication is usually phatic, that is, it concentrates on the relationship rather than on the caregiving activity; for example, while changing a nappy the adult might say, 'What a good boy.'

The structure of the interaction at this level has three major forms. The first, seen during feeding, is the 'burst-pause' pattern, where researchers have recorded an increase in the length of the infant's pauses during sucking if mothers fill the pauses with actions and speech. The second is when

> in their early dialogues, the mother imparts the child's behaviour with social significance. She provides an opportunity for the child to take a conversational or pseudo-conversational turn. Initially any child response is treated as a meaningful filling of that turn. If the child gives no response, the mother proceeds with her next conversational turn. (Owens 1984)

The above are both reciprocal patterns, but many sequences of interaction are seen as 'coactive' with mother and child acting simultaneously. It has often been suggested that this causes a conflict since, unlike reciprocity, coactions do not look like later dialogue patterns. However, Bullowa (1979) says communication as an act is continuous, behaviour in individual modalities may have an on-off character, e.g. mutual gaze or vocalisation, or be episodic. The message may be carried in multiple channels or switch channels without interrupting communication. Once the hierarchical organisation of behaviour, interaction and communication is recognised, the problem of coaction versus reciprocity takes its place as a relatively superficial issue.

Overall, as Brazelton (1979) says, 'We have come to feel that the newborn infant comes equipped with a series of complex behaviours for communication and for eliciting the appropriate nurturing responses from the adults around him.' Our description of level 1 draws heavily on contemporary theories of normal infant development which we feel allow us to assess and intervene primarily with children and adults with profound and multiple handicaps.

The Level 1 stage of communicative functioning for people with SLD or PMLD can be summarised as follows:

Social significance is assigned by the adult to a small range of very early behaviours, sounds and reflexes produced by the person in response to a limited range of internal and external stimuli. The person may receive and orient to input from all available sensory channels. Adults tend to respond instinctively to the person's behaviours and attend to the relationship rather than the caregiving activity, e.g. intense periods of eye-to-eye, face-to-face contact. The person is more likely to orient to events which are controlled by another.

N.B. As many behaviours of this level relate to visual responses, assessment may prove complex for those with additional visual impairments.

Level 2: Pre-intentional: reactive level

The child is reacting to stimuli from all senses and is beginning to react to objects as well as to people. For responses the child has a wider range of voluntary behaviours which can act as signals to the caregiver as early reflexes disappear.

Vocally, the child still cries, but gradually adds open vowels, glottals, plosives, nasals and, eventually, reduplicated babble. 'Sounds in the form of vocalisations appear early in the infant's development to have a major effect on the mother's behaviours and become, in fact, a focal point for much of mother's responses and activity concerning the infant' (Harding 1983). The child has an expanded repertoire of body and limb movements; trunk-turning/orientation, whole-body stiffening, changes in overall activity levels, hand-to-mouth movements, mouthing and holding. A variety of facial movements are evident, for example mouth puckering and tongue movement. Of particular importance at this level is the appearance of the smile (for further information see Schaffer 1971). In the area of visual functioning the child is visually inspecting people and objects and giving eye contact. Mutual gaze is changing. 'At about three months, mutual gaze may be modified occasionally into gaze coupling, a turntaking interaction resembling later gaze patterns observed in mature conversation' (Jaffe *et al.* 1973).

Receptively, the child is beginning to respond more to the affective messages from the caregiver, such as tone of voice and facial expression (Trevarthen 1979) as well as to early adult non-verbal communications, notably by the end of this level, line of regard, especially accompanied by vocalisation (Bruner 1974–5). The child's auditory responses now include searching for sound sources by eye and head movements, particularly for speech. The child's registering of speech will often produce vocalisation, paving the way for the development of vocal play and dialogues. The caregiver's following of the child's line of regard and eventually the child's response to the adult's gaze direction leads to the development of shared attention. 'A great deal of work on interaction with infants during their first half year considers shared attention. This is probably the key to the rhythm sharing underlying also fully elaborated inter-adult communication' (Bullowa 1979).

During interactions at this level the child is now likely to show anticipation of their turn and to fill it so that, while initiation is still in the hands of the adult, the child can actively maintain the interaction. 'The stimuli children provide not only occasion various adult responses, but they also maintain or alter adult responses. To maintain the care giving and the social interaction of the parent, the child must produce reinforcing feedback that is contingent on the parents' behaviour' (Ramey *et al.* 1978). These turns are increasingly filled by vocalisation and movements of the head and hands rather than body movements, which is important as handling decreases sharply during these months. Interactions increase and change in nature to include rituals and game playing (Bateson 1975), for example peek-a-boo. Daily routines such as feeding, bathing and changing 'provide predictable patterns of behaviour, which aid interpretation' (Owens 1984). This sets up a stimulus response sequence and so the child 'develops an expectation that he can change the environment or control the environment' (Owens 1984).

The Level 2 stage of communicative functioning for people with SLD or PMLD can be summarised as follows:

Social significance is assigned by the communicative partner to repertoires of changes in behaviour, reactive behaviours, produced in response to a wide range of stimuli. These include events and people within the environment, and the person is receiving and distinguishing input from all available sensory channels (McLean and Snyder-McLean 1987). The adult here tends to concentrate on aspects of the caregiving activity and will place more value on sounds produced than physical behaviours. Within a turn-taking interaction the person is expected to fill a turn with increasing vocalisation and movement of the head, body and hands. The adult will follow the person's line of visual regard. At this level, the person will respond to some familiar, non-verbal communication by the adult, such as following the adult's line of regard, and begins to respond to affective messages such as tone of voice, facial expression.

Level 3: Pre-intentional: proactive level

The child is beginning to act purposefully on objects, events and people in the environment. The repertoire of behaviours, mostly occurring as a result of these actions, which can be construed as communicative by an adult, has expanded. The child searches for and reaches for desired objects and people. They hit, shake and explore objects and let go of one item to examine a novel one. However, adults are increasingly selective in those behaviours they respond to and so reinforce; that is, they will place more communicative value on a vocalisation than a hand movement. During her research, Harding (1983) looked at mothers' reactions to their infants' behaviour:

> A second characteristic that was predicted to be significant in communication development was the consistent reaction of the mother to behaviours which will become communicative . . . It has been hypothesised that the mother's consistent communicative reaction to behaviours such as vocalisations, looking and reaching enable the infant to identify these behaviours as first instrumental in achieving goals and then as means to communicate.

This hypothesis was confirmed by her study, with particular attention being paid by mothers to eye contact accompanied by vocalisation.

Adults are becoming more selective as to which behaviours they reinforce, helping to shape the child towards more sophisticated communicative behaviours, for example responding to a hand movement rather than gross body movement. 'It may be that as mothers require certain communicative behaviours before they react, they are not only encouraging those specific behaviours but also "teaching" the infant that a mutual means of communication exists' (Harding 1983). The caregiver is still decoding the meanings outlined in Level 2, but the content of the communication now concentrates on aspects of the caregiving activities: for instance, while feeding, the adult might say, 'Here comes the spoon.' 'Much of this early pre-linguistic dialogue occurs in specific situations, the mother attempts to divide the incoming stimuli into more readily comprehensible segments to which the child can attach meaning' (Owens 1984).

At this level the vocal repertoire includes cries, screams, laughs, consonants and vowels, as before, with the addition of non-reduplicated babble. The child vocalises to self, especially to their reflection, people, toys, objects and pictures. Vocal productions vary in pitch, volume, stress and quality, giving emotional colouring to the voice, such as anger, eagerness, satisfaction, and differing intonation patterns, for example rising or questioning. Caregivers and children have dialogues of sounds with both spontaneous and imitated vocalisations from which the child learns 'the rudiments of initiation and termination of conversation, alternation and interruption, pacing and interspersing of verbal and non-verbal elements' (Bateson 1975). These dialogues often take place in set routines of interaction.

Previously, most interaction was centred on caregiving activities and people but now the emphasis shifts towards toys and objects, making the dyad of adult and child a triad of adult, child and object. Routines with joint attention and joint action allow the child to build up expectations of what will happen next and foster their initiations of interactions. Harding and Golinkoff (1980) found that babies whose mothers shared interactional initiations with their infants were more advanced communicatively than those whose parents did not. Harding (1983) states that 'shared initiations may have a positive effect on communication development'. The child also learns to repair and terminate both interactions and proto-conversations as they become a more equal partner. During these interchanges the caregiver increasingly talks about some person, object or event in the immediate environment, filling their turn with verbalisations and vocalisations.

The child is more able to abstract meaning from the caregiver's intonation patterns, voice quality, facial expression and actions. They now listen to sounds as well as searching for them from sources to the side and below ear level.

> During these first six months of life the infant begins to lay the foundations of one of his most highly developed areas of expertise, namely, 'reading' the signals and expressions of other people's behaviours. By the end of this short period of life he will be able to discriminate most of the basic human expressive displays. (Stern 1977)

Despite the child's increasing skill, the adult is still inferring communicative and cognitive intentionality and the same meanings and functions as at Level 2. Bruner (1974–5) confirms that in his study mothers can be seen to be 'inferring the baby's intentions or other directive states'. He draws attention to two types of maternal interpretation. First, 'an interpretation of the infant's behaviour as an intention to carry out some action'. Mothers therefore facilitate this action, possibly shaping the proto-imperative function. Second, an interpretation 'as trying to find out about something'. When the parent focuses on the object in view, usually saying, 'look' and its name, this fosters the proto-declarative function.

The Level 3 stage of communicative functioning for people with SLD or PMLD can be summarised as follows:

> Repertoires of behaviour become signals to the adult, who then assigns communicative intent and meaning. Adults become increasingly selective in the behaviours they respond to. They still respond to vocalisations but also to looking and reaching behaviours. First, they interpret 'the infant's behaviour as an "intention" to carry out some "action" and, secondly, they interpret the infant's behaviour as trying to "find out about" something' (Bruner 1977). The adult shapes the person towards intentional communication and tends to reference an object, person or event in close proximity. The person at this level makes efforts physically to explore and act on the environment and the reach is for real. The general focus of attention shifts from caregiving activities towards a focus on objects and toys. The person can now abstract meaning from the adult's intonation patterns, voice and facial expressions.

Level 4: Intentional: primitive level

Cognitive intention, where an child acts on their environment to create a specific effect, is now established, and communicative intention is developing. According to Bates (1976), the intention to communicate will be inferred from:

1. a context indicating that a goal desired by the child is operating,
2. the emission of some movement or sound, in which eye contact is alternated between the object and the adult,
3. the persistence of the behaviour until the inferred goal is reached,
4. consummatory behaviour confirming that the child did indeed have that goal in mind.

Level 4, therefore, represents the transition from pre-intentional to intentional communication. Similar radical changes are occurring in the form of the child's communications. They now comprise mainly primitive (McLean and Snyder-McLean 1985) motor acts. Very common is the movement of objects, for example reaching for a cup while looking at the adult, that is reach-for-signal (Bruner

1978); pushing a cup off the table while looking at the adult; trying to manipulate an object while looking at the adult, viewing its functional side, dropping, throwing or combining objects. Adults can also be moved or manipulated, for example, leading the adult to a desired location, putting the adult's hand on to handles, books and so on. The child can use whole-body action by pulling away, cooperating, going limp, stiffening and hugging. Facial expressions are now used to communicate intentionally as are other emotional displays, such as squeals, shouts, frowns, cries and hits. Vocalisations are predominantly babble and other vocalic consonant forms. With their infants, the mothers' preference for word-like sounds and vocalisations is such that Harding (1983) states 'early in development, mothers begin to selectively "teach" their infants to become word users'.

The adult needs to rely heavily on the context to understand the content and function of the communication. According to Bullowa (1979), 'Mutual attention or orientation is the context for communication based on conscious intention. Attention may be expressed by combinations of gaze, by facial expressions of interest and posturally and kinesically by orienting posture and movements.'

Two main functions are intentionally communicated at this level, marking the emergence of pragmatics out of social interaction. These are the proto-imperative, 'the insertion of the adult as a means to attaining objects or other goals' and the proto-declarative, 'the use of an object in giving, pointing, showing as a means to obtaining attention from the adult' (Bates 1976). Nelson (1978) says functions are the 'central subject matter of pragmatics'. Bates also draws attention to presupposition or shared knowledge and says: 'It is suggested that presupposing is a very early activity, a process inherent in the selection of one element from an organised context to be encoded at the exclusion of other elements.' A further area is the social organisation of discourse, which incorporates turn-taking skills (see Chapter 8).

Earlier we noted the emergence of sound play between mother and infant. At Level 3 many of these vocalisations were simultaneous, but by 12 months there is very little overlap (Schaffer *et al.* 1977) giving a more mature dialogue pattern. Receptively the child is beginning to respond more and more to adults' non-verbal communication. They will take a proffered neutral object or a held-out hand and will follow a point. The child pauses in response to 'No!' and will progressively respond to commands incorporating situational cues and gestures, for example 'give me', 'come here', 'go away', 'sit down', 'stand up' (all in context). Moore and Meltzoff (1978) write:

> If the infant is to learn to use language meaningfully he must understand how adults use it meaningfully. This implies that until the infant understands those aspects of a situation to which an adult is referring, in much the same way as the adult does, he will not be able to determine any systematic correspondence between adult words and their referents.

The child is learning to understand cognitively these early meanings which are encoded in adults' communication, for instance existence, location, disappearance, recurrence, non-existence, agent, action and object. 'Infants learn language by first determining, independent of the language, the meanings which the speaker intends to convey to them and thereby working out the relationship between the meanings and the language' (Macnamara 1972).

The Level 4 stage of communicative functioning for people with SLD or PMLD can be summarised as follows:

> Two main functions emerge as the person begins to communicate with intention. Firstly, the person uses the adult to gain an object or event, the proto-imperative function (Bates *et al.* 1975) and secondly, the person uses an object or event to gain attention from the adult, the proto-declarative function (Bates *et al.* 1975). At this stage the 'reach-for-real' becomes a 'reach-for-signal' (Bruner 1975). These communications reflect a limited range of functions or intentions and the form is context-bound, being usually situation-specific. The content is still reliant on some interpretation by the adult and the form is generally unconventional or idiosyncratic to the person. Also during this level the person may vocalise to self, reflection, people, objects, toys and pictures. Vocalisations vary in stress, volume and pitch, and intonational patterns are used. The person utilises direct imitation and begins to use some deferred imitation to solve problems.

By the end of this level, a cognitive understanding of semantic roles will be established. Here, 'the child possesses a set of co-ordinations of action schemes which can be shown to have certain structural properties which will make it possible for him to start comprehending and producing language' (Owens 1984). The person will also respond more to the adult's non-verbal communication, e.g. will take a proffered hand. In general, the person will respond to commands which incorporate gestures or situational cues.

Level 5: Intentional: conventional level

The child is now operating on the environment in a more sophisticated way. Similarly their communication is becoming more conventional and less reliant on context or 'context-mobile' (Bruner 1983), more precise and easily decoded by the receiver: 'The signalling becomes more conventional and can be comprehended with less contextual support' (Bruner 1974–5). The predominant forms of communication at this level are gestures, vocalisations (such as jargon) and verbalisations (for instance protowords) and early words. Gestures, that is motor acts or actions not involving physical contact with objects or people, are very common. They include nodding and shaking the head, waving, requesting (an open palm), showing (object is proffered but not released), giving (object is proffered and released) and pointing. Novel gestures may be created by the child which repeat part of a motor act, for example a lid-opening gesture. Alternatively, the child may use objects in a way which reflects their knowledge of the function, such as giving a straw for a drink. These actions are used specifically for communication, unlike the more general use seen at Level 4. Gestures are often combined with vocalisations, protowords and early words which 'are initially intention specific and may not be used referentially by children for several months thereafter' (Coggins and Carpenter 1981). The meanings which are conveyed by the child now expand rapidly as those notions understood cognitively at Level 4 can now be communicated (see Chapter 5).

A similar broadening of functions has occurred. The following are some of the reasons for which the child might communicate: drawing attention to self, events, objects, people and for communication; requesting objects, actions, information and recurrence; greeting, protesting, rejecting objects, events or people; informing about self and the world; responding/acknowledging (see Roth and Speckman 1984a, 1984b). The central nature of pragmatic development is highlighted by Coggins and Carpenter (1981): 'during sensori-motor IV and V a child's development may be manifest more by the number of communicative intentions used than by either lexical or structural advances'. Bruner (1983) states that in the transition from pre-linguistic to linguistic communication, the 'continuity of functions provides an important scaffold for the development of both referential and requestive procedures . . . in certain respects, indeed, the continuity of function provides a basis for progress by substitution'.

The skills acquired during interpersonal interaction are underpinning the skills developing for conversation or discourse management. The child has a variety of strategies that can initiate an exchange, for instance proximity, eye contact and vocalisation. The interchange can be extended over a 'question and answer' or a 'statement and reply' as the child learns to maintain the topic and the conversation. They also have the ability to terminate a discourse by, for example, moving away or breaking eye contact. Of particular note are the child's attempts to repair a breakdown in communication by repetition with emphasis, rephrasing or resorting to context (Roth and Speckman 1984a). Another aspect of pragmatics, which is achieving intentionality, is presupposition, previously mentioned as occurring as a feature of the child's attentional system (Bates 1976). The child will actively communicate about the changing facets of their environment rather than the static which are assumed to have been processed by both or all partners. Presupposition at this level is really the act of deciding what is shared knowledge in a particular context and what is information.

As the child's output has become more vocal, their comprehension has become more verbal. They process information from situationally cued words, such as 'wash your hands', said when standing next to the sink before dinner. Later the linguistic input alone is sufficient with the child comprehending early words, for instance 'hands', 'kick', 'car', especially in relation to the child themself and to familiar objects.

The Level 5 stage of communicative functioning for people with SLD or PMLD can be summarised as follows:

> The person intentionally communicates a range of meanings as semantic roles using more conventional signals such as gestures, vocalisations (including jargon) and protowords, which are easier to decode. The number of communicative functions conveyed increases rapidly as their knowledge of discourse expands. The person begins to decode shared knowledge with another person and actively communicates about new or changing aspects of the environment. Situationally cued words are processed and the individual understands a range of early words, particularly those which relate to self or familiar objects and people. Gestures are used and repertoires of physical action are used specifically for communication. Deferred imitation is acquired so that the model need not be present.

Areas of communicative functioning

(N.B. Not every area commences at Level 1 or continues to Level 5.)

Affective communication

Affective communication is concerned with the adult's sensitive interpretation of the person's external and internal emotional responses to changes in the environment and the people within it. The adult can then attach meaning to them and respond as if they were a communicative signal. Thus a two-way process of communication can be facilitated which will incorporate some consistent responses to the child's feelings of like, dislike, want and reject. Through observations of the child's behaviours it is possible for the adult to identify those consistent repertoires of behaviours which express feelings and responses.

Affective communication can be conceptualised at three levels of pre-intentional communication. At Level 1, the reflexive level, social significance is assigned by adults to a small range of very early behaviours and reflexes produced by the individual in response to a limited range of internal and external stimuli (Thoman 1981). Adults tend to respond instinctively to the individual's output and attend to the relationship rather than to caregiving activity. At Level 2, the reactive level, social significance is assigned by the adults to repertoires of changes in behaviour in response to a wide range of stimuli (McLean and Snyder-McLean 1987). The adult here tends to concentrate on aspects of the caregiving activities (Snow 1972). The third level, the proactive level, is concerned with the person's efforts to act on the environment. Repertoires of behaviour become signals to the adult who then assigns communicative intent and meaning (Harding 1983). Here, adults become increasingly selective in those behaviours they respond to. Firstly, they interpret 'the infant's behaviour as an "intention" to carry out some "action"' and, secondly, they interpret 'the infant's behaviour as trying to "find out about" something' (Bruner 1977). Adults are considered to be preparing and shaping the person towards proto-imperative and proto-declarative functions of communicative intentions (Bates 1976, McLean and Snyder-McLean 1978).

At each level, assessment of an individual should focus on the four crucial meanings of like, dislike, want and reject which are identified by Thoman (1981). However, by Level 3 many variations and extremes of these meanings can be interpreted, as can other meanings such as request, frustration, greeting and surprise (Ricks 1979). Izard (1978) finds surprise and interest to be observable from birth. Assessment will need to identify the stimulus presented, the consistent repertoire of behaviours by the person in response to the stimulus and the optimum setting conditions for obtaining the behaviour.

Mutual gaze

'Mutual gaze is the context for a great deal of communication in other modalities at the beginning as well as throughout life. It should be considered a very fundamental form of human communicative behaviour' (Robson 1967). The early development of vision at the reflexive level allows mutual regard to occur. Periods of mutual gaze commence with the individual and adult spending periods of time in eye contact. Brazelton (1979) notes that the 'adult interactant becomes aware of his own involvement with the infant, as he too maintains an intense period of eye to eye, face to face communication'.

In Level 2, the reactive level, 'Mutual gaze may be modified occasionally into gaze coupling, a turn taking interaction resembling the later gaze patterns observed in mature conversation' (Jaffe *et al.* 1973).

At Level 4, the primitive level of communication: 'Mutual attention or orientation is the context for communication based on conscious intention. Attention may be expressed by combinations of gaze, by facial expression of interest and kinesically by orienting posture and movements' (Bullowa 1979). Mutual regard is considered by Bullowa (1979) to be 'probably the key to the rhythm sharing underlying also fully elaborated inter adult communication'. Hence, use of gaze at Level 4 is incorporated in the area of communicative intentions. See also Owens (1984).

Social organisation of communication

From the early levels 'shared initiations may have a positive effect on communication development' (Harding 1983). As individuals become more equal partners in the interaction, and later in discourse, so they begin to repair and terminate interactions and proto-conversations. Dialogues of sound between the adult and person incorporate spontaneous and imitated vocalisations. From this the individual learns the 'rudiments of initiation and termination of conversation, alternation and interruption, pacing and interspersing of verbal and non-verbal elements' (Bateson 1975).

'The skills acquired during interpersonal interaction are underpinning the skills developing for conversational and discourse management,' state Coupe and Jolliffe (1988), who go on to identify examples of ways in which an individual can employ a variety of organisational strategies for communication. Influenced by Roth and Speckman (1984a, 1984b) they suggest that the individual can initiate communication by such strategies as eye contact, proximity and vocalisation. This can lead to people learning to maintain the topic by, for instance, question and answer, statement and reply strategies, and to terminate a communication by, for example, moving away or breaking eye contact. An attempt may also be made to repair a breakdown in communication by, for instance, repetition with emphasis, rephrasing or resorting to context. See also Bruner (1974–5), Bullowa (1979), Owens (1984) and Tronick *et al.* (1979).

Joint reference

'Joint reference is one of the earliest opportunities for the infant to engage in a truly communicative act of sharing information' (Owens 1984). It is about how 'one individual manages to get another to share, attend to, zero upon a topic that is occupying him' (Bruner 1978).

The individual's line of visual regard is followed by the adult in Level 2, the reactive level, and this leads to the development of shared attention and joint reference. At this level the person can respond to the adult's line of regard, particularly when it is accompanied by adult vocalisation (Bruner 1974–5).

In Level 3, individuals will be unable to integrate themselves with the other person and the object or event. They will be able to reference either the adult or the object or event. At this proactive level, attention shifts from caregiving activities, e.g. nappy changing, feeding, towards a focus on toys and objects. The adults tend to reference a person, object or event in close proximity to the person and fill their turn with verbal and vocal utterances.

Integrating attention is essentially something the person does when looking to the adult and some object or event, when really just opening up a channel of communication. Joint reference, however, results from the individual directing the other person's attention to the object, event or a person. See also Scaife and Bruner (1975).

Turn-taking and social interaction

In the early stages, Level 2, turn-taking is adult-directed where adults leave spaces for children to fill their turn with sounds or actions. The individual's behaviours are accepted as a response and the dialogue continues. It is important for the adult to give time for a response from the person so that they will gradually learn to anticipate their turn. 'The dialogue-like turn taking . . . in very early feeding sessions is a matter of the mother fitting her behaviour to the infant's natural rhythm' (Kaye 1979). At Level 2, they can be expected to begin to fill a turn with increasing vocalisations and movements of the head and hands rather than whole-body movements. The adult can utilise the individual's existing repertoire of behaviours by imitating them or using novel behaviours. The behaviours thus produced by the individual 'not only occasion various adult responses but they also maintain and alter adult responses. To maintain the care giving and the social interaction of the parent, the child must produce reinforcing feedback that is contingent on the parent's behaviour' (Ramey *et al.* 1978).

Owens (1984) identifies two concepts. One is the reciprocal concept where the adult provides an opportunity for the child to take a conversational turn or pseudo-conversational turn. If the child gives no response, the mother proceeds with her next conversational turn. Alternatively, coactive turn-taking is when the adult and child act simultaneously. These situations sometimes do not seem like dialogues. However, it is important to consider Bullowa's (1979) notion that communication is continuous. 'Once the hierarchical organisation of behaviour, interaction and communication is recognised, the problem of coaction versus reciprocity takes its place as a relatively superficial issue' (Bullowa 1979). At first many of the person's vocalisations are simultaneous with the adult but by the developmental stage of 12 months there is little overlap (Schaffer *et al.* 1977), and a more mature dialogue pattern is evident. See also Ainsworth and Bell (1969), Bell and Ainsworth (1972), Bruner (1974–5), Condon (1979), Trevarthen (1979), Trevarthen and Hubley (1978), Tronick *et al.* (1979) and Uzgiris (1972).

Comprehension in context

In the very early stages of life, Newson (1979) suggests that infants are 'biologically tuned to react to "person mediated" events'. At this reflexive level individuals will orient to both strange and familiar voices and to speech sounds rather than non-speech sounds. Condon and Sander (1974) also highlight 'neonatal synchrony of movement to adult speech'. During the first six months of life infants begin to lay the foundations of one of their most highly developed areas of expertise, namely 'reading' the signals and expressions of other people's behaviours. According to Stern (1977), by the end of this short period they will be able to discriminate between most of the basic human expressive displays. In Level 2, the person will respond to non-verbal communication by an adult, e.g. following a line of regard, and will also begin to respond to affective messages from the adult, e.g. tone of voice and facial expression (Trevarthen 1979). The individual's initiations and interactions develop and gradually they can learn to build up expectations of what will happen next. By the proactive level, they will be able to abstract meaning from the adult's intonation patterns, voice quality and facial expressions.

At Level 4, the primitive level of intentional communication, it is important to consider that 'If the infant is to learn to use language meaningfully he must understand how adults use it meaningfully. This implies that until the infant understands those aspects of a situation to which an adult is referring, in much the same way as the adult does, he will not be able to determine any systematic correspondence between adult words and their referents' (Moore and Meltzoff 1978). At this level, we can expect the person to respond more to adults' non-verbal communication, e.g. take proffered hand. Individuals will respond to commands which incorporate situational cues and gestures. Comprehension becomes more verbal when they are functioning within the conventional level. Here, situationally cued words are processed and towards the end of this stage, 'linguistic input alone is sufficient with infants comprehending early words . . . especially in relation to the child himself and familiar objects' (Coupe and Jolliffe 1988). Generally adults systematically modify speech 'so that it is comprehensible at the assumed functioning level of the child' (Owens 1984). See also Bullowa (1979).

Communicative intentions

'Neither the syntactic or semantic approach to language acquisition takes into account what the child is trying to do by communicating' (Bruner 1974–5). Communicative intent, according to Bates (1976), is inferred from

> 1) a context indicating that a goal desired by the child is operating, 2) the emission of some movement or sound, in which eye contact is alternated between the object and the adult, 3) the persistence of the behaviour until the inferred goal is reached, 4) consummatory behaviour confirming that the child did indeed have that goal in mind.

As the individual begins to communicate with intent, two main functions are conveyed and these mark the emergence of pragmatic skills. The proto-imperative relates to 'the insertion of the adult as a means to attaining objects or other goals' (Bates 1976), and the proto-declarative relates to 'the use of an object in giving, pointing, showing as a means to obtaining attention from the adult' (Bates 1976). The 'reach-for-real' identified in Level 3 now becomes a 'reach-for-signal' (Bruner 1975), but to understand the content and function of the communication, the adult needs to rely heavily on the context.

By Level 5, the signalling becomes more conventional and, according to Bruner (1974–5), 'can be comprehended with less contextual support'. At this level the gestures, vocalisations, protowords and early words are initially intention-specific and may not be used referentially by individuals for several months thereafter (Coggins and Carpenter 1981). However, a broadening of the function of communication does occur at this conventional level. Roth and Speckman (1984a, 1984b) highlight drawing attention, requesting, greeting, protesting, rejecting, informing and responding/acknowledging as some of the reasons for which a child might communicate. It is acknowledged that 'during sensorimotor IV and V a child's development may be manifest more by the number of communicative intentions used than by either lexical or structural advances' (Coggins and Carpenter 1981).

Cognitive roles

'Through experience with objects and events around him, the child begins to perceive particular objects and relationships conceptually' (Miller and Yoder 1974). For individuals to enter into the conventional level of communication, where relationships can be expressed between agents, actions and objects, certain (prerequisite) cognitive concepts are required. They will need to have developed the object concept and be able to understand that whole categories of objects can perform the same action while many actions can also be performed by one object. Fundamental to this is the established concept that people and objects can initiate change in the environment. Sinclair (1971) highlights the need for the person to possess 'a set of co-ordinations of action schemes which can be shown to have certain structural properties which make it possible for him to start comprehending and producing language'.

By Level 4, the primitive level, therefore, communicative intent is developing and the individual will be able to 'act on the environment to create a special effect' (Coupe and Jolliffe 1988). During Level 4 the person should be developing a cognitive understanding of those early meanings or semantic roles which are encoded in adults' communication. 'Infants learn language by first determining, independent of the language, the meanings which the speaker intends to convey to them and thereby working out the relationship between the meanings and the language' (Macnamara 1972). These early cognitive roles should be established by Level 5, the conventional level, where they will start to be conveyed communicatively as semantic roles.

First meanings (semantic roles)

Leonard (1984) defined semantic roles as 'aspects of cognitive structure that the child may attempt to communicate about'. Studies by Greenfield and Smith (1976), Leonard (1984) and Nelson (1973) indicate that the earliest words and protowords produced by normally developing children can be classified according to the underlying meanings of the utterance, the semantic roles, rather than the function or grammatical category. However, in Chapter 5 we suggest that people with severe learning difficulties are likely to 'have delayed or deficient development of semantic notions which, therefore, requires specific remediation', a view supported by Leonard (1984), Bloom (1973), and Brown (1973).

Imitation

Piaget (1952) views aspects of the development of imitation as being fundamental to the development of the representation of language. Bremner (1988) sees imitation 'in itself as an important source of information about infants' understanding, specifically their understanding of the relationship between self and other people'. Imitation is generally considered to be important because 'of the developing ability to construct internal representations of the behaviour of others' (Owens 1984).

It is uncertain how far individuals at Level 1, the reflexive level, can produce a repertoire which relates to adult gesture. Moore and Meltzoff (1978) found that infants of between two and three weeks were capable of imitating specific facial gestures as well as manual cues. With infants under three days old they also found evidence of imitative responses which specifically related to the gestures of tongue protrusion and mouth opening. However, further studies have failed to replicate this (Hayes and Watson 1981, Koepke *et al.* 1983, McKenzie and Over 1983).

In the case of early levels of development, imitation will tend to 'be of actions in the child's own repertoire and in addition the action to be performed must be visible to the child' (Hogg and Sebba 1987). Reichle and Yoder (1979) indicated three necessary prerequisites in order for a child to imitate physically: turn-taking, attending to the action and replicating the action's salient features.

Imitation becomes a learning tool once the person is functioning within Level 4, the primitive level. They are now capable of solving problems by imitation, direct at first, then indirect or deferred. According to Owens (1984), 'imitation is an important learning strategy and requires a degree of representational thought. The infant develops the ability to remember a behaviour in order to reproduce it.' Owens further stresses that 'this now requires a limited degree of short-term memory of motor behaviours'. By Level 5, the conventional level, the child's imitation, according to Owens (1984: 102), aids early meaning formation and is correlated with symbolic representation. True symbol functioning is assumed to occur when deferred imitation is acquired because the model need not be present. In addition, imitation is a social behaviour seen in child–parent interactions.

Most of the studies reviewed by Hogg and Sebba (1987) found deficits in imitative abilities of young children with severe learning difficulties. MacPherson and Butterworth's (1981) results suggest that this might be accounted for by recent theories of imitation which suggest the ability may be innate, and may depend on sensori-motor equivalences through an active matching process. See also Dunst (1980), Piaget (1952) and Uzgiris and Hunt (1975).

Auditory and visual behaviours

Bullowa (1979) points out that the possibilities for communication are limited by 'human motor and perceptual capacities'. Where an individual has sensory impairments their perceptual competence will be affected. Indeed, many auditory and visual behaviours are important prerequisites for intentional communication. When a person has auditory or visual impairments this area may be difficult to assess, and hence subsequent intervention will be affected. More sensitive strategies may need to be adopted and each person will need to be considered individually. Nevertheless, all attempts should be made to ascertain their optimum level of visual and auditory functioning at each communication level.

In Level 1 we are concerned with the individual who is 'registering input from his sensorium with particular impact from auditory and visual stimuli' (Coupe and Jolliffe 1988). By the time the person has reached the proactive level, adults will be consistently reacting to their looking behaviours in combination with vocalisations and reaching.

Vocal production

Many reflexive behaviours are evident in Level 1, along with a small number of more voluntary sounds. As a wider range of vocalisations emerge in Level 2, the reactive level, these appear to have 'a major effect on the mother's behaviour' (Harding 1983). Adults tend to place more value on vocalisation than physical behaviours such as hand movements. The adult in Level 3 still responds consistently to the person's vocalisations but also responds to looking and reaching behaviours. Harding (1983) confirmed the hypothesis that eye contact and vocalisations draw particular attention from mothers to their infants at this level.

Gradually the individual extends their repertoire of vocalisations and vocalises to self, their reflection, people, toys, objects and pictures. At the primitive level a person's 'vocal productions vary in pitch, volume, stress and quality giving emotional colouring to the voice such as anger, eagerness, satisfaction and differing intonation patterns, for example rising and questioning' (Coupe and Jolliffe 1988). Vocalisations, e.g. jargon, verbalisations, protowords and early words, are predominant forms of communication at the conventional level.

Physical production

Many of the behaviours in Level 1 are reflexive. Facial expressions reflect the 'high degree of maturity of the neuromuscular system' (Owens 1984). An expanding repertoire of physical movement, together with a variety of facial movements, develop at Level 2: 'Of particular importance is the emergence of the smile' (Coupe and Jolliffe 1988). While the person physically explores and acts on the environment at the third level, the proactive level, the adult consistently reacts to their reaching responses in addition to vocalisations and looking.

The 'reach-for-signal' grows out of the 'reach-for-real' (Bruner 1975) at the Primitive Level of intentional communication. Movement of objects and people becomes very common, these behaviours often being used to manipulate the adult. Facial expressions are not intentionally used to communicate. At the conventional level, gesture then becomes a predominant form of communication, i.e. 'motor acts or actions not involving physical contact with object or people' (Coupe and Jolliffe 1988). The child may create novel gestures which repeat part of the motor act. Certainly repertoires of physical action here are used specifically for communication.

Bullowa (1979) points out that motor and perceptual capacities can limit the possibilities for communication. Where a person has physical disabilities, assessment may be difficult. However, it is important to create setting conditions, using aids or modern technology if necessary, which enable individuals to perform at their highest level of competence. See also Bates *et al.* (1975) and Schaffer (1971).

The ECA: Where do we go from here?

In principle, the ECA would appear to fill a much needed gap for those who are involved in assessing early communicative functioning of children and adults with serious communication delay. There is generally a dearth of sound, detailed, sensitive and reliable assessment materials available which will inform intervention for those who function within the early stages of development in communication.

It is crucial that an assessment such as the ECA is available to inform teachers, therapists, carers and other staff of relevant and appropriate intervention, and to provide a means to document even very modest progress. Indeed, without such a resource it is likely that those who are committed to supporting such people will appear to be floundering, which might provoke a retrograde step of pointing to a minority population of people who are considered to be ineducable. This would be unacceptable to the majority of parents and professionals who have fought so long to provide education and appropriate provision for this population, as their right. Therefore, the need to carry out research to further develop the ECA along the lines described in Appendix B is great.

Chapter 7

From assessment to intervention: examples of the use of the Early Communication Assessment (ECA)

Using the Early Communication Assessment

Saffia is a nine-year-old child with profound and multiple learning difficulties. Her communication is within the pre-intentional levels and she responds well to adult intervention. In the past, the Affective Communication Assessment (Coupe *et al.* 1985) has proved the only really useful tool to assist her teacher in identifying her needs and planning appropriate intervention. From her assessments, it is clear that she has a wide repertoire of affective communication within Levels 2 and 3 and is making efforts to act on her environment.

In a video recording of Saffia and her teacher, Saffia is on her teacher's knee having a story read to her. The teacher uses a variety of facial expressions, frowns, laughs, smiles, along with a wide range of pitch, volume and intonation, including a squawking bird and different animal noises. In the ten-minute session, Saffia's responses can clearly be interpreted as ranging from animated delight (extremes of like, want) to quiet, still, concentrated listening.

This video was used to assess Saffia on the Early Communication Assessment. Indeed, she was seen to be communicating across nine out of the 13 areas of communicative functioning where a total of 66 different behaviours were observed.

Assessment profile of Saffia on the ECA

Affective communication

Level 2: Reactive level
4. Will consistently use a repertoire of changes in behaviours in response to a range of stimuli which is interpreted as conveying *like*.
6. Will consistently use a repertoire of changes in behaviours in response to a range of stimuli which is interpreted as conveying *want*.
8. Will consistently use a repertoire of changes in behaviours in response to a range of stimuli which is interpreted as conveying meanings and information about states such as *discomfort, surprise, interest, recognition*.

Level 3: Proactive level
9. Will make efforts to act on the environment which become signals to the adult who then assigns communicative intent and interprets the meaning of *like*.
11. Will make efforts to act on the environment which become signals to the adult who then assigns communicative intent and interprets the meaning of *want*.
13. Will make efforts to act on the environment which become signals to the adult who then assigns communicative intent and interprets the meaning of *discomfort, surprise, interest, recognition*.

Mutual gaze

Level 1: Reflexive level
1. Will join in mutual gaze with adult.
2. Will fixate on an adult's face when it appears in midline at a distance of 20–25 cms.

Level 2: Reactive level
3. Will shift gaze to an object or person.
4. Will give eye contact to adult.
5. Will look intently at adult's face while being talked to.
6. Will turn head deliberately to source of voice.
7. Will mainly maintain eye contact with an adult whilst participating in activities such as feeding, dressing, being changed.
8. Will begin to use gaze coupling similar to gaze patterns in mature conversation, e.g. mutual and intermittent gaze, initiation and termination.

Social organisation of communication

Level 1: Reflexive level
1. Will fill a turn in response to an adult's pause in an interaction when given time.
3. Will share an exchange with an adult, adapting the behaviours as the adult does, e.g. adult vocal, child vocal.
4. Will act simultaneously with adult though not necessarily using the same physical action.

Level 2: Reactive level
5. Will maintain an interaction, after responding to an adult's initiation.

Level 3: Proactive level
6. Will initiate an interaction with success.
8. Will maintain an interaction which is adult-structured but child anticipates turn.

Turn-taking and social interaction

Level 2: Reactive level
1. Will anticipate and fill a turn with adult, e.g. smiles, increased arm movement.
2. Will elicit behaviours which produce responses from an adult.
3. Will elicit responses which, in turn, alter the adult's responses.
4. Will maintain an interaction by giving rewarding feedback which relates to the adult's behaviour.
5. Will increasingly fill turns by vocalisations and movements of the head and hands.
7. Will vocalise in response to human voice.
8. Will smile in response to a smile.

Level 3: Proactive level
9. Will use many vocalisations which are simultaneous with adult.

Comprehension in context

Level 1: Reflexive level
2. Will orient to a person.

3. Will shape or control adult's behaviour, although this is not intentional control: e.g. intense periods of eye-to-eye/face-to-face contact.
5. Will move in synchrony to adult speech.

Level 2: Reactive level
7. Will increase limb movements with attention from an adult.
8. Will respond to affective messages from the adult and react to adult's behaviours, e.g. tone of voice, facial expression.

Level 3: Proactive level
9. Will show differential responses to adult intonation and voice quality, e.g. angry voice, verbal praise.

Imitation

Level 2: Reactive level
1. Will smile or frown in response to an adult's frown or smile.
2. Will vocalise in response to a human voice. N.B. Tends to imitate the mode/channel and not the exact behaviour.

Level 3: Proactive level
4. Will imitate mouth movements.

Auditory and visual behaviours

Level 2: Reactive level
1. Will visually inspect people and objects.
2. Will give eye contact to adult.
4. Will search for sound with eyes.
5. Will search for sound with head movement or orientation of the body.
6. Will stop an activity in response to sounds.
7. Will show preference for certain sounds.
8. Will respond to intense noise.
9. Will glance at noisy object.

Level 3: Proactive level
10. Will listen to sounds.
11. Will look for a fallen object.

Vocal production

Level 1: Reflexive level
2. Will produce vegetative sounds, e.g. burp, smacking lips, gurgling noises.

Level 2: Reactive level
3. Will laugh.
5. Will produce open vowels, e.g. 'oh' and 'ah'.

Level 3: Proactive level
   9. Will vocalise during play with adults.
   12. Will vocalise to people.
   14. Will use vocalisations which vary in pitch, volume, stress and quality to express anger, eagerness, satisfaction, etc.

Physical production

Level 1: Reflexive level
   3. Will head turn.
   4. Will open/close mouth.
   6. Will relax body.
   8. Will move trunk or other body parts.

Level 2: Reactive level
   11. Will smile.
   12. Will show trunk-turning/orientation to adult or other stimulus.
   14. Will produce changes in activity level.
   18. Will produce facial movements, e.g. mouth puckering, tongue movement.

Level 3: Proactive level
   23. Will orientate body posture towards desired object or adult.

Using the ECA – Daniel

At 11 years of age, Daniel was assessed on the ECA during a class English lesson where the focus was on first meanings. While he clearly functions within the communicative Levels 4 and 5, like Saffia, the range of communicative functions observed and behaviours identified is extensive and provides an extremely positive guide for drawing up future teaching priorities.

Mutual gaze

Level 3: Proactive level
   9. Will use a mature, i.e. broken, pattern of eye contact during an interaction.

Social organisation of communication

Level 3: Proactive level
   7. Will maintain an interaction which is adult-directed.
   8. Will maintain an interaction which is adult-structured but child anticipates turn.

Level 4: Primitive level
   10. Will integrate attention between self, adult and object, e.g. by gaze, gesture and touch, establishing joint reference.
   12. Will turn-take.
   13. Will terminate an interaction.

Level 5: Conventional level
14. Will repair a misunderstanding non-verbally by repetition.
15. Will repair a misunderstanding non-verbally by rephrasing with a different pitch or novel gesture.

Joint reference

Level 4: Primitive level
8. Will establish integrating joint reference by coordinating attention to self and a person with an object, event or other person.

Turn-taking and social interaction

Level 3: Proactive level
13. Will refer to a person, object or activity in
    (a) immediate proximity
    (b) distance.

Level 4: Primitive level
15. Will repeat a behaviour which has just produced a response, e.g. laughter.
20. Will 'reach-for-signal', i.e. reaches or points to object, person or event while looking at the adult.
25. Will cooperate with adult's lead in simple play routines.

Comprehension in context

Level 3: Proactive level
9. Will show differential responses to adult intonation and voice quality, e.g. angry voice, verbal praise.
10. Will show differential responses to facial expressions, e.g. smiles, angry expressions.
11. Will show differential responses to adult actions, e.g. arms held out for a hug. N.B. May respond to tone of voice in 'no' but might not hold adult hand in response to proffered hand.

Level 4: Primitive level
12. Will respond appropriately to adult's non-verbal communication, e.g. takes proferred neutral object, takes held-out hand, follows a point.
14. Will respond to commands incorporating situational cues when in context, e.g. give me, come here, sit down.
15. Will watch adult's face and gestures for cues.

Level 5: Conventional level
16. Will respond when the answer is visually apparent, e.g. when asked to show familiar object which is clearly on view.
18. Will come when called.
19. Will respond to a familiar word in adult conversation.
23. Will respond to request to give object in possession.
24. Will show understanding of a number of early words which relate to familiar situations, e.g. dinner, clap, ball, no.

Communicative intentions

Level 4: Primitive level
1. Will use a vocal and/or physical repertoire of behaviours to get a person to obtain objects (proto-imperative).
2. Will use a vocal and/or physical repertoire of behaviours to get a person to create/provide events and actions (proto-imperative).
3. Will use a vocal and/or physical repertoire of behaviours to get a person to satisfy states and conditions (proto-imperative).
4. Will use an object, action or event to get adult attention and draw it to self (proto-declarative).
5. Will produce physical and vocal messages to convey request.

Level 5: Conventional level
10. Will draw attention to an object.
18. Will reject an action.
19. Will reject an object.
21. Will protest.
25. Will respond to a question.

Cognitive roles

Level 4: Primitive level
1. Will use objects in a way which reflects the knowledge of their functions.
2. Will demonstrate the cognitive concept of the *existence* of objects, events and people.
6. Will demonstrate the cognitive concept of *location*, i.e. the position of the object, person or event or the relationship between two objects or people.
7. Will demonstrate the cognitive concept of *possession*, i.e. the relationship between an object or person and themself.
8. Will demonstrate the cognitive concept of *rejection*, i.e. not wanting an object, adult or event, or wanting an activity to cease.
9. Will demonstrate the cognitive concept of *denial* of a proposition.
10. Will demonstrate the cognitive concept of *agent*, i.e. the person or object that causes an action to occur.
11. Will demonstrate the cognitive concept of *object*, i.e. the object or person that may be affected by an action.
13. Will demonstrate the cognitive concept of *attribute*, i.e. the property of an object or person.

First meanings (semantic roles)

Level 5: Conventional level
1. Will communicate *existence* by acknowledging that an object exists.
5. Will communicate *location* by commenting on the position of an object, person or event or the special relationship between two objects, or requesting that an object is placed in a certain location.
6. Will communicate *possession* by conveying the relationship between an object, person and themself or another.
7. Will communicate *rejection* by conveying not wanting an object, adult or event, or wanting an activity to cease.

Imitation

Level 4: Primitive level
8. Will imitate actions/gestures of adult spontaneously.

Vocal production

Level 4: Primitive level
18. Will use consonant-vowel and vowel-consonant-vowel structures, e.g. 'ta', 'de', 'da', 'ada', 'aga', 'iya'.
19. Will squeal, shout, scream.
21. Will use vocalisation plus action to attain an object/event, etc.
24. Will generally use only those sounds which occur in the phonological system of their home language.

Physical production

Level 4: Primitive level
25. Will use whole-body action, e.g. to pull away from adult.
27. Will use eye or hand to point at, or indicate, an object, person or event.
28. Will use facial expressions and eye contact with adult.
29. Will reach-for-signal, e.g. reaches for, or indicates, cup while looking at adult.
31. Will manipulate objects, people or events and make eye contact with the adult, e.g. drops toy and looks at adult, turns door handle and looks at adult.

Level 5: Conventional level
33. Will shake head.
37. Will point using eye, hand or finger.
38. Will gesture to express 'gone' or 'where'.

Assessment to intervention – Level 1: Sam

Sam is a six-year-old boy with microcephaly and severe learning difficulties. He has cerebral palsy and low muscle tone. He is non-ambulant, but can sit unsupported on the floor with limited head control. Sam has severely impaired auditory and visual functioning, being fairly unresponsive to sound and all but faces and yellow visual input. He has a range of reflexes – gag, rooting – but others are absent, for instance, stepping and grasp. Sam's output comprises cries, whines, burps, clicks, frowns, opening and closing his eyes, body movements, particularly patting his tummy, and varying states of wakefulness. He actively interacts with his environment only when prompted.

Sam's lack of movement and alertness combined with the production of behaviours which can only be interpreted as *dislike* or *reject* make it difficult for staff to interact with him. Our main concern was to capitalise on any signs which could be interpreted as *like* or *want*, giving positive feedback to the staff and so prolonging interaction. A teaching priority was determined from the communicative area of affective communication, item 1, Level 1: will consistently use a repertoire of changes in behaviours in response to a range of stimuli which is interpreted by adults as conveying *like*.

The priority for Sam was:

- *In response to being rocked, cuddled or bounced on a familiar adult's knee, Sam will relax his body and this will be interpreted by the adult as conveying 'like'.*

For this to become an integral, generalised part of Sam's repertoire and for it to occur spontaneously, it may be necessary to define further priorities, altering the setting conditions, such as an active classroom, different people or extending the stimuli. For Sam, within this first level, it may be particularly appropriate to draw behaviours from the communicative areas of mutual gaze (item 2) and social organisation of communication (item 1):

- *Given no auditory stimuli from the adult, Sam will fixate on the adult's face when it appears in the midline at a distance of 25–27 cms from him.*
- *In response to an adult's pause in an interaction, Sam will fill his turn with any unspecified behaviour.*

Assessment to intervention – Level 2: Rita

Rita is a ten-year-old with severe learning difficulties, microcephaly and hypotonic cerebral palsy. She has some head and trunk control and can side-sit unsupported despite scoliosis. Rita has limited arm and hand movement especially across the midline. She is non-ambulant and cannot move independently, since she is hampered by being very overweight. Rita has good acuity and functional use of both vision and hearing, although she has a corrected squint. She responds to sounds, especially repetitions of her own noises – open vowels, laughs, 'b', 'da' and mixed sound strings. Physically she will turn her head, extend her trunk and hand but to no purpose, wave her hands and arms especially behind her head, and kick her legs in hydrotherapy. She habitually flexes both her arms and legs. Rita enjoys mutual regard, interaction, especially vocal, and being held, music and light stimulation. She does not like food or drinks, particularly water.

Rita reacts well to stimuli but not consistently, so a priority was devised from item 4, Level 2 in the area of affective communication: will consistently use a repertoire of changes in behaviours in response to a range of stimuli which is interpreted by adults as conveying *like*.

The priority for Rita was:

- *Rita will respond to tickles, trills, blowing and fluorescent toys with smiling and vocalisation strengthening the interpretation of her 'like' responses.*

Other priorities were also determined from the communicative functions of turn-taking and social interaction (item 5) and auditory and visual behaviours (item 5):

- *In a turn-taking situation Rita will use smiles, vocalisations and hand-to-mouth movement in response to an adult's pause.*
- *When seated in her Rifton chair and with no visual clues Rita will turn towards a range of sounds, for instance bells, voice, musical toys, when each sound is presented in line with the left or right ear.*

Assessment to intervention – Level 3: Roger

Roger is a 24-year-old with profound learning difficulties. At present he is ambulant only with help but gets around independently by bottom shuffling at great speed. He has accurate and functional hearing and vision. Roger can finger-feed or use a spoon if it is loaded for him. He is not discriminating in what he eats or drinks. Roger has few objects or people that interest him spontaneously. He responds positively to many auditory stimuli (for example speech, bells, music), some visual stimuli (for example snooker and cartoons on the television) and a variety of tactile stimuli (such as shaving foam and tickles), but he is predominantly motivated by food or drink.

Despite being able to grasp and manipulate objects, hitting, shaking, feeling and exploring, Roger's most common scheme is still mouthing. He also spends a considerable amount of time in self-stimulatory behaviour, such as rocking. Roger vocalises quite frequently, laughs and cries. He displays strong signs of frustration if interesting items are unavailable or out of reach, for example mugs, balls, sleigh bells, biscuits. His frustration is manifested by head banging and face thumping.

Because of this a priority was drawn up for Roger from item 11, Level 3 in the area of affective communication: will make efforts to act on the environment which become signals to the adult who then assigns communicative intent and interprets the meaning of *want*.

For Roger the priority was:

● *He will be interpreted as signalling 'want' by moving towards a desired object when the object is in view, which the adult then gives him.*

A further priority for Roger might come from the area of turn-taking and social interaction (item 11), thus consolidating his skills at this level:

● *Roger will initiate a vocal dialogue with a staff member by giving eye contact and vocalising when the staff member is in close proximity.*

Assessment to intervention – Level 4: Anne

Anne is a 20-year-old with severe learning difficulties and microcephaly. She is ambulant, has good hearing and is slightly short-sighted. Her major mode of communication is affective – for example, cries, frowns, smiles – but she exhibits some intentional communication when highly motivated: for example, looking at, or touching, another person to request a drink or music. She is very fond of music to listen and dance to, and is discriminating in which records she likes. She also enjoys curries, rocking-chairs and the jacuzzi. Anne can self-feed with a spoon but needs her food cut up into bite-sized pieces. She has some comprehension of actions in context, that is, she will place an object in another's proffered hand, and responds to common situationally cued commands with gestures. She also has a few set phrases which are used non-functionally, such as 'head down', and will vocalise in response to music or speech. If Anne is not actively occupied by the staff she habitually sits down and rocks or takes her clothes off.

Her priority in communication is drawn from item 1, Level 4, in the area of communicative intentions encoding the proto-imperative function: will use a vocal and/or physical repertoire of behaviours to get a person to obtain objects.

The priority is:

● *Anne will gain eye contact with and lead an adult towards a visible desired object that is out of reach or requires activating, for instance a radio.*

A further skill appropriate for Anne at this level comes from the communicative function of comprehension in context, item 12.

● *Anne will take a proffered object from a known adult in response to the instruction 'take it'.*

Assessment to intervention – Level 5: Tony

Tony is a five-year-old with severe learning difficulties and a moderate conductive hearing loss, but fully functioning vision. He has Down's syndrome and is fully ambulant. He is a very active and friendly child, interested in most people and events in his environment. A few of his favourite activities are music, musical instruments, wind-up and mechanical toys, tickles, swings, slides, the home corner and eating. Tony understands a wide range of common nouns and verbs in relation to himself and objects, and can understand phrases by decoding one key word. He communicates with gestures supplemented by vocalisations and has recently said his first situation-specific word.

Tony is highly motivated to communicate but has tended to perseverate on a limited range of meanings, for instance agent and recurrence, and on particular functions, such as requests. His communication priorities were devised from the following items in two communicative areas. The first is first meanings (semantic roles), item 4: will communicate non-existence by indicating that an object does not exist where it is expected to be.

- *Tony will communicate non-existence by a 'gone' gesture in the following situations: an empty biscuit tin expected to be full; dinner aprons not in the usual cupboard; no knives and forks at the dinner table.*

The second is communicative intentions, item 24: will give information about the environment and the people within it.

- *Using vocalisations and gestures, Tony will inform the adult about the following: a child finishing his crisps or drink; a child putting on the wrong clothes; a child hurting himself.*

Assessment to intervention – first meanings: Hajra

Assessment

Within the communicative area of first meanings, Hajra has achieved eight skills. Using a combination of look, vocalisation, gesture, sign and word, she can now communicate and generalise her use of the semantic notions of existence, disappearance, recurrence, location, possession, agent, object and action.

Priority teaching

The information collated during the assessment must be utilised to identify what needs to be taught next. For Hajra, the assessment shows that she is not yet competent in communicating non-existence, rejection, denial or attribute in functionally appropriate contexts. However, the assessment clearly indicates that she understands the cognitive concept of non-existence, so that, for instance, when her coat is not in its expected place she will search other locations to find it. We know from the assessment that, with prompting, she can use look, gesture and vocalisation to communicate about this concept of non-existence. Hence, for Hajra the following teaching priority was drawn up:

- *She will use a combination of look, vocalisation and gesture to communicate the meaning of non-existence in the milk-time situation.*

It may be that, for some pupils, the identified skill will prove too big a step, in which case smaller steps, which may be of graded difficulty, will be required. In this way the learning will be made easier and the steps will be more reasonable and realistic for the individual pupil. Not all skills will require such a task analysis and because no skill can have a set number of task-analysed steps, how these are determined is dependent on the strengths and needs of each pupil. For Hajra, the following steps were drawn up:

Step 1: Using a combination of look, gesture and vocalisation, will communicate the non-existence of biscuits when she expects them to be in the biscuit tin.
Step 2: Using a combination of look, gesture and vocalisation, will communicate the non-existence of straws when she expects them to be in the box.
Step 3: Using a combination of look, gesture and vocalisation, will communicate the non-existence of the milk bottles when she expects them to be in the crate.

For Hajra, communication of non-existence was considered to be best taught in a natural situation where each step identifies the non-existence of different specified materials, so that each step is not taught in isolation. Indeed, at a later stage this could be generalised to different activities, such as dressing, cookery, dolls house, play and so on.

Recording

When recording Hajra's performance for communicating non-existence it is possible to score

L = look
G = gesture
V = vocalisation.

Physical or verbal assistance and physical or verbal models for her to imitate could be considered to be a prompt, and this will be scored by prefixing the behaviour with a P.

From assessment to intervention – Affective communication: Louise

Assessment

When assessed in the area of affective communication, Louise was identified as consistently being interpreted to convey the four meanings of like, dislike want and reject at two levels. She is competent at Level 1, reflexive level, where social significance can be assigned by the adult to her reflexive (signalling) responses to internal and external stimuli. Also, at Level 2, the reactive level, social significance can be assigned by adults to her reactive behaviours – the way she reacts to events and people within her environment. Only some of her efforts to act on her environment at the third level, proactive level, are interpreted as signals to adults who then assign communicative intent. As yet she shows no evidence of Level 4 behaviours, the primitive level of intentional communication.

Teaching priorities

The assessment of Louise demonstrated that some of her efforts to act on her environment at the proactive level have become signals to adults who then assign communicative intent. Before considering Level 4, where she would be taught to signal communicative intentions to others, it will be necessary to establish consistent and generalised competence at Level 3, the proactive level. A priority for Louise therefore will be:

- *When being held by an adult in the classroom setting Louise will use a repertoire of smile and vocalisation which will be interpreted as an intention and a signal for her to 'want' the familiar adult to swing her from side to side.*
  (To be generalised to different locations, for instance soft play room, hall, corridor and with less familiar adults.)

Having achieved this, however, it cannot be assumed that Louise has reached full mastery of the skill, where the pupils' repertoire of behaviours during efforts to act on the environment are reliably interpretable by adults as a signal to convey 'want'. It may be necessary to present new priorities incorporating different wants, for example adult sneezing, adult banging the surface next to her, a drink of tea, chocolate drops and so on.

Chapter 8

Accessing and extending pragmatics: the functional use of communication[1]

What is pragmatics?

There seem to be as many definitions of the term 'pragmatics' as there are authors. One particularly informative model was that expounded by Roth and Speckman in two articles (1984a, 1984b). They outline an organisational framework for assessment which can be used to describe pragmatic abilities. Roth and Speckman discuss analysing people's messages at three levels:

- the communicative *intentions* of the speaker;
- the *social organisation of the discourse* in which the message is sent;
- the speaker's message in relation to the information needs of their listener and the context, i.e. *presupposition*.

They emphasise that any one message or utterance can be analysed at each level. For example:

message – 'Hiya';
communicative intention – to greet;
discourse structure – an initiation;
presupposition – I know this person well enough to say hiya instead of hello.

Pragmatics can, therefore, be defined as the study of communication use in context. Figure 8.1 is adapted from Roth and Speckman (1984a).

The following sections discuss each of the levels in Figure 8.1 in more detail and are broadly based on the work of the Manchester Functional Communication Working Party. The working party was a joint venture between health service and education service staff to investigate current practice in the assessment and remediation of pragmatic disabilities and to devise a user-friendly assessment primarily for teachers and speech and language therapists. The resultant Manchester Pragmatics Profile is presented in Appendix C.

N.B. For convention during this chapter the respondent is generally referred to as the *listener* and the communicator as the *speaker*.

Why is pragmatics important?

Traditionally, communication assessment focused on the way messages were sent, i.e. the form and the content of these messages. While this assessment can lead to valuable information about a person's communication, it cannot fully explain the difficulties they have on a day-to-day basis communicating with other people. Researchers and practitioners have all recognised that the study of pragmatics provides some insight into these difficulties and opens up the possibility of intervention to help people cope with their difficulties.

Harasty *et al.* (1994) addressed the issue of pragmatic difficulties, primarily in the area of presupposition, and found that pragmatic deficits did indeed affect judgements about the person's

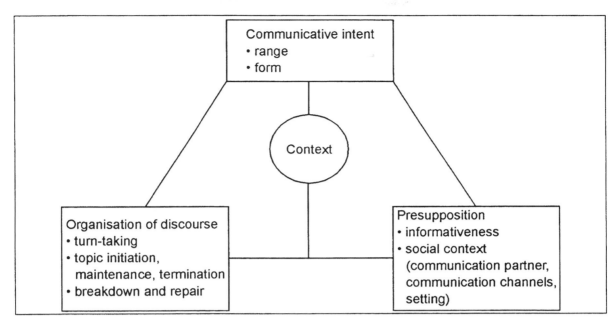

Figure 8.1 Three-level message analysis

communication impairment. They found that 'communicative flexibility is a factor in judgements of children's communicative competence and its lack increases the perception of communication disorder'. So people who have functional communication impairments are seen to be communication-impaired as much as people who have problems with, for example, their speech sounds or their grammar. It is therefore imperative that clinicians find a way to assess pragmatic skills and to promote their development.

What are communicative intentions?

An intention is the communicative goal or purpose in the mind of the speaker, the reasons why we communicate; for example, the intention to draw someone's attention to an object, to make a request for an event to happen, to greet or give information about yourself, etc.

Intentions vary in range and form. The range extends from the intention simply to gain someone's attention to complex concepts such as the intention to deceive another person. The form is the way the intention is expressed, e.g. by speaking, by paralinguistic features, such as tone of voice, stress on certain words, by non-verbal means, such as looking, pointing, nodding. The intentions finally included in the Manchester Pragmatics Profile were those considered to be needed by a competent communicator. The earliest intentions can be communicated by non-symbolic and symbolic systems; the later developing intentions require a symbolic system, e.g. speech, signs, to express them. The full range of communicative intentions from the Manchester Profile is listed in Appendix C. All intentions may be expressed spontaneously, as initiations or as responses to other people's communication.

The intentions of drawing attention to, requesting, rejecting and giving information are separated into component intentions depending on whether the intention is directed towards a person or self, object, event, action or information. For example:

request a person – asking for someone by name;
request an object – asking for a drink;
request an action or event – asking someone to sit down beside you;
request information – asking the time;
request recurrence – asking for more dinner;
request confirmation of information – asking if someone's tea is still hot.

This was necessary as members of the working party had frequently found that people with SLD displayed different levels of skill based on these categories. For example, it was common to find a speaker who could request and reject an object but not an action or event.

Most communicative intentions are self-explanatory but some require further explanation:

- *proto-imperative* – the use of another person to obtain a desired object, event, person or state;
- *proto-declarative* – the use of an object or action to obtain joint attention with another person;
- *gain attention for communication* – a communication prior to the main message to alert the listener that they are about to be given a message, e.g. by a tap on the shoulder, by saying 'Oh Caroline';
- *draw attention to objects/people/states and events* – communications which point out something to another person and are the equivalent of saying 'Oh look';
- *protest* – a person making their dislike of an activity/person known while allowing the activity/contact to continue, e.g. saying 'I wish you'd stop' or frowning and wriggling;
- *comment on or draw attention to available information* – a communication about something already present either in the environment or in the communication, e.g. hears thunders and says 'Oh, thunder';
- *describe* – giving information gained from a sense, e.g. hearing, vision, touch; this intention would cover the use of metaphors for description, e.g. 'The cloud was like cotton wool';
- *promise* – the intention to commit yourself to a course of action, e.g. 'I promise to ring';
- *metalinguistic* – the intention used when people communicate about language and the rules that govern it, e.g. asking 'What does pragmatics mean?', 'Red rhymes with bed', 'Is it rude to interrupt?';
- *regulate* – the intention to regulate social contact; these could be classified as requests for actions but are aimed specifically at controlling the interaction, e.g. 'Please go away' (regulating) versus 'Please give me that' (request for action);
- *pretend* – communication relating to pretending, for example offering someone a plate of sand as if it were food and miming eating, saying 'Let's be robots';
- *reason* – the communication of a problem and its possible solutions, e.g. saying 'Repairmen come, telly broke';
- *tease* – the intention to tease, i.e. make fun without intending to cause hurt;
- *provoke* – the intention to use communication to upset or provoke another person because that response in itself is rewarding for the communicator, e.g. by talking about someone's weight.

Occasionally the communicative intention of the speaker is masked because of the way speakers expresses themselves, e.g. making things up or confabulating, to draw attention to self. It can be difficult to distinguish between a communicative intention and a social intention – e.g. to impress, to gain social status – even for experienced communicators. It is important that difficulties such as these are identified and documented as they can have serious consequences for the individual. Many people with learning difficulties are the victims of abuse, whether financial, physical, verbal or sexual. They are often considered by investigators to be poor and unreliable witnesses when giving testimony about their experiences. People's testimony is further devalued if they are perceived to be highly acquiescent or confabulatory. It is easy for an inexperienced investigator to interpret acquiescence as fulfilling the intention 'to give information about events' and to interpret confabulation as the intention 'to lie'.

Development of intentions

A number of researchers have provided information about the development of communicative intentions (Halliday 1975, Bates 1976, Dore 1978, Roth and Speckman 1984a, McTear and Conti-Ramsden 1992, Dewart and Summers 1995). All researchers agree that infants from birth demonstrate a range of vocalisations, e.g. cries, coos, squeals, and other behaviours, e.g. smiles, eye gazing. These behaviours do not have a specific communicative intention but are interpreted by the caring adults as having meaning. The adult's responses to these behaviours therefore shapes the behaviours to become intentional (see Chapter 1).

Bates *et al.* (1975) described the notion of the proto-imperative and proto-declarative which are included as communicative intentions. These are the earliest intentions observed in children where a child gives persistent regard to another person and a desired object or event in order to have a specific influence on the behaviour of another person (as described in Chapter 1). As described earlier, the proto-imperative is the use of another person to obtain a desired object or event, the proto-declarative is the use of an object or action to obtain the attention of another person. The specific point when these behaviours become intentional and develop from their basic form of 'dual regard' to more specific and communicative acts is not clear. However most researchers agree that they describe a transitional stage between the infant's affective and intentional communication.

From about nine months old the child's developing repertoire of gestures, vocalisations and eventually words begins to be used to express a range of specific intentions. These early intentions are generally agreed to include:

- drawing attention to self, other people, objects and events;
- requesting objects, events, information and recurrence;
- greeting;
- rejecting;
- protesting;
- naming and informing.

The information on the normal development of later intentions is patchy, with some intentions studied in depth and others hardly at all. Dore (1978) observed three-year-old children describing, and Astington (1990) found five-year-olds were able to promise. However, the children were not able to judge whether other people had made a promise until they were nine or older.

There is a substantial body of research looking at the development of request for information. As Przetacznik-Gierowska and Ligeza (1990) write, 'Children asking questions often seek information about their world, and their intention is to fill a gap in their representation of reality or to acquire better orientation in an actual situation.' So the acquisition of sophisticated question forms – i.e. being able to ask 'why' and 'how' as well as 'what', 'who', 'where' and 'when' – will feed into the person's cognitive development as well as allowing them to discuss, for example, emotions, reasons etc.

As children develop their range of functions, linguistic or symbolic communications 'map on' to the already existing non-verbal and vocal repertoires (McLean and Snyder-McLean 1978). For example, requesting an object may be communicated by the following messages:

a point and eye contact with a carer and the desired object;
'da' + a point and eye contact;
'bibi' + a point and eye contact;
'biscuit please';
'chocolate biscuit please';
'two chocolate biscuits please mum'.

For a range of intentions to develop, the child needs to experience a variety of situations. These situations should stimulate the need to express certain intentions and involve observing the expression of the intentions modelled by more skilled communicators. For example, a child who has never needed to greet people is unlikely to have this intention in their repertoire. Naturally occurring models and opportunities may be sufficient for a child without any disabilities. However, for children and adults with sensory and/or learning disabilities a more structured approach may be necessary. Many people with communication impairments do not develop the full range of intentions needed to be a successful communicator. The authors and their colleagues have worked with many people with learning disabilities of all ages and, from observations and assessments, the following problems have been found to occur frequently:

- only being able to make a request in response to a question;
- being unable to use communication to focus another person's attention;
- being able to request objects but not events, states or people;
- being unable to communicate 'no', i.e. rejection using intentional communication;
- being unable to narrate or use other more mature intentions;
- overuse of rejecting and protesting and underuse of requesting.

What is the social organisation of communication?

The working party changed the title of this section from 'social organisation of discourse' to 'social organisation of communication' to remind users of the profile that all communication is not speech.

Communication is highly structured. Most people learn the rules that govern this structure without being aware of them. The skills needed to communicate effectively are usually only recognised when they are absent or when the rules are broken, for example, by people who jump from topic to topic or who interrupt inappropriately. The core skill is the ability to gain another person's attention in order to begin to convey a message. Attention needs to be gained regardless of whether you are the initiator or the respondent in a particular exchange. Vocal and verbal people may gain attention by a variety of means, e.g. use of a name, 'hey', 'oy', throat-clearing. Non-vocal ways of gaining attention include placing self in the line of gaze of the intended communication partner, touching or tapping arms and shoulders, flicking the lights on and off, waving.

Once the partner's attention is gained, they can be focused on the topic of the conversation. This is far easier for a speaker as words can be used. Users of non-verbal communication, e.g. finger, hand or eye pointing, will have difficulties in certain contexts, for example, when the object they want to point to is not there. After the message is conveyed, by whatever means, i.e. a communication initiated, there must be a swap to the listener's role. The listener's role is an active one. It involves giving feedback to the 'speaker' to reassure them that attention is being paid to their message. This is often done through eye contact, nodding murmurs of assent, short phrases, e.g. 'I know'. The speaker also relies on the listener to give feedback on their understanding of the message. To do this the listener has to be able to recognise when and what they have and have not understood. If the listener does not understand, they need to signal this need for clarification, e.g. by a puzzled look, a raised eyebrow, 'You what?', 'Pardon?' etc., the communicator then needs to exercise their skills in repairing misunderstandings. There are three common ways of repairing a misunderstanding:

- repeating – repeating the message in the same way;
- rephrasing – repeating the message altering the part that seemed to cause the problem, e.g. using a different word/sign, simplifying the grammar;
- elaborating – adding additional information to illustrate the message; elaboration can range from the simple, e.g. a gesture, to the complex, e.g. an explanation.

Once the repair has been successfully completed the speaker will be back in the listener's role.

In an exchange such as this the two people continue to take turns. The lengths of their turns, that is their talk-time, will vary greatly, but if one partner exceeds the limit they are likely to experience an interruption. Appropriate interruption is one of the hardest skills to learn and one which many people do not perfect. Both the timing and the form of the interruption are crucial to the successful outcome of getting your turn. Many conversations last a significant period of time, e.g. up to several minutes or hours. During this time it is unlikely that only one topic will be discussed. A range of topics is more likely, with the change of topic seemingly achieved effortlessly and without conscious control. There are three specific skills required: topic maintenance, topic change and adapting to new topics. The most basic skill is to carry on talking about a topic introduced by the partner but from a personal perspective. Smoothly introducing a new topic is more difficult and people often resort to explicit links e.g. 'Talking of the weather . . .'. People still developing skills in topic control frequently just change topic without any link. When a conversation is over, the interaction needs terminating. This can be done explicitly by saying 'I've had enough', 'Thanks for that', 'Bye', or with an action or gesture, such as handing someone their coat. Termination can also be implicit because the topic has been fully covered or because the participants resume or start other activities.

The development of the social organisation of communication

Again researchers have concentrated their efforts on some skills in conversational management, notably turn-taking, gaining attention, repair, but not others such as talk-time or interruptions. The fundamental skill of establishing joint reference has been addressed by Akhtar *et al.* (1991) in their study of the vocabulary development of 13-month-old toddlers. They found the single most influential factor was the mothers following and attending to the subject of their child's focus, that is establishing a period of joint attention. The mothers then usually gave a directive, a request for action associated with the toy etc., e.g. 'Pick up the brick', 'Say all fall down!' Directives given after attempts to focus the children on the subject of the mothers' attention were unsuccessful in developing the children's vocabulary. Early mother–infant interactions involve taking turns and often become formalised into games like peek-a-boo. This seems to establish the pattern of turn-taking so important in communication.

Mueller (1972) showed that children need to develop good strategies to gain attention for communication during the pre-school years. Children's communicative attempts failed, for many different reasons, because:

- they had not learnt how to engage their potential listener's interest;
- they were not close enough and did not use enough eye contact;
- their own speech was difficult to understand and their grammar insufficient to carry their message clearly.

Many researchers have studied the development of repair strategies in children. The type of repair strategies differ with the linguistic maturity and age of the child and with the type of request for clarification used by their conversational partner. Prather *et al.* (1989) looked at normally developing children aged between four and five and a half years, and found that they primarily used elaboration to repair breakdowns. This strategy was used when their partners made a general request for clarification, e.g. 'What?', or a request for confirmation, e.g. 'You want more?' When the request for clarification was specific, e.g. 'What did you want?', the children used elaboration and correction of their partner as well as rephrasing their utterances. In their discussion Prather *et al.* state that their findings are similar to those of Brinton *et al.* (1986) who studied children aged from two years seven months to ten years. They found that the ability to add information and the complexity of this information – i.e. the ability to elaborate – increased with age. Prather *et al.* felt that their findings and those of Gallagher (1977) illustrated the development of repair strategies from revision to elaborations. The revisions were most commonly phonetic changes (i.e. changing a sound in a word), reductions (i.e. losing a word from a sentence) and substitutions (i.e. replacement of a word(s) with another). Once again this study shows the influence of the conversational partner in facilitating the development of more effective repair strategies. However it may be that specific requests for clarification are not naturally used by more able partners. Gallagher (1981) showed that the most common request used was for confirmation only, i.e. 'Did you say John?', 'Did you ask for a biscuit?' The use of confirmation requests was unlikely to stimulate the development of more sophisticated repair strategies, as the speaker could resort to saying just 'yes' or 'no' in their reply.

Roth and Speckman (1994) discuss how many researchers in the 1970s studied the ability of young children to maintain topics of conversation. They found a great deal of variability and found that the main predictor of successful topic control was when 'the child initiated the topic and when the conversational focus is an object present in the environment'. This echoes the findings of Akhtar *et al.* (1991) mentioned earlier.

People with learning disabilities and communication impairments often have difficulties acquiring the full range of skills required to organise their communications successfully. After completing many communication assessments the following difficulties emerged as those most commonly seen:

- skills as a respondent but not as an initiator;
- an inability to identify the topic of the conversation by establishing joint reference;
- an inability to maintain a topic leading to frequent topic changes;
- insufficient feedback as a listener about continued interest, e.g. no head nodding or saying 'mm';
- insufficient feedback to the speaker about understanding the content of the communication, i.e. no requests for confirmation or clarification such as 'What do you mean?', 'Uh?';
- interruptions inappropriate in timing and in content;
- inability to extend a communication after an initial turn as initiator and respondent;
- termination often premature and communicated ineffectively;
- inability to recognise and repair breakdowns in communication.

What is presupposition?

Presupposition is the ability to see the listener's viewpoint and to adjust communication to that viewpoint and to the situation. This can be illustrated as a series of questions the communicator may need to ask:

Does my partner know this information or do I need to tell them this?
Does my partner understand this word or do I need to explain it?
Do I want to impress my partner with the way I am communicating?
Have we had any previous conversations about this issue?
Am I being unambiguous?
Have I taken into account any problems my listener has?
Am I being appropriate to the situation we are in?
Is my listener interested in what I have to say?

The answers to these questions should be reflected in the person's ability to communicate effectively with a variety of communication partners in a range of settings. Lyons (1977) lists the following elements as being essential:

- knowledge of role and status;
- knowledge of the physical location;
- knowledge of the formality level;
- knowledge of the most appropriate channel for communication – the medium;
- knowledge about the most appropriate subject matter for the communication;
- knowledge about the required register, i.e. vocabulary to use, politeness level required, volume etc.

There are also a set of 'unwritten rules' about communication that people have to learn in order to communicate successfully. These rules are covered in the work of Grice (1975). The rules state that our communications should be:

- cooperative – communication at the appropriate point in the exchange and with the content following the general direction of the exchange;
- of quality – the content of the communication should be factually accurate;
- of an appropriate quantity – giving sufficient information but not too much;
- relevant – to the current exchange;
- unambiguous and clear.

People with symbolic communication systems, that is those using speech, sign or other symbols, show evidence of skills in presupposition by appropriately using the following grammatical features:

- deixis – the use of words/phrases that 'point out' people, objects and locations, e.g. 'I', 'you', 'this', 'that', 'here', 'there'. Deixis is reliant on context and the speaker and listener's perspective on it; e.g. what is 'here' to me is 'there' to you;
- proforms – words that stand in for words already used, e.g. pronouns ('he', 'she', 'it') and pro-verbs ('do', 'go'); for example: 'I'm seeing John tonight, he's meeting me at the pub'; 'Tidy your room, go and do it';
- definite and indefinite articles – 'the' and 'a', 'an'. 'The' is only used when the subject of the sentence is known to both the listener and the speaker: e.g. 'I saw the film last night' refers to a specific film known to both people; 'I saw a film last night' does not and will probably be followed by the question 'What film?'
- ellipsis – a linguistic device used to reduce repetition by the omission of shared or known information: e.g. question – 'Where's Joan?', reply – ' In the bathroom' rather than 'She's in the bathroom'.
- referents – the speaker must give all the information necessary for their listener to understand their message. If the subject has not already been mentioned, it must have explicit reference made to it, e.g. 'I saw Joan last night'. If 'Joan' has already been mentioned – i.e. a referent has been given – the sentence could be 'I saw her last night'. Referents can also be established non-verbally, e.g. saying 'Like' + a point to a pair of shoes in a shop window.

Errors in presupposition often cause communication breakdown. For example, listeners are less likely to understand:

- if a communicator uses jargon (i.e. vocabulary that is exclusive to one situation or group of people) outside that group;
- if the communicator assumes shared knowledge of a situation and gives too little information;
- if the speaker does not take account of their partner's hearing or vision loss;
- if the communicator uses linguistic forms which refer back to previous information, e.g. 'I saw that', 'I know the man'.

People mainly make these errors owing to lack of skill, experience or awareness of the context. However, occasionally people select a particular message structure, vocabulary item, tone of voice etc. because of the effect it will have on their listener; for example, being deliberately over-familiar to cause a listener to become uncomfortable, or using jargon to confuse and control a listener. These choices may reflect the speaker's decision not to 'go along with' the principle described by Stalnater (1991): 'Communication, whether linguistic or not, normally takes place against a background of beliefs and assumptions which are shared by the audience, and which are recognised by them as shared.'

The development of presupposition

It could be argued that some elements of presupposition are seen in very early communicative behaviours. For example, a child crying to get their own way shows some understanding that this behaviour will produce an emotive response in the listener. Golinkoff (1993) would support this view. There is also a connection between cognitive development and the development of presupposition even more than with the acquisition of other pragmatic skills. People have to be aware of others and their environment if presupposition skills are to develop. If there is a lack of awareness and empathy with others, e.g. because of autism, presupposition skills are likely to be impaired.

Restricted experience may also impair the development of these skills; for example, a young child used to talking to one person only for prolonged periods of time may well show no ability to adapt to new people's verbal styles or to deal with the information needs of these new people. Roberts and Patterson (1983) asked children of four to five years of age to take part in referential communication tasks. Referential communication tasks involve asking the speaker to describe something to their listener so that they can select an item from a selection available. There is often a physical barrier between the speaker and their listener such as a screen, thus requiring a description rather than a point or 'Get that one'. They found that most children could take the listener's perspective in that they knew that the listener would not know what to select unless they told them. However this did not mean that the children were able to assess the precise information required by their listener; in other words, their messages were not informative enough. Roberts and Patterson found that children who were good at judging other people's communication as successful or unsuccessful when watching referential communication tasks were themselves the most skilled communicators.

Skills in presupposition are rarely explicitly taught. Children learn by watching others and by extracting the skills without being aware of the process. Research, for example Hausendorf and Quasthoff (1992), supports the view that parents model appropriate interaction skills and language use instinctively. They also found that parents systematically adapted their models as the child became more competent. Becker (1990) gives information on the other methods caregivers use to teach and shape pragmatic skills as well as other communication skills:

- reinforcement of appropriate communication, e.g. 'You said that well';
- correction of errors, e.g. 'Say it quietly';
- comments on omissions, e.g. 'Say please';
- discussion of other people's communication, e.g. 'Did he wait his turn?';
- prompting, e.g. 'Say hello to the lady';
- talking through rules, e.g. 'What do we say when we get a present?'

Adults continue to refine their skills as they experience and become practised in new situations, chairing meetings for example. It may be said that we never acquire all the skills in presupposition as we can never have met all our potential conversational partners or been in all possible situations and contexts with them. People with learning disabilities frequently have extreme difficulty learning about presupposition in the way that those without a cognitive disability do. They find it hard to extract the necessary information and rules from experience alone. Even those people who have an effective communication system in terms of their range of intentions and organisational ability may have difficulty with the complex knowledge and rules governing our interactions. This inability to understand the requirement of different listeners in varying contexts leads to situations where the speaker:

- communicates ambiguously;
- communicates too informally or inappropriately in the degree of politeness for the context;
- does not give all the information their partner needs;
- misuses pronouns and so does not clearly establish the referents for their listener;
- uses inappropriate vocabulary for the situation;
- responds at length to simple requests for information, i.e. exceeds their talk-time;
- misuses paralinguistic features, e.g. their speech is monotonous with little or no intonation, words are stressed inappropriately.

How do we assess pragmatic skills?

An assessment of pragmatic skills should collect data about the repertoire of different communicative behaviours the person uses and the contexts in which the communication occurs. The assessment should clearly record both the person's intentional and their affective communication. The recording must include the communication of the other people present which is directed towards the person who is being assessed, i.e. the communication context, along with the environmental context of the communication, i.e. the physical environment. The time, the surrounding or preceding events are also essential. Ideally, video footage should be collected but, if this is not practical, observational recordings should be made.

Assessment primarily provides information about an individual's expressive skills. However, during the assessment, evidence will be gathered about the individual's understanding of other people's pragmatic skills, e.g. their understanding of questions, requests for clarification. It should also highlight instances of misunderstanding by more able communicators, e.g. misunderstanding 'drawing attention to self' as attention-seeking behaviour, or not recognising a non-verbal request for clarification signalled by a puzzled look and a frown.

These observations can then be analysed for evidence of skills in communicative intentions, social organisation of communication and presupposition. These might include having skills in both requesting and rejecting, being able to initiate as well as respond, making judgements about appropriacy of the communication to the context and the participants. It is essential that the person is observed in as many situations as possible and with as many different communication partners as possible. Only in this way can the assessor begin to identify:

- the person's success in getting their messages across;
- the range of skills the person possesses;
- which skills are communicated intentionally and which are conveyed by affective communication only;
- the difficulties they are experiencing;
- the consequences of these difficulties;
- the factors that affect their performance;
- the frequency of communication.

Recordings over time often give unexpected information. They can identify, for example, the speaker who is verbally skilled but unable to use these skills functionally in everyday situations, or the non-verbal communicator who is skilled in meeting their needs and engaging in dialogues.

The factors which influence the person's performance may include:

- their communication partner;
- the time of day – tiredness and alertness;
- their state of health;
- the noise levels in the environment;
- the degree of urgency of the communication;
- the skills of their partners in communication/conversation;
- the number of people in the communication.

Recording the communications of both parties allows assessors to identify features of the communication which influence the individual, e.g. their partner always initiating, habitually requesting old or known information, overlong talk-time, demanding acquiescence, pre-empting communication. It is important that the data collection includes other people's responses to any 'errors' made by the person being assessed:

- Does the partner disregard the 'error'?
- Does the partner give constructive feedback, e.g. 'Oh you mean . . .'?
- Does the partner initiate a repair strategy, e.g. 'Tell me again'?
- Does the partner become irritated?
- Does the partner become dismissive or even make a disparaging remark? e.g. 'What are you talking about?'
- Does the partner give up and walk away?

The subsequent response of the person being profiled should be recorded to see how they coped. Information from these observations and prior information about both partners in the communication is essential for intervention, e.g. staff training to reduce pre-empting etc. An extensive assessment should also identify those factors which produce the most effective communication more truly reflecting the person's capability. If, after several observational sessions, it seems that the current situations do not allow the person to demonstrate their skills, new contexts or structured situations may have to be introduced to gather information on competence as well as performance. Structured tasks such as referential communication tasks may be useful in gauging people's skills in presupposition. Roth and Speckman (1984b) give more information on how referential communication tasks can be manipulated to get information on a range of skills.

The Manchester Functional Communication Working Party used the grid format in Appendix C to record their findings. Each skill is illustrated by a real-life example that has been collected through observation. This profile, based on the issues discussed above, can be used to guide intervention and monitor change. The content of the Manchester Pragmatics Profile, as outlined in the preceding sections, was based loosely on a developmental perspective drawing on the early work of Bates (1976), Dore (1977, 1978) and Halliday (1975). Information was sought concerning the sequence of development, rather than seeking age-related normative data. This confirms the view of Smith and Leinonen (1992) that while there is a lack of adequate normative data, 'accountability to the clients themselves is well served by pragmatic assessment . . . since it is able to reveal generally accepted areas of strength and need in the client'.

Recording communications

The key to an assessment of pragmatic skills is the accurate recording of the observed communications. It is important to decide how you will record the different kinds of means that may be combined in any one message.

The form of the communication can be grouped into three types – the linguistic, the paralinguistic and the non-verbal. The person may use one or all of these means depending on their ability and the context, e.g. John points to a towel using an excited tone of voice to tell you he's 'going swimming'.

Linguistic refers to the words, phrases or sentences a person may use, usually spoken but alternatively signed or communicated via a symbol system, word board or communication aid with a voice output. The exact form used varies with the context. A request for information can be conveyed at many levels, 'Where's the hospital?', 'Would you mind telling me the way to the hospital?', 'Have you got a map?' The same words, phrases or sentences can also be used to express a range of intentions, and context will be a major determiner of the listeners' recognition of the speaker's intention: for example, 'Can I have some sugar?' is a request for an object to a waiter but a request for information if said to a dietician.

Paralinguistic refers to the changes in 'stress patterns, duration, intonation, pitch and intensity levels' (Roth and Speckman 1984a) which accompany our utterances or are used as a substitute for those utterances. For example, rejecting a person may be expressed by 'Go away' said forcefully and with high stress on both words or by a angry tone with the stress on 'away'. Both these examples would probably be accompanied by non-verbal communication such as facial expression, pushing away etc.

Non-verbal refers chiefly to the range of movements and actions that can be used communicatively. Kiernan and Reid (1987a, 1987b) in the Pre-Verbal Communication Schedule list helpful descriptions of non-verbal communications:

- manipulation – taking people to desired objects and places;
- looking – looking from a desired object to a partner;
- pointing – pointing to request an object or to draw attention to something of interest;
- whole-body action – stiffening, pulling away;
- gestures – waving, nodding, shaking etc.

It is also important to record examples of the person's affective communication when they have no intentional communication. Indeed, the unintentional communication may serve to reject a person, draw attention to self, initiate or terminate an interaction.

What to do next?

After assessment and analysis of the person's difficulties the question is 'What to do next?' It is our view that intervention should focus on the person with the communication impairment, and on their environment and the people who live and work with them. This mirrors work carried out on other aspects of communication skills where the objective of increasing an individual's capability may not be feasible or desirable, e.g. increasing receptive vocabulary. For example a person with severe learning disabilities may find it hard to acquire new skills, a person with autism may find a high level of interaction aversive. This does not mean however that intervention will not have positive benefits for the person being supported or their carers.

Guiding principles of intervention

1. Only intervene if the person is experiencing communication failure and breakdown.
2. Intervene on skills necessary to enable the person to satisfy their basic needs and to give them a 'survival kit' of skills. This could be described as minimum skills for maximum communicative competence.
3. Try and assume the person's perspective to identify skills of importance to them, reflecting their interests and preferences. Intervention focused in this way should increase motivation and success as well as providing opportunities to practise skills which are likely to occur naturally.
4. Intervention can be guided by the broad developmental sequence, the person's cognitive competence and their world knowledge.
5. Use of existing skills should be maximised. People should be encouraged to feel confident in using their existing skills in a variety of situations and to view themselves as successful communicators.
6. The most flexible resource for intervention is more skilled communicators, whether these are staff, carers or peers.
7. People need to be prepared to experiment to utilise situations which will encourage the use of existing skills and support the development of new skills for each individual. If such situations do not already occur, they may need to be created. Manufactured opportunities should reflect real-life situations and genuine communication needs, e.g. to ask where the toilet is in an unfamiliar shopping arcade.
8. It is important to focus on what is 'normal' so that our intervention does not develop maladaptive skills, e.g. eye contact programmes that produce staring children who don't know why they are making eye contact.

When an individual has progressed as far as they are able at that time, it is important for people to accept their system as it is and be consistent in their responses to it. For example, it is common for people with learning disabilities to have no intentional communication to convey information about their health spontaneously and, indeed, they are often unaware that this is valued information to give. In these circumstances their affective methods of communicating about their health, such as crying, feeling tired and irritable, looking pale etc., must be identified and responded to.

Methods of intervention

As with all teaching a range of methods might be useful depending on the individual and their circumstances. These include:

- use of gentle teaching and intensive interaction techniques;
- use of models;
- use of routines;

- use of environmental manipulation;
- use of role play;
- use of feedback to the individual;
- practice and experience in community settings;
- prompting;
- explanations.

The purpose of intervention

The aim of intervention may be to develop a person's pragmatic skills through direct teaching. Skills that respond well to direct teaching are turn-taking, interruption and intentions. Many everyday situations and activities can be adapted to provide opportunities to practise skills, for example hide and seek. This provides the context for practising – describing, requesting information, requesting recurrence, initiating, responding, turn-taking, working on shared knowledge etc.

Intervention should occur alongside actions taken to make the communicative environment more supportive for the development of communication. This may relate to the people within the environment or the environment itself and might include discussing the need to encourage people with SLD to accept their right to say 'no' and to appreciate that this is a vital skill. This can be particularly difficult in situations where this skill might challenge an existing relationship, e.g. between pupil and teacher, parent and child, student and therapist.

People can also be asked to be less directive and follow their partner's lead more often. For example: people may spend much of their time in very routine-orientated environments where there is almost no need to communicate because everything happens like 'clockwork'. These contexts are often perceived as being supported and stress-free for people with restricted communication. However, they are also often communication-free zones. Relatively simple changes can make a huge impact; for instance, serving meals and letting the children choose which meal they want, providing opportunities to choose and ask for toys rather than allowing free access, involving people in choosing which household chores need to be done each day rather than sticking to a strict rota.

Many of the environments experienced by people with learning disabilities will need adjusting to reimpose the normal communicative restraints. A frequently observed example is when the communicative partner uses information given by a third party, e.g. people's names or personal preferences, without the person themselves giving that information, hearing it being given or having the source of the information made explicit. The need to avoid this should be explained to carers and significant others.

Work with the person on their skills and an analysis of their environment should help to raise other people's awareness of functional communication skills and the difficulties the person is experiencing. For example: people often complain about individuals who 'hover'. After completing an assessment of their pragmatic skills it may become clear that they have no intentional means of initiating a communication and, therefore, need people to respond to the hovering if they are not to miss out.

People may learn to ignore interruptions they previously found irritating once they are aware how complex the skill of interrupting appropriately is. Many people with learning disabilities do not make the reference clear in their communication. This can lead to fraught exchanges following statements like 'I saw him there.' Once staff or carers are aware that the individual is currently unable to establish the referents verbally, they can compensate with the use of questions (e.g. 'Who did you see?') or look at developing a photographic system (a book of photos of people and places of importance) to support the individual's information-giving.

When staff have a good knowledge of functional communication and insight into a person's difficulties, work can begin on introducing compensatory strategies for unresolved difficulties. These may be strategies for the person with the communication impairment or for their staff and family. For example: a person can be taught to use a buzzer/single message button such as a Big Mac to draw attention to themselves or to gain attention for communication as an initiation. They will, of course, have to learn about how far away their listeners can hear their buzzer. Staff can learn to modify their verbal input or questions to match more closely the person's level of understanding. Sometimes these compensatory strategies themselves which are a skill change in the more able partner bring about a change of skill in their communication partners (cf. Brinton *et al.*1986).

As well as expressing views similar to ours, Smith and Leinonen (1992) raise the issue of increasing knowledge. They feel that 'Changing what a person knows, thinks and feels will be as influential in improving that person's communicative success as attempting to change that person's behaviour.' The idea that increasing knowledge will have an impact on the development of communication skills was confirmed by Farrar *et al.* (1993) in their study of two-year-olds. They found that, as the children learnt about events through play, they could begin to communicate about aspects of, and feelings about, these events based on that knowledge. See Chapters 3 and 4 for further discussion.

Case studies

Susan

Susan is a 16-year-old girl with severe learning disabilities. She is physically able and has complex behavioural difficulties. She seems to understand tone of voice, pointing and the presence of significant objects and some everyday phrases in context.

As already described, the methods Susan used to communicate have been identified as including body language, vocalisation etc. A pragmatic approach has been employed to see how she uses the means available to influence her environment and the people around her and to give a focus for intervention. The following information was gathered:

- *Drawing attention to self.* When arriving at school, Susan will seek people out and try and make eye contact; she will touch people and make animated noises. She will not stop her communication until she is acknowledged by people and does not communicate anything further after this initial exchange.
- *Giving information about self.* Susan will hold herself when she needs the toilet and will nurse or hold an injured or painful part of her body, e.g. her tummy. This is probably affective communication.
- *Requesting an activity.* Susan will passively accept being led by the hand, e.g. to the minibus, when she wants to join in.
- *Requesting objects.* Susan clearly wants things and will frequently take things she desires. She occasionally makes prolonged eye contact with desired objects but does not indicate this desire to anyone else. If she cannot get the object by getting it herself, she will go without.
- *Rejecting an object or event.* Susan will ignore people, stare at them and make protest noises to try and reject many everyday classroom activities which she does not seem to enjoy. If these strategies fail, she will scream, lie down, kick and push. Staff respond to early signs of rejection to try and prevent this escalation.
- *Rejecting people.* Susan rejects unwanted attempts at interaction by ignoring the person speaking to her or moving away.
- *Giving information about objects or events.* Susan stands up and screams when things go 'wrong', e.g. when something has broken, when she hasn't got all the pieces she needs in a puzzle.

Because Susan's affective communication poses problems in the classroom situation, it gets a very immediate response from staff. However, the behaviour does not necessarily get the desired result for Susan because it can be difficult to locate the source of her distress accurately. Her intentional communication to draw attention to herself and receive an acknowledgement has been characterised as 'attention-seeking' and therefore staff are reluctant to respond to it.

After discussion based around Susan's need to develop a more successful functional communication system, the following objectives were drawn up:

1. Staff will respond to Susan's communication to get their attention and acknowledge her by name. After that, depending on the situation, they would use her ability to understand pointing in order to draw her attention to something of interest going on in the classroom, or offer her an activity or object.
2. Staff will experiment with setting up situations in which Susan could safely practise getting desired objects from them using her existing skills of making eye contact with them and the object, e.g. choices of foods and activities.
3. Staff would examine their reasons for not accepting Susan's rejection of activities. They also needed to identify more clearly the reasons why she might be rejecting activities. For example, did Susan understand what was required? did she find the activities boring or too difficult? did something happen to her during activities that she disliked, e.g. sitting with another pupil who was not a friend, being pushed by another pupil etc.?
4. Susan needs an intentional and acceptable means of communicating her rejection of objects and events. Staff agreed to experiment with encouraging her to reject objects she did not want by pushing them away. If this behaviour proved not to be in her repertoire, physical guidance was to be tried, to show her the means of rejection.
5. Work on Susan's communication skills would take place alongside looking at her world knowledge, e.g. knowledge of the uses of common objects.

There was also a concerted effort made to view Susan as a person with severe communication impairment leading to behavioural challenges, rather than just as a person with behavioural difficulties.

Sabia

Sabia is a woman in her late 20s with moderate learning disabilities. She is blind and hearing-impaired with severe skeletal problems. She is bilingual in English and Punjabi with English her strongest language. She uses Punjabi with her parents and nieces and nephews. She speaks English with her peers – both friends and relatives – and with her support workers.

Sabia has very good understanding and has been actively working on improving her skills, e.g. learning to understand 'before' and 'after', learning to understand 'if'. She has also been making a conscious effort to learn new words associated with the situations she has to deal with frequently, e.g. hospital appointments with orthopaedics – 'bone', 'joint', 'muscles', 'circulation'.

After observing Sabia's communication in many different situations it has become clear that, although she is able to say whether she understands a word or not when asked directly, she will still misunderstand part of a conversation without making her misunderstanding known. Several factors appear to be involved:

- can Sabia identify the exact word or phrase that she has misunderstood?
- does Sabia have a form of words she is comfortable saying, e.g. 'I don't understand', 'Can you say that again', depending on the situation?
- can Sabia deal with issues of familiarity and power when dealing with unfamiliar people or people perceived as having a more powerful status, e.g. doctors?

The issue of unfamiliarity here is complicated by Sabia's sensory disabilities which make it harder for her to relax with people she is unused to, for many reasons such as acclimatising to their accent. The issue of power is further complicated by Sabia's upbringing in quite a traditional Muslim family. She has a conflict between knowing that it is important to speak up and say what she may want or need, and her worry about appearing rude and troublesome. Her difficulties are, therefore, identified as:

- communicative intentions – metalinguistic
- social organisation of communication – request for clarification
- presupposition – identifying the tone and form of her communications depending on the situation and the conversational partner.

Initial intervention has been agreed, with regular one-to-one sessions with support workers focusing on:

- recognising word(s) as unknown, new or not understood;
- making this difficulty known to her conversational partner;
- requesting clarification;
- discussing ways of doing this with different people, starting with more familiar people and working towards conversation with new people;
- support during potentially difficult situations with prompting as agreed with Sabia when instances of misunderstanding occur.

In addition to this direct work, Sabia is considering joining People's First, a self advocacy group for people with learning disabilities.

Notes

1 This chapter was written by Jane Joliffe, Barbara Rossington and Ruth Miller. We would also like to thank the other members of the Manchester Functional Communication Working Party for lively debate and informative discussion during the drafting of the Manchester Pragmatics Profile: Nora Crawford, Judith Coupe O'Kane, Jane Rigby and Juliet Goldbart.

The Early Communication Assessment: ECA

Affective communication

Level 1: Reflexive level

1. Will consistently use a small range of behaviours and/or reflexes in response to a limited range of stimuli which will be interpreted by adults as conveying *like/want*.

2. Will consistently use a small range of behaviours and/or reflexes in response to a limited range of stimuli which will be interpreted as conveying *dislike/reject*.

3. Will consistently use a small range of behaviours and/or reflexes in response to a limited range of stimuli which will be interpreted as conveying inferred meanings or information about states such as *discomfort, surprise*.

Level 2: Reactive level

4. Will consistently use a repertoire of changes in behaviours in response to a range of stimuli which is interpreted as conveying *like*.

5. Will consistently use a repertoire of changes in behaviours in response to a range of stimuli which is interpreted as conveying *dislike*.

6. Will consistently use a repertoire of changes in behaviours in response to a range of stimuli which is interpreted as conveying *want*.

7. Will consistently use a repertoire of changes in behaviours in response to a range of stimuli which is interpreted as conveying *reject*.

8. Will consistently use a repertoire of changes in behaviours in response to a range of stimuli which is interpreted as conveying meanings and information about states such as *discomfort, surprise, interest, recognition*.

Level 3: Proactive level

9. Will make efforts to act on the environment which become signals to the adult who then assigns communicative intent and interprets the meaning of *like*.

10. Will make efforts to act on the environment which become signals to the adult who then assigns communicative intent and interprets the meaning of *dislike*.

11. Will make efforts to act on the environment which become signals to the adult who then assigns communicative intent and interprets the meaning of *want*.

12. Will make efforts to act on the environment which become signals to the adult who then assigns communicative intent and interprets the meaning of *reject*.

13. Will make efforts to act on the environment which become signals to the adult who then assigns communicative intent and interprets the meaning of *discomfort, surprise, interest, recognition*.

Mutual gaze

Level 1: Reflexive level

1. Will join in mutual gaze with adult.

2. Will fixate on an adult's face when it appears in midline at a distance of 20–25 cms.

Level 2: Reactive level

3. Will shift gaze to an object or person.

4. Will give eye contact to adult.

5. Will look intently at adult's face while being talked to.

6. Will turn head deliberately to source of voice.

7. Will mainly maintain eye contact with an adult while participating in activities such as feeding, dressing, being changed.

8. Will begin to use gaze coupling similar to gaze patterns in mature conversation, e.g. mutual and intermittent gaze, initiation and termination.

Level 3: Proactive level

9. Will use a mature – i.e. broken – pattern of eye contact during an interaction.

Social organisation of communication

Level 1: Reflexive level

1. Will fill a turn in response to an adult's pause in an interaction when given time.

2. Will join in mutual vocalisation with an adult, although not necessarily using the same vocalisation.

3. Will share an exchange with an adult, adapting the behaviours as the adult does, e.g. adult vocal, child vocal.

4. Will act simultaneously with adult, though not necessarily using the same physical action.

Level 2: Reactive level

5. Will maintain an interaction, after responding to an adult's initiation.

Level 3: Proactive level

6. Will initiate an interaction with success.

7. Will maintain an interaction which is adult-directed.

8. Will maintain an interaction which is adult-structured but child anticipates turn.

9. Will attempt to repair an interaction which the adult has terminated.

Level 4: Primitive level

10. Will integrate attention between self, adult and object, e.g. by gaze, gesture and touch, establishing joint reference.

11. Will initiate communication.

12. Will turn-take.

13. Will terminate an interaction.

Level 5: Conventional level

14. Will repair a misunderstanding non-verbally by repetition.

15. Will repair a misunderstanding non-verbally by rephrasing with a different pitch or novel gesture.

16. Will repair a misunderstanding non-verbally by elaborating to give more information or to stress the information given.

Joint reference

Level 2: Reactive level

1. Will follow adult's line of regard when accompanied by attention-getting strategies.

2. Will respond to direction of adult's gaze resulting in shared attention on object, person or event, i.e. they come to attend to stimulus jointly.

3. Will follow adult's line of regard.

4. Will establish a line of regard which can then be followed, and commented on, by an adult.

Level 3: Proactive level

5. Will follow the point/gesture of another person to an object, event or person nearby.

6. Will follow the point/gesture of another person to an object or event or person in the distance, e.g. aeroplane.

7. Will express attention to a person or an object, event or other person by gaze, facial expression and interest, but cannot integrate these.

Level 4: Primitive level

8. Will establish integrated joint reference by coordinating attention to self and a person with an object, event or other person.

Turn-taking and social interaction

Level 2: Reactive level

1. Will anticipate and fill a turn with adult, e.g. smiles, increased arm movement.
2. Will elicit behaviours which produce responses from an adult.
3. Will elicit responses which, in turn, alter the adult's responses.
4. Will maintain an interaction by giving rewarding feedback which relates to the adult's behaviour.
5. Will increasingly fill turns by vocalisations and movements of the head and hands.
6. Will respond to social turn-taking games, e.g. peek-a-boo.
7. Will vocalise in response to human voice.
8. Will smile in response to a smile.

Level 3: Proactive level

9. Will use many vocalisations which are simultaneous with adult.
10. Will use many actions which are simultaneous with adult.
11. Will use dialogues of sound with adult (spontaneous and imitated vocalisations).
12. Will use dialogues of action with adult.
13. Will refer to a person, object or activity in (a) immediate proximity, (b) distance.

Level 4: Primitive level

14. Will initiate an interaction with a familiar adult, e.g. comes for cuddles, hugs.
15. Will repeat a behaviour which has just produced a response, e.g. laughter.
16. Will repeat ritualised game sequences such as peek-a-boo.
17. Will express recognition of familiar persons.
18. Will play near other children – orienting to where they play.
19. Will initiate and join in rough-and-tumble play with adult.
20. Will reach-for-signal, i.e. reaches or points to object, person or event while looking at the adult.
21. Will play with toys as long as adult is attending.
22. Will regain adult's attention if adult turns away from children's play with toys.
23. Will show signs of distress when sequences of communication end.
24. Will use adult to play game or action.
25. Will cooperate with adult's lead in simple play routines.

26. Will attempt to manipulate adults to get own way, e.g. goes to touch plug, cries to get own way.

27. Will react with frustration when adult says 'No', e.g. when touching plug or TV switches.

28. Will initiate an interaction with another child, e.g. will take toy, look at face and smile.

29. Will join in turn-taking sequence with another child.

30. Will show signs of distress when misunderstandings occur.

Comprehension in context

Level 1: Reflexive level

1. Will quieten when picked up or comforted.

2. Will orient to a person.

3. Will shape or control adult's behaviour although this is not intentional control, e.g. intense periods of eye-to-eye/face-to-face contact.

4. Will look at object when cued (object must be within optimum focusing distance).

5. Will move in synchrony to adult speech.

Level 2: Reactive level

6. Will anticipate food and drink by opening mouth.

7. Will increase limb movements with attention from an adult.

8. Will respond to affective messages from the adult and react to adult's behaviours, e.g. tone of voice, facial expression.

Level 3: Proactive level

9. Will show differential responses to adult intonation and voice quality, e.g. angry voice, verbal praise.

10. Will show differential responses to facial expressions, e.g. smiles, angry expressions.

11. Will show differential responses to adult actions, such as arms held out for a hug. N.B. May respond to tone of voice in 'no' but might not hold adult hand in response to proffered hand.

Level 4: Primitive level

12. Will respond appropriately to adult's non-verbal communication, e.g. takes proffered neutral object, takes held-out hand, follows a point.

13. Will pause in response to 'no' with intonation.

14. Will respond to commands incorporating situational cues when in context, e.g. *give me, come here, sit down.*

15. Will watch adult's face and gestures for cues.

Level 5: Conventional level

16. Will respond when the answer is visually apparent, e.g. when asked to show familiar object which is clearly on view.

17. Will point to a familiar body part when named/requested.

18. Will come when called.

19. Will respond to a familiar word in adult conversation.

20. Will go to known place or person on request, e.g. 'Go to mummy', 'Go to car'.

21. Will obtain familiar object on request – particularly if this request is made during a familiar routine: e.g. when washing, 'Get the towel'; when preparing a drink, 'Get the milk' or 'Get the cup'.

22. Points to self when asked 'Where's . . .?'

23. Will respond to request to give object in possession.

24. Will show understanding of a number of early words which relate to familiar situations, e.g. *dinner, clap, teddy, no.*

25. Will respond to a request to show the object in possession.

Communicative intentions

Level 4: Primitive level

1. Will use a vocal and/or physical repertoire of behaviours to get a person to obtain objects (proto-imperative).

2. Will use a vocal and/or physical repertoire of behaviours to get a person to create/provide events and actions (proto-imperative).

3. Will use a vocal and/or physical repertoire of behaviours to get a person to satisfy states and conditions (proto-imperative).

4. Will use an object, action or event to get adult attention and draw it to self (proto-declarative).

5. Will produce physical and vocal messages to convey request.

6. Will produce physical and vocal messages to convey frustration.

7. Will produce physical and vocal messages to convey greeting.

8. Will produce physical and vocal messages to convey pleasant surprise.

Level 5: Conventional level

N.B. *Some of these behaviours will have been evident at Level 4, but it is necessary to ascertain that the pupil can demonstrate the behaviour in a more conventional form in order to be judged as functioning within Level 5.*

9. Will draw attention to an event or action.

10. Will draw attention to an object.

11. Will draw attention to other people.

12. Will gain attention for communication.

13. Will request a person.

14. Will request an object.

15. Will request an action or event.

16. Will request information.

17. Will request recurrence.

18. Will reject an action.

19. Will reject an object.

20. Will reject a person.

21. Will protest.

22. Will greet (social).

23. Will give information about self.

24. Will give information about the environment and the people within it.

25. Will respond to a question.

Cognitive roles

Level 4: Primitive level

1. Will use objects in a way which reflects knowledge of their functions.

2. Will demonstrate the cognitive concept of the *existence* of objects, events and people.

3. Will demonstrate the cognitive concept of *disappearance* of objects and people.

4. Will demonstrate the cognitive concept of *recurrence*, i.e. re-representation of an object or person that existed but disappeared, or repetition of an action that occurred and then stopped.

5. Will demonstrate the cognitive concept of *non-existence*, i.e. object or person does not exist where it is expected to be.

6. Will demonstrate the cognitive concept of *location*, i.e. the position of the object, person or event or the relationship between two objects or people.

7. Will demonstrate the cognitive concept of *possession*, i.e. the relationship between an object or person and themself.

8. Will demonstrate the cognitive concept of *rejection*, i.e. not wanting an object, adult or event or wanting an activity to cease.

9. Will demonstrate the cognitive concept of *denial* of a proposition.

10. Will demonstrate the cognitive concept of *agent*, i.e. the person or object that causes an action to occur.

11. Will demonstrate the cognitive concept of *object*, i.e. the object or person that may be affected by an action.

12. Will demonstrate the cognitive concept of *action*, i.e. any observable activity or change of state.

13. Will demonstrate the cognitive concept of *attribute*, i.e. the property of an object or person.

Level 5: Conventional level

14. Will relate objects appropriately and functionally or combine, e.g. putting straw in cup to drink.

15. Will repeat part of an action using novel gestures, e.g. actions in 'wind a bobbin', lid-opening gesture to open lid of bubbles.

First meanings (semantic roles)

Level 5: Conventional level

1. Will communicate *existence* by acknowledging that an object exists.

2. Will communicate *disappearance* by commenting on or requesting the disappearance of a person or object.

3. Will communicate *recurrence* by commenting on or requesting the return of an object that existed but disappeared, or a repetition of an action that occurred and then stopped.

4. Will communicate *non-existence* by indicating that an object does not exist where it is expected to be.

5. Will communicate *location* by commenting on the position of an object, person or event or the spatial relationship between two objects, or requesting that an object is placed in a certain location.

6. Will communicate *possession* by conveying the relationship between an object, person and themselves or another.

7. Will communicate *rejection* by conveying not wanting an object, adult or event or wanting an activity to cease.

8. Will communicate *denial* by denying another person's proposition or assertion.

9. Will communicate *agent* as the person (or animate or entity) that causes an action to occur.

10. Will communicate *object* as the object or person (or animate or entity) that may be affected by an action.

11. Will communicate *action* as any observable activity or change of state.

12. Will communicate *attribute* by commenting on or requesting to know a property of an object, person or event.

Imitation

Level 2: Reactive level

1. Will smile or frown in response to an adult's frown or smile.

2. Will vocalise in response to a human voice.
N.B. Tends to imitate the mode/channel and not the exact behaviour.

Level 3: Proactive level

3. Will imitate behaviours already in physical or verbal repertoire.

4. Will imitate mouth movements.

5. Will imitate sounds, e.g. clicks, tut tut, babble, etc., which are in the existing repertoire.

Level 4: Primitive level

6. Will imitate intonational contours used in adult's speech.

7. Will imitate a physical behaviour which is not in the existing repertoire but where own actions are visible.

8. Will imitate actions/gestures of adult spontaneously.

Level 5: Conventional level

9. Will imitate adult intonation for greeting, giving, etc., such as 'here you are', 'hiya', 'ta'.

10. Will imitate actions with objects, e.g. pushing car, feeding dolly.

Auditory and visual behaviours

Level 2: Reactive level

1. Will visually inspect people and objects.

2. Will give eye contact to adult.

3. Will grasp object when in view with hand, or when hand is touching object.

4. Will search for sound with eyes.

5. Will search for sound with head movement or orientation of the body.

6. Will stop an activity in response to sounds.

7. Will show preference for certain sounds.

8. Will respond to intense noise.

9. Will glance at noisy object.

Level 3: Proactive level

10. Will listen to sounds.

11. Will look for a fallen object.

12. Will visually fixate on object or person which is near.

13. Will use visually directed reaching, i.e. visually locates object and shapes hand in anticipation when picking up an object.

14. Will use alternating glance.

Vocal production

Level 1: Reflexive level

N.B. Items at Level 1 are behaviours to observe for assessment, not intervention.

1. Will cry.

2. Will produce vegetative sounds, e.g. burp, smacking lips, gurgling noises.

Level 2: Reactive level

3. Will laugh.

4. Will produce glottal, e.g. 'h'.

5. Will produce open vowels, e.g. 'oh' and 'ah'.

6. Will produce nasals, e.g. 'm', 'n', 'ng'.

7. Will produce plosives, e.g. 'p', 'b', 't', 'd', 'k', 'g'.

8. Will produce reduplicated babble, e.g. 'ba-ba-ba', 'ma-ma-ma', 'tee-tee'.

Level 3: Proactive level

9. Will vocalise during play with adults.

10. Will vocalise to self.

11. Will vocalise to own reflection.

12. Will vocalise to people.

13. Will vocalise to toys and objects.

14. Will use vocalisations which vary in pitch, volume, stress and quality to express anger, eagerness, satisfaction, etc.

15. Will use vocalisations which become more differentiated for different situations, e.g. noise while on the toilet, while eating or when mum appears.

16. Will use vocalisations which reflect adult patterns of intonation for questions and statements.

17. Will produce consonants.and vowels as in Level 2, but non-reduplicated babble, e.g. 'ba da', 'ada ma'.

Level 4: Primitive level

18. Will use consonant-vowel and vowel-consonant-vowel structures, e.g. 'ta', 'de', 'da', 'ada', 'aga', 'iya'.

19. Will squeal, shout, scream.

20. Will use vocalisation plus action to gain attention.

21. Will use vocalisation plus action to obttain an object/event, etc.

22. Will use vocalisation plus action while acting on an object, e.g. sharing, putting objects into a container.

23. Will vocalise while acting on objects, while eating.

24. Will generally use only those sounds which occur in the phonological system of their home language.

Level 5: Conventional level

25. Will produce speech sounds, vowels and consonants such as 'm', 'n', 'b', 'p', 't', 'd', 'w', 'oh', 'ah', 'ooh'.

26. Will use sound sequences which stand for an activity/object.

27. Will use specific sounds which are integral with an activity: 'brum' when being swung; 'boo' in peek-a-boo.

28. Will use a vocabulary of between ten and 20 words including protowords.

Physical production

Level 1: Reflexive level

N.B. *Many items at Level 1 are behaviours to observe for assessment, not intervention.*

1. Will frown.

2. Will suck.

3. Will head-turn.

4. Will open/close mouth.

5. Will show finger activity.

6. Will relax body.

7. Will stiffen body.

8. Will move trunk or other body parts.

9. Will grasp when palm is stimulated.

10. Will show reflex rooting.

Level 2: Reactive level

11. Will smile.

12. Will show trunk-turning/orientation to adult or other stimulus.

13. Will stiffen whole body.

14. Will produce changes in activity level.

15. Will show hand-to-mouth movement.

16. Will mouth.

17. Will hold.

18. Will produce facial movements, e.g. mouth puckering, tongue movement.

19. Will touch object when cued by adult.

Level 3: Proactive level

20. Will reach for object or person using visually directed reaching.

21. Will let go of object to examine a new object.

22. Will use complex behaviours on objects, i.e. physically explores (hitting, shaking) and visually examines.

23. Will orientate body posture towards desired object or adult.

24. Will use simple actions on others, e.g. pushing, looking.

Level 4: Primitive level

25. Will use whole-body action, e.g. to pull away from adult.

26. Will place adult's hands on objects, e.g. on clockwork toy to activate.

27. Will use eye or hand to point at, or indicate, an object, person or event.

28. Will use facial expressions and eye contact with adult.

29. Will reach-for-signal, e.g. reaches for, or indicates, cup while looking at adult.

30. Will intentionally use movement and eye contact towards a presumed desired goal, e.g. takes adult to the door and gives eye contact.

31. Will manipulate objects, people or events and make eye contact with the adult, e.g. drops toy and looks at adult, turns door handle and looks at adult.

Level 5: Conventional level

32. Will nod.

33. Will shake head.

34. Will wave.

35. Will show an object.

36. Will give an object.

37. Will point using eye, hand or finger.

38. Will gesture to express 'gone' or 'where'.

39. Will perform novel gestures which represent part of a motor act, e.g. tickling own hand for 'Round and round the garden . . .'

40. Will try to manipulate adult while acting on an object, e.g. moves object towards edge of table while looking at adult.

Appendix B

Consideration of reliability of the ECA

Reliability is a complex measurement issue which encompasses accuracy and stability of measures as well as, and importantly for the development of this assessment of early communication, the actual conditions under which observations are made. In other words, reliability involves the aspects of dependability and predictability. Having arrived at a working assessment instrument, it was thought that some preliminary investigations of measure of reliability might be helpful in ascertaining its dependability. Could, for example, an experienced observer identify children's behaviours following the ECA? Furthermore, could there be agreement in the observations of two or more observers? In addition, it was thought that such a preliminary reliability phase would aid the final selection of items.

While observer agreement was used as an estimate of reliability, it is the case that observer agreement does not, by itself, assess observer accuracy unless it is compared with some previously established standard. Similarly, observer agreement does not assess stability unless it is measured over repeated trials (Sackett 1978). Thus, it is important to understand that it is entirely possible to obtain very high observer agreement with close to no reliability in terms of accuracy and stability. Simply, all agreeing observers could be applying the same incorrect definitions. Having acknowledged those important limitations for observer agreement, it has to be argued that it is the most frequently used reliability procedure in the observational literature (Sackett 1978) and it was also considered to be the most practical approach for the ECA.

This reliability study employed observer agreement in order to 'mimic' what would naturally happen in the classroom where teachers/classroom assistants might be observing the same behaviour. Furthermore, the technique of calculating the percentage of observer agreement was considered useful, first because of its relatively straightforward calculation and second because of a desire to share this information with the observers involved. It was thought that the concept of percentage agreement could be relatively simply described and illustrated to the teachers involved in the study.

Finally, the initial draft of the ECA offered a number of levels, none of which could confidently and definitely be ordered in a developmental sequence such that any child who demonstrates Level 2 competence will also demonstrate Level 1 competence.

In addition, one could not confidently and definitely argue that the step between one level and the next was the same size as that between the following level and the next; that is, the data in this particular study had neither ordinal nor interval properties. Thus it has been desirable to settle for a procedure where agreement was possible with 'no measurement scale'; hence the use of percentage agreement as opposed to correlations or coefficients of concordance.

With those concerns in mind, a two-phased procedure was designed to preliminarily ascertain the reliability of the initial draft of the ECA via the use of percentage agreement, and the following formula suggested by Sackett (1978) was used:

$$\text{percentage agreement} = \frac{\text{(agreements)}}{\text{(agreements + disagreements)}} \times 100$$

Reliability study: Phase 1

The two authors of this book, both of whom were thoroughly familiar with the assessment, the underlying theories and the children involved, independently analysed 11 selected video observations of children functioning within early stages of communicative development. Most of the children involved had severe or profound and multiple learning difficulties, although three normally developing infants were also included. The video observations were not prepared specifically for the analysis; instead, pre-existing recordings of children in classroom and family interactions were used. In this way, contrived situations were avoided and more natural content and contexts were ensured. This required the concession that a small number of behaviours included in the assessment might not be included in the reliability calculations.

After viewing each video-taped observation in turn, the observers decided which areas of communicative functioning were relevant to that particular video observation. Thus, the areas of communication and items were defined for that particular session. Once each session was observed in this manner, they then independently rated the behaviours of the children involved at the appropriate levels. In this way all areas of communicative functioning were assessed and each behaviour item, where possible, was observed at least once. While there could be no control for frequency of the behaviours observed, given the natural nature of the situations, some assessment items were inevitably exhibited more frequently than others. Nevertheless, this was not thought to be a disadvantage. On the contrary, it was thought to be advantageous, as such situations would parallel normal life where everyday situations would provide a natural frequency of communicative behaviour.

A discussion follows of each of the areas in terms of the percentage agreements. The reliability information included percentage agreement on observed items as well as a description of those items which were agreed not to have been observed but which belong to the area being tested for reliability (for tables of reliability data for items, observations and levels, see Coupe O'Kane 1994). This provides indirect evidence for reliability, although the actual absent items were not tested as such.

Areas of communicative functioning reaching 100 per cent agreement

The following six areas of communicative functioning obtained 100 per cent agreement by the two observers across 11 video observations.

Affective communication
There was 100 per cent agreement between the two observers for 12 items observed across four of the 11 video observations. Items were observed on one or two occasions. The six items which were agreed as not being observed in the four video observations were:

> Level 1: 'want', 'reject' and 'recognition'.
> Level 2: 'reject' and 'recognition'.
> Level 3: 'recognition'.

Mutual gaze
All nine items were viewed once by each observer across two of the 11 video observations.

Joint reference
Seven of the nine items were viewed once by each observer and item 9 was viewed on four occasions by each across six of the 11 video observations. Item 2, 'will lead adult to follow line of regard (non-intentional)', was agreed not to have been observed.

Cognitive roles
Three of the 15 items were agreed by each observer on one occasion only, with the remaining 12 being observed by each on up to four occasions across four of the 11 video observations.

First meanings (semantic roles)
One item was agreed not to have been observed, 'non-existence'. The 11 items agreed were viewed up to three times across three of the 11 video observations.

Presupposition
Agreement was reached that none of the four behaviours identified within this area were observed across the 11 video observations.

Areas of communicative functioning reaching less than 100 per cent agreement

The following eight areas of communicative functioning obtained less than 100 per cent agreement by the two observers across 11 video observations.

Social organisation of communication
Out of the 19 items included in this area of communicative functioning, three were agreed as not being observed across six of the 11 video observations. These were items 6, 10 and 12. One hundred per cent agreement was reached on 13 items with some behaviours being viewed up to four times across four different video observations.

Disagreements occurred for three items. For item 7, at Level 3, 'will initiate an interaction with success', nought per cent agreement was reached as the behaviour was considered to have occurred once in observation by one observer only. The other observer failed to see this behaviour. Within Level 4, item 13 was agreed as occurring on four occasions, but only one observer considered it to be evident on a fifth occasion. Similarly, item 14 was agreed twice but agreement was not reached on a third occasion. Ninety-one per cent agreement of observations of items across levels within this area was reached.

Turn-taking and social interaction
Of the four levels included in this area, 100 per cent agreement was reached across Levels 2, 3 and 5 on individual items. One hundred per cent agreement was reached for 28 out of the 29 items observed across eight of the 11 video observations, and four items were not observed. Disagreement was reached over item 23, 'will reach-for-signal', where the behaviour was agreed once but viewed by one observer only, on a further occasion. Ninety-seven per cent agreement of observations of items across levels within this area was reached.

Comprehension in context
Of the 31 items included in this area, 21 items had 100 per cent agreement and were viewed up to three times across seven of the 11 video observations, and eight items were agreed as not occurring. Of the two items where disagreement occurred, item 26, 'will go to known place or person on request', was seen by one observer and not the other, hence nought per cent agreement was reached. Item 27, however, was agreed once but seen by only one observer on a second observation. Both items came within Level 5, hence only 81 per cent agreement was achieved within this level. Ninety-one per cent agreement across observations within this area was reached.

Communicative intentions
Two levels are included in communicative intentions. For Level 4, 100 per cent agreement was reached and 92 per cent for Level 5. Twenty-three out of the 25 items included were observed across six of the 11 video observations with 100 per cent agreement reached for all but two. Some behaviours were agreed to be observed on up to five occasions. However, items 9 and 11 were viewed only once each by one observer. Hence nought per cent agreement was reached for these items. Only two items were agreed not to have been observed. Ninety-five per cent agreement of observations of items across levels within this area was reached.

Imitation

Levels 2, 3, 4 and 5 are incorporated in the area of imitation and 100 per cent agreement was achieved for Levels 4 and 5. Between one and two agreed observations provided 100 per cent reliability for seven items. Item 2, 'will vocalise in response to a human voice', was agreed once but viewed by one observer only on a second occasion. Item 5, 'will imitate sounds which are in existing repertoire', was seen by only one observer. One hundred per cent agreement was reached across six of the 11 video observations on all but observation 8. Eighty-three per cent agreement of observations of items across levels within this area was reached.

Auditory and visual behaviours

Twenty-one items are included in this area and, of the 14 items observed across three of the 11 video observations, 100 per cent agreement was reached for 12. For the two items where agreement did not occur, the behaviour was seen each time by only one observer. Nought per cent agreement for those two items resulted in 78 per cent agreement for Level 2, while for Level 3 100 per cent agreement was obtained. Eighty-seven per cent agreement of observations of items across levels within this area was reached.

Vocal production

Fourteen out of 36 items were agreed as not being observed across eight of the 11 video observations. Some of these involved reflex behaviours such as 'cough', 'sneeze', which would occur by chance. Others relied heavily on the eliciting contexts which, across the 11 observations, could not be guaranteed, e.g. item 35, 'will sing to music using own words'. All five levels are included in this area and 100 per cent agreement was reached on all but Level 3, on which 88 per cent agreement was obtained.

Only one of the eight video observations failed to achieve 100 per cent agreement, and this is reflected in the fact that, of the 22 items observed, 21 obtained 100 per cent reliability. Item 14, 'will vocalise in response to environmental sounds', was acknowledged as observed by only one observer. Items were agreed on up to three occasions. Ninety-seven per cent agreement of observations of items across levels within this area was reached.

Physical production

Forty-eight items in physical production were observed across ten of the 11 video observations. Of these, 100 per cent agreement was reached on 38 items. Two items within level 5 were observed on one occasion by one observer only. This gives 100 per cent reliability on Levels 1 to 4 with 82 per cent agreement being reached in Level 5. Agreement was reached that eight items were not observed: four of those were more reflex responses such as 'will show reflex cardinal points that stimulate sucking', 'show reflex stepping', 'yawn' and 'will stiffen whole body', which leaves only a further four items within Levels 3, 4 and 5 which are not included in the video observations. Ninety-seven per cent agreement of observations of items across levels within this area was reached.

Summary of Phase 1

The percentage agreements attained for each of the five levels included in the ECA are presented in Table B.1. Although 100 per cent agreement is only obtained for Level 1, agreement is over 90 per cent for all levels. There appears to be no trend for agreement to be higher or lower within increasing developmental levels. In total, 95 per cent agreement was reached across all items in the ECA (Table B.2). Of the total 295 items, 56 were agreed as not observed.

Table B.1 Summary of Phase 1 ECA levels: percentage agreement of observations of items within levels

level	%	number of agreements
1	100	37/37
2	95	53/56
3	94	46/49
4	98	129/132
5	92	90/98

Table B.2 Summary of Phase 1 ECA items

Agreement of observations across all items in the ECA	355/372
% agreement of observations across all items in the ECA	95%
Total number of items in the ECA	295
Total number of items agreed as not observed	56

Within Phase 1, percentage agreement between the two observers was high. This is not surprising given the familiarity of the observers with the ECA. Furthermore, Phase 1 raised interesting information about possible problematic items presented in the ECA, as well as an overall measure of the reliability of the observed items in Levels 1–5 in the assessment.

Reliability study: Phase 2

The second phase of the study involved examining the level of agreement obtained by the Phase 1 assessors against two groups of experienced SLD teachers. Two of these teachers were familiar with the initial draft of the ECA and two were not. However, it has to be noted that experienced teachers of SLD tend to be sensitive to the needs of pupils who function within the early stages of communication, utilise published assessments such as the Affective Communication Assessment (Coupe *et al*. 1985) and are familiar with underlying theories. Thus, this preliminary look at the reliability of the ECA involved experienced teachers who were familiar with the ECA (teachers A and B), and others who were not familiar with the ECA (teachers C and D). Data were obtained by comparing the ratings of these teachers with the standard rating agreed by the two observers involved in Phase 1.

First, the aim of Phase 2 and their part in the study was explained to the four observers. The areas of communicative functioning and levels of the ECA were described for the benefit of teachers C and D, and all four teachers were encouraged to read through the assessment thoroughly in order to be conversant with its range and progression. In order to practise, short video observations were viewed, analysed together and discussed. Next, each of the 11 selected video observations was viewed and analysed in turn using modified versions of the ECA.

These modified assessments each included the items actually assessed in Phase 1 across all areas and levels, plus the inclusion of confuser items. These confuser items included behaviours which were agreed not to have occurred on the selected video observations but which were similar behaviours at a different level, or related behaviours within the same level. For example, in video observation 3, social organisation of communication was one of the areas of communicative functioning identified by Phase 1 observers, with agreement reached that four of the 19 items were observed. When observing video observation 3, in Phase 2, the two pairs of teacher observers considered whether any of five items in this area were present, that is four items agreed in Phase 1 (items 13, 14, 15 and 16) and a confuser item (item 17), i.e.:

13. Will integrate attention between self, adult and object, e.g. gaze, gesture and touch, establishing joint reference.
14. Will initiate communication.
15. Will turn-take.
16. Will terminate an interaction.
17. Will repair a misunderstanding non-verbally by rephrasing with a different pitch and novel gesture.

Similarly in video observation 1, seven items involved in the area of social organisation of communication were agreed to be observed by Phase 1 observers. For Phase 2 observers these seen items along with three confuser items (items 8, 11 and 13) were presented for consideration, i.e.:

1. Will fill a turn in response to an adult's pause in an interaction when given time.
2. Will share in an exchange with an adult, adapting the behaviours as the adult does, e.g. adult vocal, child vocal.
3. Will act simultaneously with adult, although not necessarily using the same physical action.
4. Will join in mutual vocalisation with an adult, although not necessarily using the same vocalisation.
5. Will maintain an interaction, after responding to an adult's initiation.
6. Will initiate an interaction with success.
8. Will maintain an interaction which is adult-directed.
9. Will maintain an interaction which is adult-structured but pupil anticipates turn.
11. Will attempt to repair an interaction which the adult has terminated.
13. Will integrate attention between self, adult and object, e.g. by gaze, gesture and touch, establishing joint reference.

In the light of items and confuser items presented to Phase 2 observers in the example of social organisation of communication in video observation 3, it is apparent that item 13 might potentially be agreed as being observed as both an item and a confuser item. The confusers were included in order to ensure that the observers involved in the study would be making judgements about the items in question and not simply identifying behaviours seen on the video. In other words, it was thought that the introduction of the confuser items and the teachers' knowledge that such items were included provided teachers with an 'observe–decide' strategy instead of a 'record' strategy.

For tables of reliability data across items, confuser items and items and confuser items, see Coupe O'Kane 1994.

Areas of communicative functioning reaching 100 per cent agreement

Of the 14 areas of communicative functioning included in the initial draft of the ECA, affective communication and joint reference obtained 100 per cent agreement by the two pairs of observers (that is A/B, experienced teachers who were familiar with the ECA, and C/D, experienced teachers who were not familiar with the ECA) for items and confuser items. For affective communication, eight items were observed, and for joint reference, one item and no confuser items were included across one video observation.

Areas of communicative functioning reaching 90 per cent agreement or above

Of the 13 areas of communicative functioning included in the initial draft of the ECA, nine reached 90–99 per cent agreement for items and confuser items. These items were observed across 11 different video observations: see Table B.3.

Table B.3   Phase 2 percentage agreement across items and confuser items

	%
Comprehension in context	99
Mutual gaze	98
Physical production	98
Cognitive roles	95
First meanings	94
Vocal production	94
Communicative intentions	92
Social organisation of communication	90
Auditory and visual behaviours	90

Comprehension in context

Ninety-nine per cent agreement was reached for the area of comprehension in context. On only one occasion one of the teachers experienced with the assessment acknowledged seeing item 19, 'will pause in response to "no" with intonation'.

Mutual gaze

For all nine items involved in this area across three levels, 100 per cent agreement was reached. In one of the video observations item 9 was included as a confuser item. One of the two teachers familiar with the assessment felt that this behaviour occurred, i.e. 'will use a mature – i.e. broken – pattern of eye contact during an observation'. Hence, 98 per cent agreement was reached across items and confusers within the area.

Physical production

Ninety-eight per cent agreement was reached for items and confusers within this area; 17 items were incorporated together with six confuser items. One teacher familiar with the assessment failed to see item 37, and one teacher not familiar with the assessment acknowledged seeing a confuser item. Hence, 75 per cent agreement was reached for each of those items.

Cognitive roles

One hundred per cent agreement was reached for the nine items included as being observed. However, the two assessors who were familiar with the assessment acknowledged observing one of the confuser items. Hence, 95 per cent agreement across items and confusers was reached.

First meanings (semantic roles)

The agreement across items within this area was 100 per cent and this included eight of the 12 items. The two teachers experienced with the assessment however, included item 2, the confuser item, as being viewed. Hence, only 50 per cent agreement that behaviours did not occur was reached. Ninety-four per cent overall agreement across items and confusers within this area was established.

Vocal production

Of the 11 items present, all but three achieved 100 per cent agreement. A teacher unfamiliar with the assessment considered that items 3, 9 and 26 were not present. Five confuser items were included and all but one reached 100 per cent agreement. Here, one of the teachers familiar with the assessment acknowledged seeing the behaviour. Ninety-four per cent agreement was, therefore, reached across items and confusers within this area.

Communicative intentions

For this area 92 per cent agreement was reached. All three confuser items were agreed not to have occurred. The teachers experienced with the assessment both failed to see item 3, 'will use a vocal and/or physical repertoire of behaviours to get a person to satisfy states and conditions'. On two other occasions a teacher from this group also failed to see the behaviours for items 2 and 4.

Social organisation of communication

Within this area 90 per cent agreement was reached across items and confusers. One hundred per cent agreement was obtained for nine of the 13 items involved. On three occasions one of the teachers familiar with the assessment did not assess an item as occurring while the other assessors did. For item 7, 'will initiate an interaction with success', nought per cent agreement was reached. In the case of all four confuser items, 100 per cent agreement was reached that they did not occur.

Auditory and visual behaviours

Agreement across items and confusers within this area was 90 per cent. For the two confuser items included, 100 per cent agreement was reached. Of the ten items incorporated within this area, 100 per cent agreement was reached for seven. On one occasion a teacher familiar with the assessment did not see the behaviour. Hence, 75 per cent agreement was obtained for this item. For items 10, 'will respond to intense noise' and 11, 'will glance at noisy object', the two teachers not familiar with the assessment failed to see the behaviours. Hence, 50 per cent agreement was reached for each.

Areas of communicative functioning reaching less than 90 per cent agreement

Two of the 14 areas of communicative functioning reached an agreement of below 90 per cent by the pair of observers for items and confuser items.

Turn-taking and social interaction

One hundred per cent agreement was reached for ten of the 13 items included in the area of turn-taking and social interaction. On two occasions a teacher experienced with the assessment failed to agree that a behaviour was seen. For item 16, 'will initiate an interaction with a familiar adult', there was nought per cent agreement. It is interesting to note that this matches with the same decision made in social organisation of communication for item 7, 'will initiate an interaction with success'.

With the five confuser items involved, 100 per cent agreement that the behaviour did not occur was twice reached. A teacher familiar with the assessment acknowledged observing three of these behaviours on three occasions. One of these items was also seen by a teacher unfamiliar with the assessment.

Imitation

Seventy-nine per cent agreement was reached across the six items and confusers within this area. For item 1, 'will imitate adult's smile and frown', only 25 per cent agreement was reached. Just one of the teachers experienced with the assessment acknowledged seeing this behaviour. Of the four items included as being seen by the Phase 1 assessors, items 2 and 10 were agreed by all. For item 4, however, the two teachers not familiar with the assessment failed to see the behaviour.

Summary of Phase 2

Phase 2 was organised in order to determine the level of agreement reached between the Phase 1 observers and four experienced SLD teachers, two of whom had prior experience of using the assessment. In assessing the ECA items actually agreed to have been observed by Phase 1 observers, combined with a number of confuser items, it is clear that a high degree of agreement was reached overall. Table B.4 shows that, of the 13 areas of communicative functions included, agreement of 90 per cent or over was reached for 11 areas, with affective communication and joint reference gaining 100 per cent agreement. The two areas which fell below this were turn-taking and imitation, which obtained 86 per cent and 79 per cent agreement respectively.

Table B.4   Phase 2 percentage agreement across items and confuser items

Areas of communicative functioning	A/B %	C/D %	A/B & C/D %
Affective communication	100	100	100
Mutual gaze	95	100	90
Social organisation of communication	86	94	90
Joint reference	100	100	100
Turn-taking	81	92	86
Comprehension in context	98	100	99
Communicative intentions	85	100	92
Cognitive roles	91	100	95
First meanings (semantic notions)	89	100	94
Imitation	86	71	79
Auditory and visual behaviours	96	83	90
Vocal production	97	88	94
Physical production	98	98	98

There were some differences in agreement between the two groups of experienced SLD teachers, A/B who were familiar with the assessment and C/D who were not. Of the 13 areas involved, A/B achieved 90 per cent or over on eight occasions, whilst C/D teachers achieved this on ten occasions. Group C/D teachers, in fact, had 100 per cent agreement for seven areas, whilst A/B gained this on only two occasions. It is evident that there was agreement between teachers but with C/D even more so. For teachers A/B this may well be partly due to their keenness and particular emphasis on detail. Hence they became more conservative in their judgements and did not count items as observed if they were not 100 per cent sure. Teachers C/D perhaps became more firm with their judgements and were able to make distinctions between items and confusers more easily. Nonetheless, it needs to be re-emphasised that the differences between the two groups of teachers was small and that overall, both sets of teachers obtained high percentages of agreement.

Summary of Phases 1 and 2

The present preliminary findings outlined in this appendix indicate that the ECA has a great deal of potential as an assessment/curriculum instrument for people who function at an early stage of development. It is apparent, nonetheless, that a number of questions and issues need to be addressed before its possible adoption. Although the present study has gone some way to show the consistency of observations of very experienced teachers using the ECA, the question 'To what extent can "naive" teachers who have no knowledge of the ECA use this scale?' has yet to be answered. There is little doubt that further refinements and broader reliability measures are needed which involve not only consistency but also the important 'ordering' or 'developmental' question. In addition, it needs to be noted, the agreements reached were high but were obviously influenced by the number of occasions on which items were assessed. Frequently, where nought per cent agreement was reached, the behaviour was seen only once by an observer. Similarly, the same occurred on the occasion where 100 per cent was reached, although many behaviours were viewed on more than one occasion. Future research concerning the ECA should attempt to include more presentations per item and keep this number relatively consistent across the entire ECA.

Changes in the ECA

In the light of the results of the reliability study, a final version of the ECA was established. This final version includes 13 of the 14 original areas of communicative functioning. In addition, a number of items were deleted from the new ECA. Following is a discussion of the arguments leading to these decisions. The rationale for deleting items from this second version of the ECA was addressed in two stages. Firstly, items were assessed on the grounds of low percentage agreement obtained by Phase 2 observers, and in cases where behaviours did not appear on the video observations and hence there was no percentage agreement available by Phase 2 observers. Once these items had been identified they were further considered by the second stage of criteria, i.e.:

- Research and theoretical support for the item.
- The author's experience (Coupe O'Kane 1994) gained by observing a range of children through Phases 1 and 2, along with practically utilising the ECA in the classroom.
- The need to assess these behaviours in naturally occurring situations only (since, for ethical reasons, contexts would not be created to elicit them).
- Whether behaviours were likely to be found in communicative interactions. In many instances reference is also made to research and theoretical support for items where a high percentage agreement is reached so as to substantiate their retention in the final version of the ECA (see Appendix A).

Affective communication: initial draft assessment

Level 1: Reflexive level
1. Will consistently use a small range of behaviours and/or reflexes in response to a limited range of stimuli which will be interpreted by adults as conveying *like*.
2. Will consistently use a small range of behaviours and/or reflexes in response to a limited range of stimuli which will be interpreted as conveying *dislike*.
3. Will consistently use a small range of behaviours and/or reflexes in response to a limited range of stimuli which will be interpreted as conveying *want*.
4. Will consistently use a small range of behaviours and/or reflexes in response to a limited range of stimuli which will be interpreted as conveying *reject*.
5. Will consistently use a small range of behaviours and/or reflexes in response to a limited range of stimuli which will be interpreted as conveying *recognition*.
6. Will consistently use a small range of behaviours and/or reflexes in response to a limited range of stimuli which will be interpreted as conveying inferred meanings or information about states such as *discomfort, surprise*.

Level 2: Reactive level
7. Will consistently use a repertoire of changes in behaviours in response to a range of stimuli which is interpreted as conveying *like*.
8. Will consistently use a repertoire of changes in behaviours in response to a range of stimuli which is interpreted as conveying *dislike*.
9. Will consistently use a repertoire of changes in behaviours in response to a range of stimuli which is interpreted as conveying *want*.
10. Will consistently use a repertoire of changes in behaviours in response to a range of stimuli which is interpreted as conveying *reject*.
11. Will consistently use a repertoire of changes in behaviours in response to a range of stimuli which is interpreted as conveying *recognition*.
12. Will consistently use a repertoire of changes in behaviours in response to a range of stimuli which is interpreted as conveying meanings and information about states such as *discomfort, surprise, interest*.

Level 3: Proactive level
13. Will make efforts to act on the environment which become signals to the adult who then assigns communicative intent and interprets the meaning of *like*.
14. Will make efforts to act on the environment which become signals to the adult who then assigns communicative intent and interprets the meaning of *dislike*.
15. Will make efforts to act on the environment which become signals to the adult who then assigns communicative intent and interprets the meaning of *want*.
16. Will make efforts to act on the environment which become signals to the adult who then assigns communicative intent and interprets the meaning of *reject*.
17. Will make efforts to act on the environment which become signals to the adult who then assigns communicative intent and interprets the meaning of *recognition*.
18. Will make efforts to act on the environment which become signals to the adult who then assigns communicative intent and interprets the meaning of *discomfort, interest*, etc.

On reflection it was considered that where a person is functioning within Level 1, responding to a limited range of stimuli with a small repertoire of behaviours and reflexes, it may be extremely difficult for an observer to differentiate between *like* and *want* or *dislike* and *reject*. Thus, in the final version, no distinction is made between *like/want* and *dislike/reject* at Level 1. At this level also, it is the author's experience that it may be unrealistic to expect to interpret *recognition*. It was considered that adult interpretation of the child conveying *discomfort, alarm* or *surprise* might be realistic at Level 1, but did not happen to appear on the particular video observations used. For ethical reasons, contexts would not have been created to elicit these behaviours simply for the purpose of this study.

Within Level 2, *reject* was agreed as not being viewed, as was *recognition* within Levels 2 and 3. These behaviours did not happen to appear on the video observations used. However, preferences such as *like, dislike, want* and *reject* are identified at this pre-intentional stage (Thoman 1981) as are *request, frustration, greeting* and *surprise* (Ricks 1979). Also, *surprise* and *interest* are observed from birth (Izard 1978). Hence item 10, whilst not observed, was retained in the assessment. Taking these issues into account, a number of items were combined. Within Level 1, these were items 1 and 3, *like* and *want*, items 2 and 4, *dislike* and *reject* and items 5, *recognition*, and 6, states such as *discomfort, surprise*. In Level 2, items 11, *recognition*, and 12, states such as *discomfort, surprise* and in Level 3, items 17, *recognition*, and 18, states such as *discomfort* and *surprise*. Although item 10, *reject* at Level 2, was not observed, it was considered important to keep it in the assessment, as such behaviour provides the assessor with information which can be very useful in setting up a comfortable communicative environment for the child.

Mutual gaze: initial draft assessment

Level 1: Reflexive level
1. Will join in mutual gaze with adult.
2. Will fixate on adult's face when it appears in midline at a distance of 8–10 inches.

Level 2: Reactive level
3. Will modify gaze to an object or person.
4. Will give eye contact to adult.
5. Will look intently at adult's face while being talked to.
6. Will turn head deliberately to source of voice.
7. Will mainly maintain eye contact with an adult while participating in activities such as feeding, dressing, being changed.
8. Will begin to use gaze coupling similar to gaze patterns in immature conversation, e.g. mutual and intermittent gaze initiation and termination.

Level 3: Proactive level
9. Will use a mature – i.e. broken – pattern of eye contact during an interaction.

One hundred per cent reliability was gained across all items in this section. Furthermore there is support in the literature related to mutual gaze for each of the items used in this section: e.g. item 1, will join in mutual gaze with adult (Brazelton 1979), item 2, will fixate on an adult's face when it appears in midline at a distance of 8–10 inches (Robson 1967), item 3, will shift gaze to an object or person (Bruner 1974/5), item 4, will give eye contact to adult (Jaffe *et al.* 1973), item 5, will look intently at adult's face while being talked to (Bullowa 1979), item 6, will turn head deliberately to source of voice (Bullowa 1979, Bruner 1974–5), item 7, will mainly maintain eye contact with an adult while participating in activities such as feeding, dressing, being changed (Owens 1984), item 8, will begin to use gaze coupling similar to gaze patterns in mature conversation, and item 9, will use a mature – i.e. broken – pattern of eye contact during an interaction (Jaffe *et al.* 1973). Hence, all mutual gaze items were retained in the final version of the ECA.

Social organisation of communication: initial draft assessment

Level 1: Reflexive level
1. Will fill a turn in response to an adult's pause in an interaction when given time.
2. Will join in mutual vocalisation with an adult, although not necessarily using the same vocalisation.
3. Will share in an exchange with an adult, adapting the behaviours as the adult does, e.g. adult vocal, child vocal.
4. Will act simultaneously with adult, though not necessarily using the same physical action. (This coactive behaviour is a fore-runner to joint action.)

Level 2: Reactive level

5. Will maintain an interaction, after responding to an adult's initiation.
6. Will terminate an interaction by default, e.g. looks/turns away.

Level 3: Proactive level

7. Will initiate an interaction with success.
8. Will maintain an interaction which is adult-directed.
9. Will maintain an interaction which is adult-structured but child anticipates turn.
10. Will terminate an interaction by default.
11. Will attempt to repair an interaction which the adult has terminated.
12. Will attempt to repair an interaction which child has self-terminated by default or lack of response.

Level 4: Primitive level

13. Will integrate attention between self, adult and object, e.g. gaze, gesture and touch, establishing joint reference.
14. Will initiate communication.
15. Will turn-take.
16. Will terminate an interaction.

Level 5: Conventional level

17. Will repair a misunderstanding non-verbally by repetition.
18. Will repair a misunderstanding non-verbally by rephrasing with a different pitch or novel gesture.
19. Will repair a misunderstanding non-verbally by elaborating to give more information or stress the information given.

The three items not observed by the observers, items 6, 10 and 12, all concerned terminations of interaction by default. While there is some theoretical support for this area (Roth and Speckman 1984a), in the experience of the author (Coupe O'Kane 1994) their occurrence in natural situations cannot be manipulated and they are not so frequently occurring as to warrant their inclusion. Those items were therefore withdrawn from the assessment.

Agreement for item 7, will initiate an interaction with success, was very low at nought per cent. This was partly due to the fact that only one occurrence of the behaviour was seen to be present on the video by one of the six observers. This argument, taken into consideration along with the theoretical support provided by the work of Roth and Speckman (1984a) on the importance of self-initiated behaviours in communicative development, led to a decision by the author (Coupe O'Kane 1994) to retain this item in the final version.

Almost all remaining items in the assessment are supported by the research literature concerned with social organisation of communication (Bruner 1974–5, Bullowa 1979, Owens 1984, Roth and Speckman 1984a, Tronick *et al.* 1979). The four remaining items, 9, 14, 15 and 16, have to be considered speculative. However, high reliability was achieved on each item over several observations. Hence these items are retained in the final version.

Joint reference: initial draft assessment

Level 2: Reactive level

1. Will follow adult's line of regard when accompanied by attention-getting strategies.
2. Will lead adult to follow line of regard (non-intentional).
3. Will respond to direction of adult's gaze resulting in shared attention on object, person or event, i.e. they come to attend stimulus jointly.
4. Will follow adult line of regard.
5. Will establish a line of regard which can then be followed and commented on by adult.

Level 3: Proactive level

6. Will follow the point/gesture of another person to an object or event near to.

7. Will follow the point/gesture of another person to an object or event in the distance, e.g. aeroplane in the sky.
8. Will express attention to a person, an object, event or other person by gaze, facial expression and interest, but cannot integrate these.

Level 4: Primitive level
9. Will establish integrating joint reference by coordinating attention to self and a person with an object, event or other person.

Despite support from research literature, item 2 was not observed in any of the 11 video observations. It was, therefore, decided to exclude it from the assessment. As a non-intentional item, item 2, will lead adult to follow line of regard (non-intentional), proved impossible to control in natural situations. One hundred per cent reliability was achieved across the other eight items related to joint reference with theoretical support from Bruner (1973, 1974–5), Owens (1984) and Scaife and Bruner (1975). Hence, items 1 and 3–9 were retained for the final version.

Turn-taking and social interaction: initial draft assessment

Level 2: Reactive level
1. Will anticipate and fill a turn with adult, e.g. smiles, increased arm movement.
2. Will produce behaviours which elicit responses from an adult.
3. Will produce responses which, in turn, alter the adult's responses.
4. Will maintain an interaction by giving rewarding feedback which relates to the adult's behaviour.
5. Will increasingly fill turns by vocalisations and movements of the head and hands.
6. Will respond to social turn-taking games, e.g. peekaboo.
7. Will vocalise in response to human voice.
8. Will smile in response to a smile.

Level 3: Proactive level
9. Will use many vocalisations which are simultaneous with adult.
10. Will use many actions which are simultaneous with adult.
11. Will use dialogues of sound with adult (spontaneous and imitated vocalisations).
12. Will use dialogues of action with adult.
13. Will fill a turn by acting on an object or paying attention to the adult.
14. Will refer to a person, object or activity in (a) immediate proximity, (b) distance.

Level 4: Primitive level
15. Will cling to adult when tired or distressed.
16. Will initiate an interaction with a familiar adult, e.g. comes for cuddles, hugs.
17. Will repeat a behaviour which has just produced a response, e.g. laughter.
18. Will repeat ritualised game sequences such as peekaboo.
19. Will express recognition of familiar persons.
20. Will use adult as a safe base from which to explore but frequently returns.
21. Will play near other children – orienting to where they play.
22. Will initiate and join in rough-and-tumble play with adult.
23. Will reach-for-signal, i.e. reaches or points to object, person or event while looking at the adult.
24. Will play with toys as long as adult is attending.
25. Will regain adult's attention if adult turns away from child's play with toys.
26. Will show signs of distress when sequences of communication end.

Level 5: Conventional level
27. Will use adult to play game or action.
28. Will cooperate with adult's lead in simple play routines.
29. Will attempt to manipulate adults to get own way, e.g. goes to touch plug, cries to get own way.

30. Will react with frustration when adult says 'No', e.g. when touching plug or TV switches.
31. Will initiate an interaction with another child, e.g. will take toy, look at face and smile.
32. Will join in turn-taking sequence with another child.
33. Will show signs of distress when misunderstandings occur.

Items 13, 15, 20 and 22 were not observed over the 11 video observations. Despite modest theoretical support related to these aspects of social interaction (item 20: Ainsworth and Bell 1969), it seemed, from the author's experience (Coupe O'Kane 1994), more rigorous to exclude these items from this area.

Good theoretical support exists for the remaining items, all of which are based on observations of natural interactions where turn-taking takes place (Ainsworth and Bell 1969, Bell and Ainsworth 1972, Bruner 1974–5, Bullowa 1979, Condon 1979, Ramey *et al.* 1978, Trevarthen 1979, Trevarthen and Hubley 1978, Tronick *et al.* 1979 and Uzgiris 1972). In Phase 1 of the study, high reliability was achieved on all remaining items, thus they were all included.

Comprehension in context: initial draft assessment

Level 1: Reflexive level
1. Will quieten when picked up or comforted.
2. Will orient to a person.
3. Will discriminate between strange and familiar voices.
4. Will respond more to speech sounds than non-speech sounds.
5. Will react to events caused by people rather than objects.
6. Will shape or control adult's behaviour although this is not intentional control, e.g. intense periods of eye-to-eye/face-to-face contact.
7. Will look at object when cued (object must be within optimum focusing distance).
8. Will move in synchrony to adult speech.

Level 2: Reactive level
9. Will anticipate food and drink by opening mouth.
10. Will increase limb movements with attention from an adult.
11. Will differentiate between pairs of stimuli, e.g. voice/non-voice, known/unknown adults, angry/friendly expressions, preferred/non-preferred adults.
12. Will show some recognition of objects as well as people.
13. Will demonstrate some expectation of changing or controlling the environment.
14. Will respond to affective messages from the adult and react to adult's behaviours, e.g. tone of voice, facial expression.

Level 3: Proactive level
15. Will show differential responses to adult intonation and voice quality, e.g. angry voice, verbal praise.
16. Will show differential responses to facial expressions, e.g. smiles, angry expressions.
17. Will show differential responses to adult actions, e.g. arms held out for a hug. N.B. May respond to tone of voice in 'no' but might not hold adult hand in response to proffered hand.

Level 4: Primitive level
18. Will respond appropriately to adult's non-verbal communication, e.g. takes proffered neutral object, takes held-out hand, follows a point.
19. Will pause in response to 'no' with intonation.
20. Will respond to commands incorporating situational cues when in context, e.g. give me, come here, sit down.
21. Will watch adult's face and gestures for cues.

Level 5: Conventional level

22. Will respond when the answer is visually apparent, e.g. when asked to show familiar object which is clearly on view.
23. Will point to a familiar body part when named/requested.
24. Will come when called.
25. Will respond to a familiar word in adult conversation.
26. Will go to known place or person on request, e.g. 'Go to mummy', 'Go to car'.
27. Will obtain familiar object on request – particularly if this request is made during a familiar routine, e.g. when washing, 'Get the towel'; when preparing a drink, 'Get the milk' or 'Get the cup'.
28. Points to self when asked 'Where's . . .?'
29. Will respond to request to give object in possession.
30. Will show understanding of a number of early words which relate to familiar situations, e.g. *dinner, clap, teddy, no.*
31. Will respond to a request to show the object in possession.

Eight items were not observed in this area, items 3, 4, 5, 7, 11, 12, 13 and 28. Despite theoretical support it was decided from the author's experience to exclude items 3, will discriminate between strange and familiar voice, 4, will respond more to speech sounds than non-speech sounds, 5, will react to event caused by people rather than objects, 11, will differentiate between pairs of stimuli, 12, will show some recognition of objects as well as people, and 13, will demonstrate some expectation of changing or controlling the environment, as involving excessive detail which made their occurrence infrequent. Item 7, will look at object when cued, supported by Bullowa (1979), and item 28, points to self when asked 'Where's . . .?', were regarded as sufficiently useful to be retained in the assessment.

One hundred per cent agreement was reached on all other items except for items 26, will go to known place or person on request, and 27, will obtain a familiar object on request (nought per cent and 50 per cent agreement respectively). These items are so regularly included in early comprehension assessment and experienced by the author (Coupe O'Kane 1994) that it was decided that their inclusion was justified, possibly with a re-wording to make them clearer. It is anticipated that a greater number of observations of children functioning within Level 5 would have yielded higher reliability, and these behaviours may well be more difficult to identify in lower functioning children. In conclusion, 25 of the original 31 items are retained in the final version of the assessment.

Communicative intentions: initial draft assessment

Level 4 : Primitive level

1. Will use a vocal and/or physical repertoire of behaviours to get a person to obtain objects (proto-imperative).
2. Will use a vocal and/or physical repertoire of behaviours to get a person to create/provide events and actions (proto-imperative).
3. Will use a vocal and/or physical repertoire of behaviours to get a person to satisfy states and conditions (proto-imperative).
4. Will use an object, action or event to get adult attention and draw it to self (proto-declarative).
5. Will produce physical and vocal messages to convey request.
6. Will produce physical and vocal messages to convey frustration.
7. Will produce physical and vocal messages to convey greeting.
8. Will produce physical and vocal messages to convey pleasant surprise.

Level 5: Conventional level

N.B. Some of these behaviours will have been evident at Level 4 but it is necessary to ascertain that the pupil can demonstrate the behaviour in a more conventional form in order to be judged as functioning within Level 5.

9. Will draw attention to an event or action.
10. Will draw attention to an object.
11. Will draw attention to other people.

12. Will gain attention for communication.
13. Will request a person.
14. Will request an object.
15. Will request an action or event.
16. Will request information.
17. Will request recurrence.
18. Will request an action.
19. Will reject an object.
20. Will reject a person.
21. Will protest.
22. Will greet (social).
23. Will give information about self.
24. Will give information about the environment and the people within it.
25. Will respond to a question.

Two items were not observed in this area, item 20, will reject a person, and 24, will give information about the environment and the people within it. However, both are, judging by the author's experience in the classroom (Coupe O'Kane 1994), frequently observed and well supported by research literature (Halliday 1979, and Roth and Speckman 1984a, 1984b). For this reason it was felt justified to retain them in the final assessment.

One hundred per cent agreement was reached on 21 of the remaining 23 items. Items 9 and 11 were confused on one occasion by the two observers, which resulted in nought per cent agreement for each. These too are retained in the light of support from Roth and Speckman (1984, 1984b) and the fact that some clarification between the items has achieved greater differentiation between them. Hence this area remains unchanged.

Presupposition: initial draft assessment

Level 5: Conventional level
1. Will generally convey new or changing aspects of self or the environment.
2. Will assume that the listener has access to certain background information during communication.
3. Will often establish the reference for the listener.
4. Will often adjust a communication to take account of a simple listener problem such as distance, object or event not in view to the listener.

Despite strong theoretical support for this area from Bates (1976), Owens (1984) and Roth and Speckman (1984a), no examples of presupposition were observed across the 11 video observations. It was concluded from the author's experience (Coupe O'Kane 1994) that this type of video observation is not the best format for assessing presupposition skills, and also that examples of items in this area of communicative functioning are difficult to ascertain. Hence, the whole of this area has been excluded from the final version of the ECA. (See Chapter 8 for further detail on assessing presupposition.)

Cognitive roles: initial draft assessment

Level 4: Primitive level
1. Will use objects in a way which reflects the knowledge of their functions.
2. Will demonstrate the cognitive concept of *existence*.
3. Will demonstrate the cognitive concept of *disappearance* of objects and people.
4. Will demonstrate the cognitive concept of *recurrence*, i.e. re-presentation of an object or person that existed but disappeared, or repetition of an action that occurred then stopped.
5. Will demonstrate the cognitive concept of *non-existence*, i.e. object or person does not exist where it is expected to be.

6. Will demonstrate the cognitive concept of *location*, i.e. the position of the object, person or event or the relationship between two objects or people.
7. Will demonstrate the cognitive concept of *possession*, i.e. the relationship between an object or person and themself.
8. Will demonstrate the cognitive concept of *rejection*, i.e. not wanting an object, adult or event, or wanting an activity to cease.
9. Will demonstrate the cognitive concept of *denial* of a proposition.
10. Will demonstrate the cognitive concept of *agent*, i.e. the person or object that causes an action to occur.
11. Will demonstrate the cognitive concept of *object*, i.e. the object or person that may be affected by an action.
12. Will demonstrate the cognitive concept of *action*, i.e. any observable activity or change of state.
13. Will demonstrate the cognitive concept of *attribute*, i.e. the property of an object or person.

Level 5: Conventional level

14. Will relate objects appropriately and functionally or combine, e.g. puts straws in cup to drink.
15. Will repeat part of an action using novel gestures, e.g. actions in 'wind a bobbin', lid-opening gesture to open lid of bubbles.

All 15 items were observed with 100 per cent agreement on up to four occasions each. Hence, this area has been retained in the final assessment in its entirety.

First meaning (semantic roles): initial draft assessment

Level 5: Conventional level

1. Will communicate *existence* by acknowledging that an object exists.
2. Will communicate *disappearance* by commenting on or requesting the disappearance of a person or object.
3. Will communicate *recurrence* by commenting on or requesting the return of an object that existed but disappeared, or a repetition of an action that occurred and then stopped.
4. Will communicate *non-existence* by indicating that an object does not exist where it is expected to be.
5. Will communicate *location* by commenting on the position of an object, person or event or the special relationship between two objects, or requesting that an object be placed in a certain location.
6. Will communicate *possession* by conveying the relationship between an object, person and themselves or another.
7. Will communicate *rejection* by conveying that they do not want an object, adult or event or that they want an activity to cease.
8. Will communicate *denial* by denying another person's proposition or assertion.
9. Will communicate *agent* as the person (or animate or entity) that causes an action to occur.
10. Will communicate *object* as the object or person (or animate or entity) that may be affected by an action.
11. Will communicate *action* as any observable activity or change of state.
12. Will communicate *attribute* by commenting on or requesting to know a property of an object, person or event.

Eleven out of 12 items were observed with 100 per cent reliability on up to three occasions. Item 4, will communicate non-existence, was not observed. However, strong support from Bloom (1973), Brown (1973) and Leonard (1984) suggests that this was a matter of the appropriate context not occurring in the situations observed. Hence, all 12 items which receive similar theoretical support were retained in the final assessment.

Imitation: initial draft assessment

Level 2: Reactive level
1. Will smile or frown in response to an adult's frown or smile.
2. Will vocalise in response to a human voice. N.B. Tends to imitate the mode/channel and not the exact behaviour.

Level 3: Proactive level
3. Will imitate behaviours already in physical or verbal repertoire.
4. Will imitate mouth movements.
5. Will imitate sounds, e.g. clicks, tut tut, babble, etc. which are in the existing repertoire.
6. Will imitate sounds, e.g. clicks, tut tut, babble, etc., which are not in the existing repertoire.

Level 4: Primitive level
7. Will imitate intonational contours used in adult's speech.
8. Will imitate using body parts which are out of view.
9. Will imitate a physical behaviour which is not in the existing repertoire but where own actions are visible.
10. Will imitate actions/gestures of adult spontaneously.

Level 5: Conventional level
11. Will imitate adult intonation for greeting, giving, etc., such as 'Here you are', 'Hiya', 'ta'.
12. Will imitate tunes sung by adult.
13. Will imitate actions with objects, e.g. pushing car, feeding dolly.
14. Will use deferred imitation.
15. Will imitate the play of other children.

Imitation at Levels 2 and 3 achieved relatively low percentage agreement. Six of the 15 items were not observed, but this seemed to have resulted from the 11 selected video observations, which included few examples of imitation. Those items not observed were 3, will vocalise in response to human voice, 6, will imitate sounds which are in the existing repertoire, 8, will imitate using body parts which are out of view, 12, will imitate tunes sung by adult, 14, will use deferred imitation, and 15, will imitate the play of other children. In attempting to assess these items, the author's classroom experience (Coupe O'Kane 1994) leads to the decision that items, 6, 8, 12, 14 and 15 be rejected from the second version of the assessment. Existing assessments of imitation which provide greater detail, e.g. Uzgiris and Hunt (1975), Dunst (1980), may be utilised. Item 3 is retained in view of strong theoretical support, e.g. Piaget (1952), Uzgiris and Hunt (1975), and because, in the author's experience (Coupe O'Kane 1994), it seems to be a useful item in relation to early communication.

The items which achieved poor reliability – item 1, will imitate adult's smile and frown, item 2, will vocalise in response to human voice, item 4, will imitate mouth movements, and item 5, will imitate sounds – are well supported by the literature (Uzgiris and Hunt 1975) and are retained because of their relevance to early communication. The area now contains ten items.

Auditory and visual behaviour: initial draft assessment

Level 2: Reactive level
1. Will visually inspect people and objects.
2. Will give eye contact to adult.
3. Will track slowly moving object jerkily through 180°.
4. Will grasp object with hand when in view, or when hand is touching object.
5. Will search for sound with eyes.
6. Will search for sound with head movement or orientation of the body.
7. Will stop an activity in response to sound.
8. Will show preference for certain sound.

9. Will search for human voice (in preference to non-voice sounds).
10. Will respond to intense noise.
11. Will glance at noisy object.

Level 3: Proactive level

12. Will listen to sounds.
13. Will search for sounds from sources to side and below ear level.
14. Will look for a fallen object.
15. Will visually fixate on object or person which is near.
16. Will visually fixate on object or person which is in the distance, e.g. aeroplane in the sky, car outside.
17. Will coordinate eyes with hand when picking up an object.
18. Will use visually directed reaching, i.e. visually locates object and shapes hand in anticipation when picking up an object.
19. Will use alternating glance.
20. Will track smoothly through 180°.
21. Will locate object appearing in visual field.

In order to focus on behaviours more likely to be found in communicative interactions, the seven items which were not observed over the range of video-taped observations used were excluded. Two items achieved low levels of reliability, items 10, will respond to intense noise, and 11, will glance at noisy object/person. In reviewing this area these items seemed to contribute little and were therefore excluded.

The remaining 12 items, over two levels, were seen as sufficient to inform the ECA and these items had obtained an adequate level of reliability.

Vocal production: initial draft assessment

Level 1: Reflexive level
N.B. Objectives at Level 1 are behaviours to observe for assessment, not intervention.
1. Will cry.
2. Will produce glottal sounds/click sounds.
3. Will produce vegetative sounds, e.g. burp, smacking lips, gurgle noises.
4. Will cough.
5. Will sneeze.

Level 2: Reactive level
6. Will laugh.
7. Will produce glottals, e.g. 'h'.
8. Will produce clicks, e.g. clip clop.
9. Will produce open vowels, e.g. 'oh' and 'ah'.
10. Will produce nasals, e.g. 'm', 'n', 'ng'.
11. Will produce plosives, e.g. 'p', 'b', 't', 'd', 'k', 'g'.
12. Will produce reduplicated babble, e.g. ba-ba-ba, ma-ma-ma, tee-tee.

Level 3: Proactive level
13. Will vocalise in response to music.
14. Will vocalise in response to environmental sounds.
15. Will vocalise during play with adults.
16. Will vocalise to self.
17. Will vocalise to own reflection.
18. Will vocalise to people.
19. Will vocalise to toys, objects and pictures.
20. Will use vocalisations which vary in pitch, volume, stress and quality to express anger,

eagerness, satisfaction, etc.
21. Will use vocalisations which become more differentiated for different situations, e.g. noise while on the toilet, while eating or when mum appears.
22. Will use vocalisations which reflect adult patterns of intonation for questions and statements.
23. Will produce consonants and vowels as in Level 2, but non-reduplicated babble, e.g. ba, da, ada, ma.

Level 4: Primitive level

24. Will use consonant-vowel and vowel-consonant-vowel structures, e.g. ta, de, do, ada, aga, iya.
25. Will squeal, shout, scream.
26. Will use vocalisation plus action to gain attention.
27. Will use vocalisation plus action to attain an object/event, etc.
28. Will use vocalisation plus action while acting on an object, e.g. sharing, putting objects into container.
29. Will vocalise while acting on objects, while eating.
30. Will generally use only those sounds which occur in the phonological system of their home language.

Level 5: Conventional level

31. Will produce speech sounds, vowels and consonants such as m, n, b, p, t, d, w, oh, ah, eeh.
32. Will use own sound to express self when having difficulty, e.g. tuts.
33. Will use sound sequences which stand for an activity/object.
34. Will use specific sounds which are integral with an activity: 'brum' when pushing car; 'whee' when being swung; 'boo' in peek-a-boo.
35. Will sing to music using own words.
36. Will use a vocabulary of 10–20 words, including protowords.

At very early stages of communication, for ethical reasons and in the experience of the author (Coupe O'Kane 1994), it is extremely difficult to elicit some aspects in the vocal production area, e.g. 'cough' and 'sneeze'. It was, therefore, not surprising that 14 of the 36 items were not observed in the eight video observations used. However, in order to ensure the breadth of this area, several items which were not observed but which have strong theoretical support were retained. These consist of items 7, will produce glottals, 11, will produce plosives, 12, will produce reduplicated babble, 22, will use vocalisations which reflect adult patterns of intonation for questions and statements, and 36, will use a vocabulary of 10–20 words, including protowords. These are behaviours which are regularly reported in the language acquisition literature (Crystal 1976, Owens 1984) and Nelson (1973) for item 36. The following items have been excluded: 2, 4, 5, 8, 13, 22, 32 and 35 (see Appendix A). Item 14, will vocalise in response to environmental sounds, was observed only once by one observer. Given the amount of detail already available at Level 3 it was, therefore, decided that this item should be excluded also and this was substantiated by the author's experience (Coupe O'Kane 1994).

Physical production: initial draft assessment

Level 1: Reflexive level

N.B. Many of these objectives are behaviours to observe for assessment, not intervention.
1. Will frown.
2. Will suck.
3. Will head-turn.
4. Will open/close mouth.
5. Will show finger activity.
6. Will relax body.
7. Will stiffen body.
8. Will move trunk or other body parts.
9. Will grasp when palm is stimulated.

10. Will show reflex rooting.
11. Will show reflex cardinal points that stimulate sucking.
12. Will show reflex stepping.
13. Will yawn.

Level 2: Reactive level
14. Will smile.
15. Will show trunk-turning/orientation to adult or other stimulus.
16. Will stiffen whole body.
17. Will produce changes in activity level.
18. Will show hand-to-mouth movement.
19. Will mouth.
20. Will hold.
21. Will produce facial movements, e.g. mouth puckering, tongue movement.
22. Will establish a controlled repertoire of physical behaviours.
23. Will touch object when cued by adult.

Level 3: Proactive level
24. Will reach for object or person using visually directed reaching.
25. Will let go of object to examine a new object.
26. Will use complex behaviours on objects, i.e. physically explores – hits, shakes – and visually examines.
27. Will make movement (noises) towards a desired goal that directs the adult to child, e.g. crawls towards door, cries if toy falls out of reach.
28. Will orientate body posture towards desired object or adult.
29. Will use simple actions on others, e.g. pushing, looking.

Level 4: Primitive level
30. Will use whole-body action, e.g. to pull away from adult.
31. Will place adult's hands on objects, e.g. clockwork toy to activate.
32. Will hug adult.
33. Will use eye or hand to point at (or indicate) an object, person or event.
34. Will use facial expressions and eye contact with adult.
35. Will reach-for-signal, e.g. reaches for or indicates cup whilst looking at adult.
36. Will intentionally use movement and eye contact towards a presumed desired goal, e.g. takes adult to the door and gives eye contact.
37. Will manipulate objects, people or events and make eye contact with the adult, e.g. drops toy and looks at adult, turns door handle and looks at adult.

Level 5: Conventional level
38. Will nod.
39. Will shake head.
40. Will wave.
41. Will open palm to request.
42. Will show an object.
43. Will give an object.
44. Will point using eye, hand or finger.
45. Will gesture to express 'gone' or 'where'.
46. Will greet familiar people.
47. Will perform novel gestures which represent part of a motor act, e.g. tickling own hand for 'Round and Round the Garden . . .'.
48. Will try to manipulate object while looking at adult, e.g. moves towards edge of table while looking at adult.

Of the 48 items incorporated in this area, only eight were not observed. Some of these items, 11, 12, 13, 22, 27, 32, 46 (see Appendix A), would prove difficult to obtain by chance or would require very artificial means of elicitation which do not necessarily relate to communication: e.g. item 12, will show reflex stepping, item 32, will hug adult. They have, therefore, been excluded from this area. Item 16, will stiffen whole body, has been retained in view of its support by Schaffer (1971) and the fact that in the experience of the author it is easily observable.

Forty items were observed, two of which, item 38, will nod, and item 41, will open palm to request, obtained nought per cent reliability. Both relate to gestural communication and are supported by Bates *et al.* (1975). Because, in the experience of the author (Coupe O'Kane 1994), they are generally considered to be commonly used gestures, it was considered valuable to maintain their inclusion.

The final version of the ECA

Appendix A presents the final, revised version of the ECA, which lists all the items included at the five different levels within 13 areas of communicative functioning.

Conclusion

In practice, the ECA's main strength has been its evolution and development; yet, as an assessment instrument, it has a number of hurdles still to overcome. In particular, the issue of reliability of items of the the ECA could be addressed more fully. The current study has been limited in both the scope and the breadth of its reliability investigations.

It would be valuable to widen the scope of future investigations involving the reliability of the ECA to include a number of considerations. One such consideration involves the extent to which staff who are unknown to the author (Coupe O'Kane 1994) or who are unfamiliar with the ECA or the ethos of the school used in this study, or who have limited experience of children and adults with severe and profound learning difficulties, can use the ECA. This issue would involve not only further reliability measures but also the need to examine training requirements for such inexperienced staff.

In addition, the scale is based upon the well-established position that there exists some sort of 'order' or 'developmental progression' in these early communicative attempts. There is little doubt that, at present, the ECA simply assumes this position. Clearly, it is desirable to test the ECA in this respect. It would be important, for example, to investigate whether those who demonstrate Level 2 skills also demonstrate Level 1 skills, and similarly whether those who demonstrate Level 3 skills also demonstrate Level 2 skills. Furthermore, the scale is influenced by Piaget's sensori-motor stages, and these stages are assumed as the framework within which communicative attempts can be analysed. This assumption should also be tested. It is necessary to investigate possible correlations in performance on items in different areas but at similar levels. For example, do those who perform at Level 2 in affective communication also perform at Level 2 in the social organisation of communication and comprehension in context? Answers to such questions would be an invaluable support for the ECA's future use.

Appendix C

The Manchester Pragmatics Profile

Intentions conveyed	Context	Repertoire of behaviours
1. Draws attention to self, i.e. wants attention: e.g. hovers near an adult/friend		
2. Draws attention to an event or action: e.g. points to a plane flying over		
3. Draws attention to an object: e.g. shows you a new watch		
4. Draws attention to other people: e.g. gets eye contact and points to someone coming into the room		
5. Gains attention for communication: e.g. taps on the shoulder before attempting to communicate		
6. Requests a person: e.g. does a 'come here' gesture to get someone to come over		

Name: Observer: Date:

Intentions conveyed	Context	Repertoire of behaviours
7. Requests an object: e.g. alternates glance between person and an object		
8. Requests an action or event: e.g. looks at adult and points to chair next to them		
9. Requests information: e.g. points to an object, looks at adult and vocalises with a questioning intonation		
10. Requests recurrence: e.g. finishes lunch, will not give plate for washing, keeps giving plate back to staff		
11. Requests confirmation of information: e.g. says 'still hot?' ten minutes after being told their drink is too hot		
12. Rejects an action, event or task: e.g. closes mouth to prevent a spoon being put in		
13. Rejects an object: e.g. puts an object back in its box while looking at the adult		

Intentions conveyed	Context	Repertoire of behaviours
14. Rejects a person: e.g. closes eyes and turns away from person initiating an interaction		
15. Protests: e.g. cries constantly while being washed		
16. Greets: e.g. says 'hiya'		
17. Gives information about self: e.g. an opinion, an experience, or shows their towel to indicate they are going swimming, or shows bus card in response to 'what's your name?', or shows a plaster on a cut finger		
18. Gives information about events and other people: e.g. takes adult to a broken milk bottle, or points to own home when travelling past, or takes adult to show cat stuck up a tree and says 'stuck'		
19. Comments or draws attention to available information: e.g. 'nice' + tugs at own new jumper		

Intentions conveyed	Context	Repertoire of behaviours
20. Directs or tells others: e.g. says 'stand up' with arm movements to get a peer to stand at the appropriate time		
21. Tells jokes: e.g. 'knock, knock . . .'		
22. Narrates: e.g. 'I opened the door, walked up the stairs and into the bedroom . . .'		
23. Describes: e.g. 'sitting next to her is like sitting next to a tiger'		
24. Uses the metalinguistic intention: e.g. 'why can you have gymnastic and not frednastic?'; 'you can't say 'lefted''		
25. Regulates a) social contact: e.g. 'come and sit next to me' b) conversation: e.g. 'let me get a word in' c) conduct/telling off: e.g. 'don't touch that'		
26. Pretends: e.g. 'let's be monsters'		

Intentions conveyed	Context	Repertoire of behaviours
27. Reasons: e.g. 'what if . . .?', 'how about . . .?', 'let's try . . .', 'will it fit if I turn it?'		
28. Deceives: e.g. says 'I didn't do it' – when they did		
29. Teases: e.g. 'your nose is getting bigger and bigger'		
30. Complains: e.g. 'this is not worth the money I paid for it', 'I didn't ask for salt and vinegar flavour, I wanted prawn'		
31. Provokes: e.g. 'you can't sit at my table!'		

Comments: Intentions conveyed

Social organisation of communication	Context	Strategies
1. Integrates attention between another person and object: i.e. alternating gaze		
2. Establishes joint reference: i.e. ensures that the other person is looking at the same thing		
3. Gains attention prior to communication		
4. Initiates a) communication b) conversation		
5. Turn-takes		
6. Maintains a conversation over more than two turns		
7. Terminates a conversation		
8. Recognises that a breakdown has occurred: e.g. says 'no, no' and looks distressed		

Social organisation of communication	Context	Strategies
9. Repairs a misunderstanding non-verbally by: a) repetition b) rephrasing c) elaboration d) enlisting the help of others		
10. Repairs a misunderstanding verbally by: a) repetition b) rephrasing c) elaboration d) enlisting the help of others		
11. Gives feedback when in the listener role: a) non-verbal b) verbal		
12. Requests clarification: a) specific, e.g 'did you say large or small?' b) non-specific, e.g. 'pardon?' c) confirmatory, e.g. 'you did say at the lights didn't you?'		
13. Maintains the topic/content: a) inappropriately, e.g. is repetitive b) appropriately		

Social organisation of communication	Context	Strategies
14. Adapts to change in topic		
15. Changes topic appropriately by: a) linking the preceding and the new topic b) introducing the new topic when the preceding one appears complete OR Generally changes the topic before the current one is complete		
16. Alters the duration of turns or 'talk-time' according to the demands of the discourse and the situation		
17. Interrupts appropriately		
18. Responds or answers appropriately, or inappropriately: e.g. says 'I don't know' when they do		

Comments: Social organisation of communication

Presupposition	Context	Examples
1. Conveys new, additional or changing aspects of the environment: i.e. is informative OR Typically offers shared or known information as though it were novel: i.e. is repetitive		
2. Communications are a) vague and ambiguous OR b) generally unambiguous: i.e. is the message or meaning understood from the context, from the shared knowledge or not at all?		
3. The referents are clearly established for the listener a) if present b) if absent		
4. Uses vocabulary which is exclusive to one situation: e.g. 'dad's' means any CD, 'Elsie' means any car		
5. Awareness of i) the listener's needs, ii) the content, iii) the previous conversation is shown in the use of the following linguistic devices: a) deixis, e.g. *here, there, then, now* b) proforms, e.g. *she, he, them, did* c) definite or indefinite forms, e.g. *the, that, a, this* d) ellipsis, e.g. 'where's mum?' 'in the bedroom' Uses correctly most of the time or has difficulty with		

Presupposition	Context	Examples
6. Communications are generally relevant to the topic under discussion OR Establishes a new topic to give a new context for communication OR Communications are frequently not relevant to the topic under discussion		
7. Shows awareness of the listener's needs by being a) appropriately concise b) not overly repetitive		
8. Adjusts communication to account for listener's problems OR Does not adjust communication		
9. Communications are generally appropriate to the communicative partner and the setting in terms of a) vocabulary, e.g. forms of address b) paralinguistic features, e.g. tone, volume of voice c) non-verbal features, e.g. facial expression		

Presupposition	Context	Examples
10. Shows understanding of the effect communication has on others by manipulating the following aspects: a) verbal, e.g. choice of words b) paralinguistic, e.g. tone, stress, volume of voice c) non-verbal features, e.g. facial expression		
11. Does or does not show an awareness of the following factors in the form of communications: a) the formality of the context b) the degree of politeness required c) the relationship or degree of familiarity between self and the listener d) the shared history with the conversational partner		
Comments: Presupposition		

References

Ainsworth, M. and Bell, S. (1969) 'Some contemporary patterns of mother–infant interaction in the feeding situation', in Ambrose, J. (ed.) *Stimulation in Early Infancy*. New York: Academic Press.

Akhtar, N., Dunham, F., Dunham, P. (1991) 'Directive interactions and early vocabulary development: the role of joint attentional focus', *Journal of Child Language* 1, 41–9.

Alegria, J. and Noirot, E. (1978) 'Neonate orientation behaviour towards human voice', *International Journal of Behavioural Development* 1, 291–312.

Astington, J. (1990) 'Metapragmatics: children's conception of promising', in Conti-Ramsden, G. and Snow, C. E. (eds) *Children's Language*. Hillsdale, NJ: Lawrence Erlbaum Associates.

Barber, M., Goldbart, J., Munley, G. (1995) 'Student initiations and staff responses: identifying optimal contexts for pupils with profound intellectual disabilities'. Paper presented to BILD Conference, Oxford, 17 September 1995.

Barton, L. and Coupe, J. (1985) 'Teaching first meanings', *Mental Handicap* 13, 67–70.

Bates, E. (1976) *Language and Context: The Acquisition of Pragmatics*. New York: Academic Press.

Bates, E., Camaioni, L., Volterra, V. (1975) 'The acquisition of performatives prior to speech', *Merrill-Palmer Quarterly* 21, 205–16.

Bates, E., Benigni, L., Bretherton, I., Camaioni, L., Volterra, V. (1979) *The Emergence of Symbols: Cognition and Communication in Infancy*. New York: Academic Press.

Bateson, M. (1975) 'Mother–infant exchanges: the epigenesis of conversational interaction', in Aaronson, D. and Rieber, R. (eds) *Developmental Psycholinguistics and Communication Disorders*. New York: New York Academy of Sciences.

Becker, J. A. (1990) 'Processes in the acquisition of pragmatic competences', in Conti-Ramsden, G. and Snow, C. E. (eds) *Children's Language*. Hillsdale, NJ: Lawrence Erlbaum Associates.

Beckman, P., Lieber, J., Strong, B. (1993) 'Influence of social partner on interactions of toddlers with disabilities', *American Journal on Mental Retardation* 98, 378–89.

Bell, I. (1985) 'Communication and language in mental handicap: 5: Don't teach – intervene', *Mental Handicap* 13, 17–19.

Bell, S. and Ainsworth, M. (1972) 'Infant crying and maternal responsiveness', *Child Development* 43, 1171–90.

Benedict, H. (1979) 'Early lexical development: comprehension and production', *Journal of Child Language* 6, 183–200.

Bennett, C. (1973) 'A four and a half year old as teacher of her hearing impaired sister: a case study', *Journal of Communication Disorders* 6, 67–75.

Beveridge, M. and Hurrell, P. (1980) 'Teachers' responses to severely mentally handicapped children's responses in the classroom', *Journal of Child Psychology and Psychiatry* 21, 175–81.

Beveridge, M., Conti-Ramsden, G., Leudar, I. (1989/97) *Language and Communication in Mentally Handicapped People*, 1st and 2nd edns. London: Chapman & Hall.

Bloom, L. (1973) *One Word at a Time: The Use of Single Word Utterances Before Speech*. The Hague: Mouton.

Bloom, L. and Lahey, M. (1978) *Language Development and Language Disorders*. New York: John Wiley.

Bloomberg, K. and West, D. (1996) *Picture It: Partners in Communication Training using Real Environments through Interactive Teaching*. St Kilda, Victoria: SCIOP/Spastic Society of Victoria.

Brazelton, T. (1979) 'Evidence of communication in neonatal behavioural assessment', in Bullowa, M. (ed.) *Before Speech*. Cambridge: Cambridge University Press.

Bremner, J. G. (1988) *Infancy*. Oxford: Blackwell.

Bricker, W. and Bricker, D. (1974) 'An early language training strategy', in Schiefelbusch, R. and Lloyd, L. (eds) *Language Perspectives: Acquisition, Retardation and Intervention*. Baltimore, MD: University Park Press.

Brinker, R. (1978) 'Teaching language in context: a feasibility study', *Le Revue de Phonetique Appliquée* 46/47, 159–203.

Brinker, R. P. and Lewis, M. (1982a) 'Discovering the competent handicapped infant: a process approach to assessment and intervention', *Topics in Early Childhood Special Education* 2, 1–16.

Brinker, R. P. and Lewis, M. (1982b) 'Making the world work with microcomputers: a learning prosthesis for handicapped infants', *Exceptional Children* 49, 163–70.

Brinton, B., Fuijiki, M., Loeb, D., Winkler, E. (1986) 'Development of conversational repair strategies in response to requests for clarification', *Journal of Speech and Hearing Research* 29, 75–81.

Brown, R. (1973) *A First Language: The Early Stages*. Cambridge, MA: Harvard University Press.

Bruner, J. (1974–5) 'From communication to language: a psychological perspective', *Cognition* 3, 255–87.

Bruner, J. (1975) 'The ontogenesis of speech acts', *Journal of Child Language* 2, 1–19.

Bruner, J. (1977) 'Early social interaction and language acquisition', in Schaffer, H. R. (ed.) *Studies in Mother–Infant Interaction: Proceedings of the Loch Lomond Symposium*. London: Academic Press.

Bruner, J. (1978) 'Learning how to do things with words', in Bruner, J. and Girton, A. (eds), *Wolfson College Lectures 1976:*

Human Growth and Development. Oxford: Oxford University Press.

Bruner, J. (1981) 'The social context of language acquisition', *Language and Communication* 1, 155–78.

Bruner, J. (1983) *Child's Talk: Learning to Use Language*. Oxford: Oxford University Press.

Bruner, J. (1985) 'Vygotsky: a historical and conceptual perspective', in Wertsch, J. (ed.) *Culture, Communication and Cognition*. Cambridge: Cambridge University Press.

Bullowa, M. (1979) 'Introduction: Prelinguistic communication: a field for scientific research', in Bullowa, M. (ed.) *Before Speech*. Cambridge: Cambridge University Press.

Butterfield, N. (1994) 'Play as an assessment and intervention strategy for children with language and intellectual difficulties', in Linfoot, K. (ed.) *Communication Strategies for People with Developmental Disabilities*. Sydney: MacLennan and Petty.

Calculator, S. and Bedrosian, J. (1988) *Communication Assessment and Intervention for Adults with Mental Retardation*. London: Taylor & Francis.

Camaioni, L. (1993) 'The development of intentional communication: a re-analysis', in Nadel, J. and Camaioni, L. (eds) *New Perspectives in Early Communicative Development*. London: Routledge.

Campbell, R. C. and Stremel-Campbell, K. (1986) 'Programming "Loose Training" as a strategy to facilitate language generalisation', *Journal of Applied Behavioral Analysis* 15, 295–301.

Carr, E., Schreibman, L., Lovaas, O. (1975) 'Control of echolalic speech in autistic children', *Journal of Abnormal Child Psychology* 3, 331–52.

Casby, M. and Ruder, K. (1983) 'Symbolic play and early language development in normal and mentally retarded children', *Journal of Speech and Hearing Research* 26, 404–11.

Cheseldine, S. and McConkey, R. (1979) 'Parental speech to young Down's syndrome children: an intervention study', *American Journal on Mental Deficiency* 83, 612–20.

Chomsky, N. (1957) *Syntactic Structures*. The Hague: Norton

Chomsky, N. (1965) *Aspects of the Theory of Syntax*. Cambridge, MA: MIT Press.

Cirrin, F. and Rowland, C. (1985) 'Communicative assessment of non–verbal youths with severe/profound mental retardation', *Mental Retardation* 23, 52–62.

Coggins, T. and Carpenter, R. (1981) 'The Communication Intention Inventory: a system for coding children's early intentional communication', *Applied Psycholinguistics* 2, 235–52.

Condon, W. (1979) 'Neonatal entrainment and enculturation', in Bullowa, M. (ed.) *Before Speech*. Cambridge: Cambridge University Press.

Condon, W. and Sander, L. (1974) 'Neonate movement is synchronised with adult speech: interactional participation and language acquisition', *Science* 183, 99–101.

Connolly, J., Doyle, A., Reznick, E. (1988) 'Social pretend play and social interaction in preschoolers', *Journal of Applied Developmental Psychology* 9, 301–13.

Conti-Ramsden, G. (1997) 'Parent–child interaction in mental handicap: a commentary', in Beveridge, M., Conti-Ramsden, G., Leudar, I. (eds) *Language and Communication in Mentally Handicapped People*. London : Chapman & Hall.

Coupe, J. (1981) *Melland School Language Survey* (unpublished). Manchester: Melland School.

Coupe, J., Barton, L., Barber, M., Collins, L., Levy, D., Murphy, D. (1985) *The Affective Communication Assessment*. Manchester: Melland School.

Coupe, J. and Jolliffe, J. (1988) 'An early communication curriculum: implications for practice', in Coupe, J. and Goldbart, J. (eds) *Communication Before Speech*, 1st edn. Beckenham: Croom Helm.

Coupe O'Kane, J. (1994) *Developing an Early Communication Assessment for Pupils with Severe Learning Difficulties* (unpublished M.Phil. thesis). University of Manchester.

Coupe O'Kane, J. and Levy, D. (1996) 'The object related scheme assessment procedure', *The SLD Experience* 14, 16–18.

Crystal, D. (1976) *Child Language, Learning and Linguistics*. London: Edward Arnold.

Cunningham, C., Glenn, S., Wilkinson, P., Sloper, P. (1985) 'Mental ability, symbolic play and receptive and expressive language of young children with Down's syndrome', *Journal of Child Psychology & Psychiatry* 26, 255–65.

Department of Education and Science (1988) *Task Group on Assessment and Testing: Report*. London: HMSO.

Dewart, H. and Summers, S. (1995) *The Pragmatic Profile of Everyday Communication Skills in Children*. Windsor: NFER-Nelson.

Donaldson, M. (1978) *Children's Minds*. London: Fontana.

Donaldson, M. and McGarrigle, J. (1974) 'Some clues to the nature of semantic development', *Journal of Child Language* 1, 185–94.

Dore, J. (1977) 'Children's illocutionary acts', in Freedle, R. (ed.) *Discourse, Production and Comprehension*. Norwood, NJ: Ablex.

Dore, J. (1978) 'Variations in pre-school children's conversational performance', in Nelson, K. (ed.) *Children's Language*. New York: Academic Press.

Dunst, C. (1980) *A Clinical and Educational Manual for Use with Uzgiris and Hunt Scales of Infant Psychological Development*. New York: Pro-Ed Inc.

Evans, P. and Ware, J. (1987) *'Special Care' Provision: The Education of Children with Profound and Multiple Learning Difficulties*. Windsor: NFER-Nelson.

Farrar, M., Friend, M., Forbes, J. (1993) 'Event knowledge and early language acquisition', *Journal of Child Language* 20, 591–606.

Fein, G. (1975) 'A transformational analysis of pretending', *Developmental Psychology* 77, 291–6.

Felce, D., Saxby, H., de Kock, U., Repp, A., Ager, A., Blunden, R. (1987) 'To what behaviours do attending adults respond?', *American Journal on Mental Deficiency* 91, 496–504.

Fewell, R. and Kaminski, R. (1988) 'Play skill development and instruction for young children with handicaps', in Odom, S. and Karnes, M. (eds) *Early Intervention for Children with Handicaps*. Baltimore, MD: P. H. Brookes.

Fischer, K. W. (1980) 'A theory of cognitive development: the control and construction of hierarchies of skills', *Psychological Review* 87, 477–531.

Gallagher, T. (1977) 'Revision behaviours in the speech of normal children developing language', *Journal of Speech and Hearing Research* 20, 308–18.

Gallagher, T. (1981) 'Contingent query within adult–child discourse', *Journal of Child Language* **8**, 51–82.

Galloway, C. and Richards, B. (1994) *Input and Interaction in Language Acquisition*. Cambridge: Cambridge University Press.

Garvey, C. (1991) *Play*, 2nd, edn. London: Fontana.

Glenn, S. M. and Cunningham, C. C. (1984) 'Special care but active learning', *Special Education: Forward Trends* **2**, 33–6.

Goldbart, J. (1985) *The Assessment of Programmed and Environmental Factors in Teaching Language to Developmentally Delayed Children* (unpublished PhD thesis). University of Manchester.

Goldbart, J. (1994) 'Playing in the zone: communication and cognition in the classroom', *The SLD Experience* **10**, 12–14.

Golinkoff, R. (1993) 'When is communication a "meeting of minds"?', *Journal of Child Language* **20**, 199–207.

Gordon, N. (1976) *Paediatric Neurology for the Clinician*. Leverham: Leverham Press.

Gowen, J., Johnson-Martin, N., Goldman, B., Hussey, B. (1992) 'Object play and exploration in children with and without disabilities: a longitudinal study', *American Journal on Mental Retardation* **97**, 21–38.

Gray, B. and Fygetakis, L. (1968) 'Mediated language acquisition for dysphasic children', *Behaviour Research and Therapy* **6**, 263–80.

Greenfield, P. and Smith, J. (1976) *The Structure of Communication in Early Language Development*. New York: Academic Press.

Greenwald, C. and Leonard, L. (1979) 'Communication and sensori-motor development of Down's syndrome children', *American Journal on Mental Deficiency* **84**, 296–303.

Grice, H. P. (1975) 'Logic and conversation', in Cole, P. and Morgan, J. (eds) *Syntax and Semantics Vol. 3: Speech Acts*. New York: Academic Press.

Guess, D., Keogh, W., Sailor, W. (1978) 'Generalisation of speech and language behavior', in Schiefelbusch, R. L. (ed.) *Bases of Language Intervention*. Baltimore, MD: University Park Press.

Gunzburg, H.C. (1973) *Progress Assessment Charts*. London: NAMH.

Haith, M. (1980) *Rules That Babies Look By*. Hillsdale, NJ: Lawrence Erlbaum.

Halle, J., (1984) 'Arranging the natural environment to occasion language: giving severely language-delayed children reasons to communicate', *Seminars in Speech and Language* **5**, 185–97.

Halle, J., Marshall, A., Spradlin, J. (1979) 'Time delay: a technique to increase language use and facilitate generalisation in retarded children', *Journal of Applied Behavioral Analysis* **12**, 431–9.

Halliday, M. (1975) *Learning How to Mean: Explorations in the Development of Language*. London: Edward Arnold.

Halliday, M. (1979) 'One child's proto-language', in Bullowa, M. (ed.) *Before Speech*. Cambridge: Cambridge University Press.

Harasty, J., Rosenthal, J., Reed, V., Jones, A. (1994) 'Communicative flexibility in children: its effect on judgments of communicative competence and communication disorder', *Clinical Linguistics and Phonetics* **8**, 141–52.

Harding, C. (1982) 'Development of the intention to communicate', *Human Development* **25**, 140–51.

Harding, C. (1983) 'Setting the stage for language acquisition: communication development in the first year', in Golinkoff, R. (ed.) *The Transition from Pre-Linguistic to Linguistic Communication*. Hillsdale, NJ: Lawrence Erlbaum Associates.

Harding, C. (1984) 'Acting with intention: a framework for examining the development of the intention to communicate', in Feagans, L,. Garvey, C., Golinkoff, R. (eds) *The Origins and Growth of Communication*. Norwood, NJ: Ablex.

Harding, C. and Golinkoff, R. (1980) 'The origins of intentional vocalisations in prelinguistic infants', *Child Development* **49**, 33–40.

Hargrave, L. and Swisher, L. (1975) 'Modifying the verbal expression of a child with autistic behaviors', *Journal of Autism and Childhood Schizophrenia* **5**, 147–54.

Harris, J. (1984a) 'Early language intervention programmes', *Association for Child Psychology and Psychiatry Newsletter* **6**, 2–20.

Harris, J. (1984b) 'Encouraging linguistic interactions between severely mentally handicapped children and teachers in special schools', *Special Education: Forward Trends* **11**, 17–24.

Harris, J. (1990) *Early Language Development: Implications for Clinical and Educational Practice*. London: Routledge.

Harris, M. (1992) *Language Experience and Early Development*. Hove: Lawrence Erlbaum Associates.

Hausendorf, H. and Quasthoff, U. (1992) 'Children's storytelling in adult–child interaction. Three dimensions in narrative development', *Journal of Narrative and Life History* **2**, 293–306 (special issue on narrative development in a social context).

Hayes, L. A. and Watson, J. S. (1981) 'Neonatal imitation: fact or artifact?', *Developmental Psychology* **17**, 655–60.

Hedge, M. and Gierut, J. (1979) 'The operant training and generalisation of pronouns and a verb form in a language delayed child', *Journal of Communication Disorders* **12**, 74–7.

Hill, P. and McCune-Nicolich, L. (1981) 'Pretend play and patterns of cognition in Down's syndrome children', *Child Development* **52**, 611–17.

Hogg, J. and Sebba, J. (1987) *Profound Retardation and Multiple Impairment Vols 1 & 2*. London: Croom Helm.

Hogg, J., Lamb, L., Cowie, J., Coxon, J. (1987) *People with Profound Retardation and Multiple Handicaps Attending Schools or Social Educational Centres*. London: Mencap.

Izard, C. E. (1978) 'On the ontogenesis of emotions and emotion-cognition relationships in infancy', in Lewis, M. and Rosenbloom, L. (eds) *The Development of Affect*. New York: Plenum Press.

Jaffe, J., Stern, R. and Peery, J. (1973) ' "Conversational" coupling of gaze behaviour in prelinguistic human development', *Journal of Psycholinguistic Research* **2**, 321–9.

Jeffree, D. and McConkey, R. (1976) 'An observation scheme for recording children's imaginative doll play', *Journal of Child Psychology and Psychiatry* **17**, 189–97.

Jones, S. (1986) *Assessing the Functional Communication Skills of People with Mental Handicaps*. Report of a One-Year Feasibility Study at St. Lawrence's Hospital, Caterham, Surrey.

Kahn, J. (1984) 'Cognitive training and initial use of referential speech', *Topics in Language Disorders* **5**, 14–28.

Kamhi, A. and Masterson, J. (1989) 'Language and cognition in mentally handicapped persons: last rites for the delay–difference controversy', in Beveridge, M., Conti-Ramsden, G., Leudar, I. (eds) *Language and Communication in Mentally Handicapped People*. London: Chapman & Hall.

Kaye, K. (1979) 'Thickening thin data: the maternal role in developing communication and language', in Bullowa, M. (ed.) *Before Speech*. Cambridge: Cambridge University Press.

Kelly, C. and Dale, P. (1989) 'Cognitive skill associated with the onset of multi word utterances', *Journal of Speech and Hearing Research* **32**, 645–56.

Kennedy, M., Sheridan, M., Radlinski, S., Beeghly, M. (1991) 'Play–language relationships in young children with developmental delays: implications for assessment', *Journal of Speech and Hearing Research* **34**, 112–22.

Kiernan, C. and Reid, B. (1987a) *The Pre-verbal Communication Schedule (PVCS) Manual*. Windsor: NFER-Nelson.

Kiernan, C. and Reid, B. (1987b) *The Pre-verbal Communication Schedule (PVCS) Assessment*. Windsor: NFER-Nelson.

Kiernan, C., Reid, B., Goldbart, J. (1987) *Foundations of Communication and Language*. Manchester: BIMH/Manchester University Press.

Kiernan, C., Reid, B., Jones, M. (1982) *Signs and Symbols: A Review of Literature and Use of Non-Vocal Communication Systems* (University of London Institute of Education Studies in Education, 11). London: Heinemann.

Knowles, W. and Masidlover, M. (1982) *Derbyshire Language Scheme*. Ripley, Derbyshire (private publication).

Koepke, J. E., Hamm, H., Legerstee, M., Russell, M. (1983) 'Neonatal imitation: two failures to replicate', *Infant Behavior and Development* **6**, 97–102.

Lacey, P., Smith, B., Tilstone, C. (1991) 'Influences on curriculum design and assessment', in Tilstone, C. (ed.) *Teaching Pupils with Severe Learning Difficulties: Practical Approaches*. London: David Fulton.

Latham, C. and Miles, A. (1997) *Assessing Communication*. London: David Fulton.

Leeming, K., Swann, W., Coupe, J., Mittler, P. (1979) *Teaching Language and Communication to the Mentally Handicapped*. London: Evans-Methuen Educational.

Leonard, L. (1974) 'A preliminary view of generalisation in language training', *Journal of Speech and Hearing Disorders* **39**, 429–33.

Leonard, L. (1984) 'Semantic considerations in early language training', in Ruder, K. and Smith, M. (eds) *Developmental Language Intervention*. Baltimore, MD: University Park Press.

Lewis, V., Boucher, J., Astell, A. (1992) 'The assessment of symbolic play in young children: a prototype test', *European Journal of Disorders of Communication* **27**, 231–45.

Linfoot, K. (ed.) (1994) *Communication Strategies for People with Developmental Disabilities*. Sydney: MacLennan and Petty.

Lovaas, O. I. (1977) *The Autistic Child: Language Development through Behavior Modification*. New York: Wiley.

Lyons, J. (1977) *Semantics Vols 1 & 2*. Cambridge: Cambridge University Press.

Macnamara, J. (1972) 'Cognitive basis of early language learning in infants', *Psychological Review* **79**, 1–13.

MacPherson, F. D. and Butterworth, G. E. (1981) *Application of a Piagetian Infant Development Scale to the Assessment of Profound Mentally Handicapped Children* (paper presented to the Annual Conference, Developmental Psychology Section), British Psychological Society, Manchester.

Manolson, A. (1992) *It Takes Two to Talk*. Toronto: Hanen.

Martin, H., McConkey, R., Martin, S. (1984) 'From acquisition theories to intervention strategies', *British Journal of Disorders of Communication* **19**, 3–14.

Matsuo-Muto, H. and Kato, T. (1994) 'Maternal speech to Japanese children with and without severe mental retardation', *Education and Training in Mental Retardation and Developmental Disabilities* **29**, 145–54.

McConkey, R. and Price, P. (1986) *Let's Talk*. London: Souvenir Press.

McConkey, R., McEvoy, J., Gallagher, F. (1982) 'Learning through play: the evaluation of a video course for parents of mentally handicapped children', *Child: Care, Health and Development* **8**, 345–59.

McCune-Nicolich, L. (1981) 'Toward symbolic functioning: structure of early pretend games and potential parallels with language', *Child Development* **52**, 785–97.

McCune-Nicolich, L. (1986) 'Play–language relationships: implications for a theory of symbolic development', in Gottfried, A. and Brown, C. (eds) *Play Interactions*. Lexington, MA: Lexington Books.

McHale, S., Simeonsson, R., Marcus, L., Olley, J. (1980) 'The social and symbolic quality of autistic children's communication', *Journal of Autism and Developmental Disorders* **10**, 299–311.

McKenzie, B. E. and Over, R. (1983) 'Young infants fail to imitate facial and manual gestures', *Infant Behavior and Development* **6**, 85–95.

McLean, J. and Snyder-McLean, L. (1978) *A Transactional Approach to Early Language Training*. Columbus, OH: Charles Merrill.

McLean, J. and Snyder-McLean, L. (1985) *Developmentally Early Communicative Behaviours Among Severely Mentally Retarded Adolescents* (seminar topic outline), Hester Adrian Research Centre, University of Manchester.

McLean, J. and Snyder-McLean, L. (1987) 'Form and function of communicative behaviour among persons with severe developmental disabilities', *Australia and New Zealand Journal of Developmental Disabilities* **13**, 83–98.

McTear, M. F. and Conti-Ramsden, G. (eds) (1992) *Pragmatic Disability in Children*. London: Whurr.

Miller, J. and Chapman, R. (1984) 'Disorders of communication: investigating the development of mentally retarded children', *American Journal on Mental Deficiency* **88**, 536–45.

Miller, J. F. and Yoder, D. (1974) 'An ontogenic language teaching strategy for retarded children', in Schiefelbusch, R. L. and Lloyd, W. L. (eds) *Language Perspectives: Acquisition, Retardation and Intervention*. New York: University Park Press.

Mitchell, S. (1994) 'Some implications of the High Scope Curriculum and the education of children with learning difficulties', in Coupe O'Kane, J. and Smith, B. (eds) *Taking Control: Enabling People with Learning Difficulties*. London: David Fulton.

Mittler, P. and Berry, P. (1977) 'Demanding language', in Mittler, P. (ed.) *Research Into Practice in Mental Retardation Vol. II: Education and Training*. Baltimore, MD: University Park Press.

Moore, K. and Meltzoff, A. (1978) 'Object permanence, imitation and language development in infancy: toward a neo-Piagetian perspective on communicative development', in Minfie, F. and Lloyd, L. (eds) *Communicative and Cognitive Abilities – Early Behavioural Assessment*. Baltimore, MD: University Park Press.

Mossler, D., Marvin, R., Greenberg, M. (1976) 'Conceptual perspective taking in 2 to 6 year-old children', *Developmental Psychology* **13**, 314–19.

Mueller, E. (1972) 'The maintenance of verbal exchanges between young children', *Child Development* **43**, 930–38.

Muma, J. (1978) *Language Handbook*. Englewood Cliffs, NJ: Prentice Hall.

Mundy, P., Seibert, J., Hogan, A. (1984) 'Relationship between sensory motor and early communication abilities in developmentally delayed children', *Merrill-Palmer Quarterly* **30**, 33–48.

Mundy, P., Sigman, M., Ungerer, J., Sherman, T. (1987) 'Nonverbal communication and play correlates of language development in autistic children', *Journal of Autism and Developmental Disorders* **17**, 349–64.

Nadel, J. and Camaioni, L. (eds) (1993) *New Perspectives in Early Communicative Development*. London: Routledge.

National Joint Committee for the Communicative Needs of Persons with Severe Disabilities (1992) 'Guidelines for meeting communication needs of persons with severe disabilities', *American Speech and Hearing Association* **34**, (March, Supp. 7), 1–8.

Nelson, K. (1973) 'Structure and strategy in learning to talk', *Monographs of the Society for Research in Child Development*, 38.

Nelson, K. (1978) 'Early speech in its communicative context', in Minifie, F. and Lloyd, L. (eds) *Communicative and Cognitive Abilities – Early Behavioural Assessment*. Baltimore, MD: University Park Press.

Newson, J. (1979) 'The growth of shared understandings between infant and care giver', in Bullowa, M. (ed.) *Before Speech*. Cambridge: Cambridge University Press.

Newton, S. (1981) *Social Aspects of Communicative Competence in Mentally Handicapped Adolescents and Non-Handicapped Children* (unpublished Ph.D. thesis), University of Manchester.

Nind, M. and Hewett, D. (1994) *Access to Communication*. London: David Fulton.

O'Brien, Y., Glenn, S., Cunningham, C. (1994) 'Contingency awareness in infants and children with severe and profound learning disabilities', *International Journal of Disability, Development and Education* **41**, 231–43.

Ogura, T. (1991) 'A longitudinal study of the relationship between early language development and play development', *Journal of Child Language* **18**, 273–94.

Owens, R. (1984) *Language Development: An Introduction*. Columbus, OH: Charles Merrill.

Owens, R. (1989) 'Cognition and language in mentally retarded population', in Beveridge, M., Conti-Ramsden, G., Leudar, I. (eds) *Language and Communication in Mentally Handicapped People*. London: Chapman & Hall.

Palermo, D. (1982) 'Theoretical issues in semantic development', in Kuczaj, S. (ed.) *Language Development Vol. 1: Syntax and Semantics*. Hillsdale, NJ: Lawrence Erlbaum Associates.

Piaget, J. (1952) *The Origins of Intelligence in Children*. New York: International Universities Press.

Piaget, J. (1962) *Play, Dreams and Imitation in Childhood*. New York: Norton.

Porter, J. (1986) 'Beyond a simple behavioural approach', in Coupe, J. and Porter, J. (eds) *The Education of Children with Severe Learning Difficulties*. London: Croom Helm.

Prather, E., Cromwell, K., Kenney, K. (1989) 'Types of repairs used by normally developing and language impaired pre-school children in response to clarification requests', *Journal of Communication Disorders* **22**, 49–64.

Pratt, M., Bumstead, D., Raynes, N. (1976) 'Attendant staff speech to the institutionalised retarded: language use as a measure of the quality of care', *Journal of Child Psychology and Psychiatry* **17**, 133–43.

Price, P. (1997) 'Language intervention and mother–child interaction', in Beveridge, M., Conti-Ramsden, G. Leudar, I. (eds) *Language and Communication in Mentally Handicapped People*, 2nd edn. London: Chapman & Hall.

Prior, J. (1997) *The Use of the ACA at St Ann's School, Surrey* (unpublished study).

Prior, M., Minnes, P., Coyne, T., Golding, B., Hendy, J., McGillivray, J. (1979) 'Verbal interactions between staff and residents in an institution for the young mentally retarded', *Mental Retardation* **17**, 65–9.

Przetacznik-Gierowska, M. P. G. and Ligeza, M. (1990) 'Cognitive and interpersonal functions of children's questions', in Conti-Ramsden, G. and Snow, C. E. (eds) *Children's Language*. Hillsdale, NJ: Lawrence Erlbaum Associates.

Ramey, C., Farron, D., Campbell, F., Finkelstein, N. (1978) 'Observation of mother–infant interaction: implications for development', in Minifie, F. and Lloyd, L. (eds) *Communicative and Cognitive Abilities – Early Behavioural Assessment*. Baltimore, MD: University Park Press.

Reddy, V. (1990) 'Humorous communication in the first year of life', paper presented to the 4th European Developmental Psychology Conference, University of Stirling, September 1990.

Reddy, V. (1991) 'Playing with others' expectations: teasing and mucking about in the first year', in Whiten, A. (ed.) *Natural Theories of Mind*. Oxford: Blackwell.

Reichle, J. and Yoder, D. (1979) 'Communication behavior of the severely and profoundly mentally retarded: assessment and early stimulation strategies', in York, R. and Edgar, E. (eds) *Teaching the Severely Handicapped Vol. 4*. Seattle: American Association for the Education of the Severely and Profoundly Handicapped.

Ricks, D. (1979) 'Making sense of experience to make sensible sounds', in Bullowa, M. (ed.) *Before Speech*. Cambridge: Cambridge University Press.

Roberts, R. and Patterson, C. (1983) 'Perspective taking and referential communication: the question of correspondence reconsidered', *Child Development* **54**, 1005–14.

Robson, K. (1967) 'The role of eye-to-eye contact in maternal–infant attachment', *Journal of Child Psychology and Psychiatry* **8**, 13–25.

Rogers, S. J. (1977) 'Characteristics of the cognitive development of profoundly retarded children', *Child Development* **48**, 837–43.

Rogers-Warren, A. and Warren, S. (1980) 'Mands for verbalization: facilitating the display of newly trained language in children', *Behavior Modification* **4**, 361–82.

Rondal, J. (1976) *Maternal Speech to Normal and Down's Syndrome Children Matched for Mean Length of Utterance* (Research Report No 98), Research Development and Demonstration Centre in Education of Handicapped Children, Minnesota: University of Minnesota.

Roth, F. and Speckman, N. (1984a) 'Assessing the pragmatic abilities of children, Part 1: Organisational framework and assessment parameters', *Journal of Speech and Hearing Disorders* **49**, 1–11.

Roth, F. and Speckman, N. (1984b) 'Assessing the pragmatic abilities of children, Part 2: Guidelines, considerations and specific evaluation procedures', *Journal of Speech and Hearing Disorders* **49**, 12–17.

Roth, F. and Speckman, N. (1994) 'Oral story production in adults with learning disabilities', in Bloom, R., Obler, L., De Santi, S. Ehrlich, J. (eds) *Discourse Analysis and Applications: Studies in Adult Clinical Populations*. Hillsdale, NJ: Lawrence Erlbaum Associates.

Rubin, K., Fein, G., Vandenberg, B. (1983) 'Play', in Mussen, P. and Hetherington, E. (eds) *Handbook of Child Psychology, Vol. 4: Socialisation, Personality and Social Development*, 4th edn. New York: Wiley.

Rutter, M. (1980) 'Language training with autistic children: how does it work and what does it achieve?', in Hersov, L. A. and Berger, M. (eds) *Language and Language Disorders in Childhood: Supplement No. 2, Journal of Child Psychology and Psychiatry*. Oxford: Pergamon Press.

Sackett, G. P. (1978) *Observing Behaviour, Vol. II*. London: University Park Press.

Scaife, M. and Bruner, J. (1975) 'The capacity of joint visual attention in the infant', *Nature* **253**, 265–6.

Schaffer, H. R. (1971) *The Origins of Human Social Relations*. New York: Academic Press.

Schaffer, H. R., Collis, G., Parsons, G. (1977) 'Vocal interchange and visual regard in verbal and pre-verbal children', in Schaffer, H. R. (ed.) *Studies in Mother–Infant Interaction*. New York: Academic Press.

Schweigert, P. (1989) 'Use of microswitch technology to facilitate social contingency awareness as a basis for early communication skills', *A.A.C. (Augmentative and Alternative Communication)* 5, 192–8.

Schweigert, P. and Rowland, C. (1992) 'Early communication and microtechnology: instructional sequence and case studies of children with severe multiple disabilities', *A.A.C. (Augmentative and Alternative Communication)* 8, 273–86.

Seibert, J. and Oller, D. (1981) 'Linguistic pragmatics and language intervention strategies', *Journal of Autism and Developmental Disorders* ll, 75–88.

Sheridan, M. D. (1973) *Children's Developmental Progress*. London: NFER.

Sinclair, M. (1971) 'Sensory motor action patterns as a condition for the acquisition of syntax', in Huxley, R. and Ingram, E. (eds) *Language Acquisition: Models and Methods*. New York: Academic Press.

Skinner, B. F. (1957) *Verbal Behaviour*. New York: Appleton-Century-Croft.

Smith, B. R. and Leinonen, E. (1992) *Clinical Pragmatics – Unravelling the Complexities of Communication Failure*. London: Chapman & Hall.

Snow, C. E. (1972) 'Mothers' speech to children learning language', *Child Development* 43, 549–65.

Snyder-McLean, L., Solomon, B., McLean, J., Sacks, S. (1984) 'Structuring joint action routines: a strategy for facilitating communication and language development in the classroom', *Seminars in Speech and Language* 5, 213–328.

Stalnater, R. (1991) 'Chapter 27', in Davis, S. (ed.) *Pragmatics: a Reader*. Oxford: Oxford University Press.

Stark, R. (1981) 'Aspects of language behavior in infancy and early childhood: summary and implications', in Stark, R. (ed.) *Language Behavior in Infancy and Early Childhood*. New York: Elsevier/North-Holland.

Stephens, B. (1977) 'A Piagetian approach to curriculum development for the severely, profoundly and multiply handicapped', in Sontag, E. (ed.) *Educational Programming for the Severely and Profoundly Handicapped*. Riston, VA: Council for Exceptional Children.

Stephenson, J. and Linfoot, K. (1996) 'Intentional communication and graphic symbol use by students with severe intellectual disability', *International Journal of Disability, Development and Education* 43, 147–65.

Stern, D. (1977) *The First Relationship*. Cambridge, MA: Harvard University Press.

Sugarman, S. (1983) 'Why talk? Comment on Savage-Rumbaugh *et al.*, J.', *Experimental Psychology – General* 112, 493–7.

Sugarman, S. (1984) 'The development of pre-verbal communication: its contribution and limits in promoting the development of language', in Schiefelbusch, R. L. and Pickar, J. P. (eds) *The Acquisition of Communicative Competence*. Baltimore, MD: University Park Press.

Thoman, E. (1981) 'Affective communication as the prelude and context for language learning', in Schiefelbusch, R. L. and Bricker, D. (eds) *Early Language Acquisition and Intervention*. Baltimore, MD: University Park Press.

Tizard, B., Cooperman, O., Joseph, A., Tizard, J. (1972) 'Environmental effects on language development: a study of young children in long stay residential nurseries', *Child Development* 43, 337–58.

Trevarthen, C. (1979) 'Communication and cooperation in early infancy: a description of primary inter-subjectivity', in Bullowa, M. (ed.) *Before Speech*. Cambridge: Cambridge University Press.

Trevarthen, C. (1993) 'The function of emotions in early infant communication and development', in Nadel, J. and Camaioni, L. (eds) *New Perspectives in Early Communicative Development*. London: Routledge.

Trevarthen, C. and Hubley, P. (1978) 'Secondary inter-subjectivity: confidence, confiding and acts of meaning in the first year', in Lock, A. (ed.) *Action, Gesture and Symbol: the Emergence of Language*. New York: Academic Press.

Tronick, E. (1981) 'Infant communicative intent: the infant's reference to social interaction', in Stark, R. (ed.) *Language Behaviour in Infancy and Early Childhood*. New York: Elsevier/North-Holland.

Tronick, E., Als, M., Adamson, L. (1979) 'Structure of early face to face communicative interactions', in Bullowa, M. (ed.) *Before Speech*. Cambridge: Cambridge University Press.

Uzgiris, I. (1972) 'Patterns of vocal and general imitation in infants', in *Proceedings of the Symposium on Genetic and Social Influences*. Basle: Karger.

Uzgiris, I. and Hunt, J. McV. (1975) *Assessment in Infancy: Ordinal Scales of Psychological Development*. Urbana, IL: University of Illinois Press.

Vygotsky, L. (1962) *Thought and Language*. Cambridge, MA: MIT Press.

Vygotsky, L. (1978) *Mind in Society: The Development of Higher Psychological Processes*. Cambridge, MA: Harvard University Press.

Ware, J. (1996) *Creating a Responsive Environment for People with Profound and Multiple Learning Difficulties*. London: David Fulton.

Warren, S. and Bambara, L. (1989) 'An experimental analysis of milieu language intervention: teaching the action-object form', *Journal of Speech and Hearing Disorders* 54, 448–61.

Watson, J. S. and Ramey, C. (1972) 'Reactions to response-contingent stimulation in early infancy', *Merrill-Palmer Quarterly* 18, 219–27.

Westby, C. (1980) 'Assessment of cognitive and language abilities through play', *Language, Speech and Hearing Services in Schools* 11, 154–68.

Wing, L., Gould, J., Yeates, S., Brierley, L. (1977) 'Symbolic play in severely mentally retarded and in autistic children', *Journal of Child Psychology and Psychiatry* 18, 167–78.

Yoder, P. J. (1987) 'Relationship between degree of infant handicap and clarity of infant cues', *American Journal on Mental Deficiency* 91, 639–41.

Zwitman, D. and Sonderman, J. (1979) 'A syntax programme designed to present base linguistic structures to language disordered children', *Journal of Communication Disorders* 12, 323–35.

Index

Printed in Great Britain
by Amazon